NARRATIVE PSYCHOLOGY AND VYGOTSKY IN DIALOGUE

This book draws together two domains of psychological theory, Vygotsky's cultural-historical theory of cognition and narrative theories of identity, to offer a way of rethinking the human subject as embodied, relational and temporal. A dialogue between these two ostensibly disparate and contested theoretical trajectories provides a new vantage point from which to explore questions of personal and political change.

In a world of deepening inequalities and increasing economic precarity, the demand for free, decolonised quality education as articulated by the South African Student Movement and in many other contexts around the world, is disrupting established institutional practices and reinvigorating possibilities for change. This context provokes new lines of hopeful thought and critical reflection on (dis)continuities across historical time, theories of (social and psychological) developmental processes and the practices of intergenerational life, particularly in the domain of education, for the making of emancipatory futures.

This is essential reading for academics and students interested in Vygotskian and narrative theory, and critical psychology, as well as those interested in the politics and praxis of higher education.

Jill Bradbury is Associate Professor of Psychology at the University of the Witwatersrand, Johannesburg, South Africa. She teaches in the fields of narrative psychology and psychosocial childhood studies. Her research focuses on intergenerational narratives, sociohistorical theories of personhood, the transformation of higher education and the (im)possibilities of individual and social change. She is a principal investigator on the interdisciplinary research project, NEST (Narrative Enquiry for Social Transformation).

Concepts for Critical Psychology: Disciplinary Boundaries Re-thought
Series editor: Ian Parker

Developments inside psychology that question the history of the discipline and the way it functions in society have led many psychologists to look outside the discipline for new ideas. This series draws on cutting-edge critiques from just outside psychology in order to complement and question critical arguments emerging inside. The authors provide new perspectives on subjectivity from disciplinary debates and cultural phenomena adjacent to traditional studies of the individual.

The books in the series are useful for advanced level undergraduate and postgraduate students, researchers and lecturers in psychology and other related disciplines such as cultural studies, geography, literary theory, philosophy, psychotherapy, social work and sociology.

Most recently published titles:

Madness and Subjectivity
A Cross-Cultural Examination of Psychosis in the West and India
Ayurdhi Dhar

Decolonial Psychoanalysis
Towards Critical Islamophobia Studies
Robert Beshara

Subjectivity and Critical Mental Health
Lessons from Brazil
Daniel Goulart

Psycurity
Colonialism, Paranoia, and the War on Imagination
Rachel Jane Liebert

NARRATIVE PSYCHOLOGY AND VYGOTSKY IN DIALOGUE

Changing Subjects

Jill Bradbury

Routledge
Taylor & Francis Group

LONDON AND NEW YORK

First published 2020
by Routledge
2 Park Square, Milton Park, Abingdon, Oxon OX14 4RN

and by Routledge
52 Vanderbilt Avenue, New York, NY 10017

Routledge is an imprint of the Taylor & Francis Group, an informa business

© 2020 Jill Bradbury

British Library Cataloguing-in-Publication Data
A catalogue record for this book is available from the British
Library

Library of Congress Cataloging-in-Publication Data
A catalog record has been requested for this book

ISBN: 978-1-138-55180-0 (hbk)
ISBN: 978-1-138-55187-9 (pbk)
ISBN: 978-1-315-14782-6 (ebk)

Typeset in Bembo
by Swales & Willis, Exeter, Devon, UK

For Siyanda Ndlovu
25 March 1982 – 5 April 2010
In memory of all your beautiful futures
Siyaqhubeka

CONTENTS

SECTION 3
Intergenerational subjects in changing worlds   **103**

SERIES EDITOR PREFACE

This book reconfigures the academic boundaries between narrative psychology and Vygotskian work by exploring in a richly contextualised reading of local institutional and state practices what it means to be "subject". Clearly the "subject" or discipline of academic and professional psychology is not up to the task, and critical psychologists who are searching for alternatives and building sub-disciplinary perspectives on the self and culture need to go well outside the discipline; to be "changing subjects" in this sense necessitates, as Jill Bradbury argues so cogently, rethinking the boundaries of psychology. The link between culture and psychology was made by Lev Vygotsky a century back and is being remade today through narrative approaches. The interweaving of those two traditions allows us to appreciate how important the meaning of "subject" as grammatical function is; we are subject to language, and the application of the two theoretical frameworks to personal and collective processes of change requires that we attend in detail to how that language works. There is a third "subject" who speaks in this text, however, the subject as agent; empowered through the process of constructing contested readings of narrative, this active acting subject is able to reflect on who they are and who they could become in relation to others.

This book, *Narrative Psychology and Vygotsky in Dialogue: Changing Subjects*, looks at first glance as if it is about an old psychologist – Vygotsky, Russian pioneer researcher into the nature of subjectivity grounded in the specific language of a dominant culture and working at the contradictions which speak of alternative conceptions of what it is to be a human being after a revolution – but it is actually as much about specific contexts of work a century later; it is as much about the way that black subjectivity is conceptualised in the work of South African phenomenologist Chabani Manganyi writing during the revolutionary struggle against the apartheid regime. That startling shift of perspective and focus as we read the book poses a question. How could it be that two specific-context writers could also be writing about something universal? The answer being that what is universal is not the psychological content of their work but the *method* they lead us to and the focus on language which narrative psychology gives us the tools to explicate.

The double-lesson of narrative and Vygotskyan critique is that different senses of subject must be situated in social context, not merely concerned with personal change – though personal change is the prerequisite and consequence of this radical work – but also concerned with changing the world, with changing worlds. Those are the stakes of the proposed synergy between Vygotsky's relational dialogical subjectivity constituted in an engagement with the African concept "Ubuntu". The boundaries that are being transgressed and traversed in this book are therefore disciplinary, grammatical and agentic; and it is then clear how and why the standard psychologised binary opposition between what is interior to the subject and what is exterior to them must also be disturbed, challenged and transcended. This necessary book teaches us not only that the conceptual resources we need are as much outside the discipline of psychology as lying hidden in our history – Vygotsky as the resource we needed always already there if we had cared to look for him – but also that the narratives we now construct as alternatives to psychology must operate at the edge of the disciplinary boundaries, as "outwith" them; in and against them.

Ian Parker
University of Manchester

AUTHOR PREFACE

A narrative of the text coming into being

This book draws together two domains of psychological theory that are generally considered quite disparate, namely, Vygotsky's cultural-historical theory of cognition, and narrative theories of identity or subjectivity. Although some concepts from Vygotsky's theory of mind have been widely taken up in educational psychology, most notably, the "zone of proximal development", the implications of Vygotsky's theory of consciousness have been less thoroughly explored or articulated in relation to the critical psychology project of reconceptualising psychological life. Conversely, while narrative theory is deployed, together with both phenomenological and discursive psychologies, for theoretical and empirical research purposes, these approaches are typically mobilised for sociopolitical purposes and often resist articulation with psychological or interior worlds. While the binary between internal and external realities is widely recognised as false, we lack the conceptual tools for speaking differently about psychosocial phenomena and processes. I suggest that there is a productive commensurability between Vygotsky's theory and Narrative theories and that linking these domains will contribute to rethinking the disciplinary boundaries of psychology, and to informing new forms of praxis. The "changing subjects" of the title therefore refers to multiple senses of the "subject" that play on its semantic and grammatical ambiguities: (1) the subject or discipline of psychology; (2) the subject as subjected (subjugated) to social life; and (3) as the agentic acting subject of social life.

The question of change needs to be engaged in all of these senses and new theoretical resources are released by placing Vygotskian theory and narrative psychology in dialogue.

Those looking for a comprehensive (or even partial) overview of these vast theoretical terrains will be disappointed. In mitigation, the loose ends and frayed edges of this text may offer readers possible threads to tug at and from which to weave new and different lines of theoretical enquiry and praxis. Narrative psychology provides not only the content but also the *method* of the text, crossing multiple time zones, the spaces of the academy and everyday life, the political and the personal. Vygotsky's theory-method that enables us to engage with changing forms and history as possibility, is part of my own narrative life history, enfolded into my educational praxis. The project to fuse aspects of these two ostensibly disparate and contested theoretical trajectories is enmeshed in the very processes of change that are the focus of my enquiry. With the benefit of hindsight, changes in understandings and practices, changes to our earlier selves, seem inevitable. Life, however, unlike textual narrative, is never complete; we are always in the middle of the story and, as I began to write this text, the higher education landscape of South Africa was radically disrupted by the emergence of the Student Movement, demanding free decolonised quality education. In the wider national and global context of deepening inequalities and increasing economic precarity, this political movement challenges the status quo, demanding accountability from the democratic state and shaking up established institutional practices. The Student Movement is continuous with previous decades of struggle as student protests around financial and academic exclusions have always been a consistent feature of higher education in South Africa and, in this sense, these are not new issues. However, this is a particular historical moment in which multiple disruptions to taken-for-granted sociopolitical life are occurring across the globe and the South African Student Movement presents new formations and articulations of critique and activism, reinvigorating possibilities for change, the effects of which are still in the making. Writing this text in this context provoked me along new lines of hopeful thought and critical reflection on (dis)continuities across historical time, theories of (social and psychological) developmental processes, and the practices of intergenerational life, particularly in the domain of education, for the making of emancipatory futures. The time-space context from which I write thus both requires and makes possible a unique critical perspective on the (im)possibilities of social and psychological change, providing interesting entangled threads from which to weave stories of changing subjects and changing worlds.

Mapping the sections of the text

I have attempted to engage multiple projected audiences in the text, psychologists and non-psychologists, South Africans and those from elsewhere, and to cross the widening generational gaps between now and then. This means that, for different readers, different aspects of the text may feel more or less familiar or foreign. The text crosses multiple disciplinary domains not only within psychology but beyond, drawing on literary work, philosophy, educational and social theory, and contemporary political commentaries beyond the academy. The text is at once a conceptual exploration and a reflexive account of personal experiences and collaborative projects in the world of learning-teaching and knowledge-making. I traverse a few decades of my own life history, working in relationship with colleagues in the South African academy in changing times, in conversation with the longer history of psychology and with international scholars who are busy with different articulations of the project of critical psychology in their own contexts.

The text is organised in three primary sections: (1) theorising human subjectivity; (2) conceptual tools for the subject (discipline) of psychology; and (3) reflections on contextual engagements in changing intergenerational worlds. In the first section, Vygotskian theory and Narrative psychology are placed in dialogue to create an alternative framework for conceptualising living subjectivities and exploring implications for the subject of psychology. Chapter 1 provides a psychosocial conceptualisation of personhood that is embodied, temporal and relational. From a Vygotskian perspective, the world is mediated by the meanings of others, providing the constraints and possibilities of culture, and subjecting each generation to the "weight" of history. However, this mediated consciousness paradoxically enables the narrative subject to generate new storylines for the future through self-regulating internal dialogues. In Chapter 2, this conceptualisation is inserted into the history and contemporary articulations of the discipline of psychology, particularly exploring points of connection to, and differentiation from, critical "turns" to discourse and more recently, embodiment and affect. The chapter draws together the two lines of Vygotsky's development, natural and cultural, to explore questions about the mutability of human "nature", and possibilities for individual and sociopolitical change. The theory of (black) subjectivity proposed by the South African psychologist, Chabani Manganyi, is juxtaposed with that of Vygotsky, highlighting productive synergies and provocations. The (social) construction of the subject of psychology, in the dual sense of how persons are conceptualised and in the constitution of the discipline, may contribute to or frustrate possibilities for change in both subjects and worlds.

In the second section, two specific concepts developed through theorising from the South are explored in more detail in dialogue with Vygotskian and narrative theory. The first is outlined in Chapter 3, in which ways of thinking about psychosocial realities are fleshed out through the African concept of "ubuntu" in synergy with Vygotskian consciousness, asserting a relational, dialogical subjectivity that challenges traditional binaries or dichotomies. The second conceptual exploration in Chapter 4 examines the possibilities and difficulties entailed in changing our minds and challenging established understandings of the world. (Mis)understandings are only partly amenable to challenge by rational argument and evidence and their functional validity is ordinarily recursively (re)established in our relations with others and the (social) structure of the world. The pedagogical and political task is to disrupt these self-perpetuating patterns.

The third and final section of the text focuses on contextual applications of theories and concepts for engaging individual and collective processes of change. These chapters present reflections on autobiographical chapters of my life as an academic, conducting research and teaching across the breach between the apartheid and democratic systems in the 1990s, through the first decade of the new century, and into the changing times of the present. These are neither neatly distinct periods nor linear progressive stages through which my thinking and practice have developed. In Oscar Wilde's witty words, "I am not young enough to know everything!". A retrospective narrative remakes earlier events and experiences rather than simply recollecting them and the story of my pedagogical and political engagements in questions of change both within and beyond the academy is inevitably partial and particular, shaped as much by my accumulated experience as by the current context in which I live, think and work.

Chapter 5 focuses on the radical possibilities of the Vygotskian concepts of potential and the zone of proximal development in the highly unequal terrain of higher education in the historical moment of change signalled by the collapse of the apartheid regime in South Africa. This (partial) history of pedagogical experiments provides critical resources for the present, particularly in relation to questions of decolonising curricula and pedagogies. Chapter 6 presents reflections on learning and teaching as processes of identity construction and subject formation, about *being* rather than solely matters of knowing and thinking. Theorising identity and subjectivity as narrative becomes infused into my theoretical and empirical projects, offering a new vantage point from which to think about processes of change, particularly in relation to history and temporality. Intergenerational educational relationships have productive potential but simultaneously have subjugating effects and in this chapter I reflect on my positionality as a teacher committed to a social justice agenda and to the emancipatory effects of education. The final chapter of the book extends the narrative to explore how traumatic memory and hopeful imagination might coalesce in the fluid landscape of the present. While the process of writing can only really capture meaning in the past tense, the book ends by articulating a version of critical hope in relation to the messiness of the changing present and possibilities for the future.

ACKNOWLEDGEMENTS

This book was a long time in the making and its shape and thematic threads have changed, unravelled and been remade through wonderfully provocative conversations and exchanges across many different times and places. I am grateful to the University of the Witwatersrand for sabbatical leave that enabled me to immerse myself in the slow processes of reading and reflection so necessary to be able to write anything at all. I am very thankful to the series editor, Ian Parker, for trusting that this book would happen even when it seemed unlikely. Thanks to the Routledge editorial and production teams for their patient attention.

I am thankful for networks of collegial scholarship and overlapping circles of friendship that have challenged my thinking and sustained my soul over the years. To Ian Parker and Erica Burman and the Discourse Unit for providing a home-away-from-home in the years of commuting between Durban and Manchester; to Michelle Fine, Susan Opotow and María Elena Torre of the Graduate Centre of the City University of New York (CUNY) for exemplary experimental and hopeful praxis; to Molly Andrews, Corinne Squire and Maria Tamboukou of the Centre for Narrative Research at the University of East London (UEL) for generating exceptionally robust narrative threads that have become woven into my thinking and life. Connections to these international circles were facilitated by two vibrant intellectual projects in the making of critical psychology in South Africa. Thanks to Grahame Hayes for sustaining the PINS (Psychology in Society) journal and network over several decades, and to Norman Duncan and Garth Stevens, and colleagues in the department of Psychology at Wits for initiating, and welcoming me into, the Apartheid Archives project. My current thinking, acting and being is only possible in and through a remarkable collaborative partnership with Bhekizizwe Peterson in the vibrant space of NEST (Narrative Enquiry for Social Transformation). Special thanks to the NEST reading group for our reading, thinking and talking together – you will read yourselves between the lines! My immense gratitude to all my students past, present and yet-to-come, the characters that give my narrative life.

Thanks to Joni Brenner for the beautiful cover image of Marigold beads that tells the story of human connectivity in the interleaving processes of continuity and change. Heartfelt thanks to Molly Andrews, Hugo Canham, Jude Clark, Peace Kiguwa, Ronnie Miller and Bhekizizwe Peterson for reading chapters along the way and giving me critical but kind feedback. To Ronnie who read every word, thank you for continuing to fix commas with only mild irritation, for decades of mediational moments that have revealed new worlds for me, and an exceptional friendship of heart and mind. Thanks to Judes, Lindelwa, Mthoko and Rejane for animated conversations about and mostly not-about the book, for sharing your inspiring and wonderful life-worlds with me, and refusing to let me give up. Finally, my love and deep thankfulness to Keith, without whom I could not narrate my-self.

SECTION 1
Changing subjects
Theorising personhood

1

VYGOTSKY'S NARRATIVE SUBJECT

Introduction

Vygotsky's subject is a storytelling animal. Reframing Vygotsky's subject (in both senses, his subject of study, but also his conceptualisation of the human "subject") in narrative terms is premised on the pivotal role of language in his theory that not only serves to carry cultural history and thus construct the social subject, but is also a natural, universal human capacity. The internalisation of the contents of social talk, the cultural baggage (or capital) of history is well recognised as constituting the "social subject", or reformulates Vygotsky's position as "society in mind". Storytelling or narration enables us to become quite other than our natural selves, quite different in kind than even our nearest animal relatives, not only in our capacity to tell stories, but also *through* our narration of life. However, this social subject constituted in the world of language and meaning remains entirely natural, embodied in the material world. There is nothing more "natural" to human life than the use of signs and the telling of stories: it is intrinsic to the kind of animal that human beings are. This first chapter will draw together the resources of Vygotskian theory and narrative psychology for rethinking personhood as embodied, temporal and relational. Several themes that will run throughout the text will be introduced, in particular, highlighting the role of language in the formation of psychosocial life through internal conversations, dialogue and the narration of the self.

Both Vygotskian theory and narrative psychology are approaches more properly described as theory-methods or innovative *ways of thinking* about persons in terms of dynamic processes rather than as circumscribed entities. In outlining Vygotsky's "enabling theory-method", Shotter (2000, p. 234) emphasises the "*responsivity* of growing and living forms, both to each and to the otherness in their surroundings, and on *their* own particular and unique ways of coming-into-Being". Narrative psychology emphasises the temporal quality of human life that biologically unfolds inexorably forwards but in psychological terms is constituted through perpetual oscillations back and forth in time in which each fleeting present moment is infused with memories of the past and tenuously connected by intention and imagination to projected futures. This emphasis on the living processes of changing subjects requires a very different conceptual and methodological approach to aspirations to science and the taxonomically descriptive language that characterises much of psychology's history. Vygotsky's theory-method attempts to trace the origins and course of development of psychosocial functions. His focus is not on the "fossilised" products of human behaviour in finished current forms but on "the very process of genesis or establishment of the higher form caught in a *living aspect*" (Vygotsky, 1997, p. 71, emphasis added). This conceptualisation of history does not refer to a static archive but to a flow of activity in which present forms of life participate: "It is here that the past and the present are fused *and the present is seen in the light of history*" (Shotter, 2000, p. 236).

These sociohistorical processes are woven through intergenerational narratives that both constrain and enable possibilities for change. While history and culture shape both the contents and forms of our narratives, it is because we are storytelling creatures that history and culture are possible at all. The subjects of psychology, human beings, are both subject to and subjects of change, but we have been slow to recognise the methodological implications of this understanding, amusingly captured in the injunction from Harré and Secord (1972, p. 84): "for scientific purposes, treat people as if they were human beings".[1]

Vygotsky's theory: society in mind

Vygotskian theory is typically understood as an account of the powerful sociohistorical and cultural effects on the formation of human mind, and his concepts of mediation and the zone of proximal development are now established received wisdoms in psychological theory and educational applications. However, as important as this contribution is in deepening our understanding of children's development in context, the more thoroughly radical and transformative implications of Vygotskian theory are often eclipsed or erased: minds are always "in society" (or social contexts) but critically, they are also always infused with the social; society is "in mind". Thus, Vygotsky provides us with a developmental account of human consciousness as articulated *in and through* sociohistorical processes. Vygotsky's approach, in similar vein to other stage theorists such as Freud, Erikson and Piaget,[2] focuses on ontogenetic development as a route to explaining the processes of psychological life.

While Vygotsky and Piaget are often understood as providing antithetical theories of cognitive development, the two theories provide divergent but complementary, rather than opposing, explanatory accounts of the human mind. Piaget explains human consciousness as constructed in and through the mental operations of mind in transaction with the material world. His purpose is to neutralise the effects of culture or the malleable historical elements of human life, which he acknowledged as *necessary* but *insufficient* for cognitive development.[3] In this way, his theoretical project is to abstract ontogenetic, species-specific universals from multiple empirical studies of children's engagement with cognitive tasks. By contrast, Vygotsky acknowledges the necessity of the material fabric of both individual mental life and collective social life, but focuses on how these resources are insufficient to either effect or explain development or change.

Collective histories inform our current individual modes of being and the traces of the past create the contours of present life, and constrain our imaginative future projections. To put this idea into the psychological language of development, into Vygotskian language, the world is always mediated. Unlike the Piagetian baby who crawls and grasps towards the object desired, the mother of Vygotsky's baby inserts herself between the baby's grasping action and the object, interpreting her baby's action and providing the desired object. By conferring meaning on the grasping action, it is transformed into a *gesture* of desire, pointing, that is a meaningful gesture of communication with another person, directing her attention to the object and "requesting" assistance. In this way, Vygotsky argues, the "[t]he path from the object to the child and from the child to the object, passes through another person" (1978, p. 30), prism-like, radically altering its quality and the form of experience.

The focus on ontogenetic development is thus a theory-method for Vygotsky, a vehicle for exploring and accounting for the dynamic historical development of cultural life *and* the intellectual actions of persons in the making of human history. Marx's visceral image of the intertwining of the past and present resonates:

> Men make their own history, but they do not make it as they please; they do not make it under self-selected circumstances, but

under circumstances existing already, given and transmitted from the past. The traditions of all dead generations weighs like a nightmare on the brains of the living.

(Marx, 1852)

The theoretical lenses of sociohistorical psychology enable us to engage with the (im)possibilities of changing our worlds and selves in the landscape of this living nightmare by recognising that social and psychological phenomena are intertwined rather than oppositional. Thinking about change entails attending to both social structure and individual agency, adopting a stance that Michelle Fine (2018) calls "critical bifocality". This requires a willingness to learn new ways of seeing, shifting our focus from persons to the social world and back again. But these alternations in focus are an analytic necessity rather than a reflection of the phenomenon of change. The domain that is currently in sharp focus (whether social or individual) remains intertwined with the blurry zone that has temporarily receded beyond our immediate attention. The key to active developmental processes of change, and to a "bifocal" vision of these processes, both within and beyond mind, is language.

Language for thought: conceptualising the world

First, I want to emphasise, following Vygotsky, that human language is *conceptual* not just expressive or communicative, although of course this is its most obvious function, in common with the languages of other social animals.

> When we meet what is called a cow and say "this is a cow," we add the act of thinking to the act of perception, bringing the given perception under a general concept. A child who first calls things by their names is making genuine discoveries. I do not see that this is a cow, for this cannot be seen. I see something big, black, moving, lowing, etc., and understand that this is a cow. And this act is an act of classification, of assigning a singular phenomenon to the class of similar phenomena, of systematizing the experience, etc.
>
> *(Vygotsky, 1987, pp. 249–250)*

This abstraction from life is what makes it possible for us to "see" multiple objects from multiple angles which are, in simple visual or perceptual terms, very different indeed, as "cows". As Vygotsky argues, we can detach the word from the world (the specific object referent) and indeed, further, detach the meaning from the word. Generalisation, systematisation and classification thus underpin all language. In other words, a kind of thinking is entailed in all language, allowing for the creation of complex systems and relations of meaning and enabling us to establish new relations between ourselves and the world. (These complex relations are extended in formal instruction, writing and other forms of symbolic representation.)

I am from a part of South Africa called KwaZulu-Natal and from there comes the beautiful book *Abundant Herds: A Celebration of the Nguni Cattle of the Zulu People* by Marguerita Poland and David Hammond-Tooke (2003). The following images of Nguni cattle from the book are by Leigh Voigt (see Figures 1.1 and 1.2).

These images offer a glimpse of an intricate story about culture and symbolic naming of the world. Cows are, throughout the world, concrete material objects of great utilitarian value for their milk and meat and skins. Moreover, in Zulu culture, as in many other African cultures, cattle are units of exchange for lobola (often crudely and inaccurately translated as "bride price" in English) and other practices (such as the payment of "damages" to repair breaches in relationships or as offerings to ancestors). In other words, cattle are central to both economic and social relations. Beyond this, the naming of these individual cows for the visual patterns of their hides speaks to questions of aesthetics and meaning and cultural history. Children in these cultural worlds encounter far more than "something big, black, moving, lowing" and also, far more than simply the synthesis of these material elements into the abstract category of "cow". Tracing a simple dialogical exchange between a 7-year-old child in the Eastern Cape of South Africa and a documentary interviewer in the BBC *Seven-Up* series (1992), provides us with a vivid instantiation of this insertion into language and meaningful histories.

INTERVIEWER: How many cattle are there at your place?

LINDA[4]: 19.

INTERVIEWER: Do you know them all?

LINDA: Yes.

INTERVIEWER: Which are your favourites? Tell me their names.

LINDA: Tamblain and Holland.

INTERVIEWER: Who names them?

LINDA: When I was born, they were already here, so I don't know who named them.

INTERVIEWER: So they were here. Don't the small ones have names?

LINDA: Yes.

INTERVIEWER: What?

LINDA: One is Wazibula. The others are calves.

FIGURE 1.1 Abundance
Reproduced by kind permission of the artist, Leigh Voigt

FIGURE 1.2 Houses
Reproduced by kind permission of the artist, Leigh Voigt

INTERVIEWER: Who named them?

LINDA: Elder brother.

INTERVIEWER: Did you name any?

LINDA: No.

INTERVIEWER: Why not?

LINDA: Elder brother says little boys give cattle bad names.

INTERVIEWER: Why?

LINDA: They don't sound right.

This little boy makes two pertinent observations about the naming of cows: first, he resists the interviewer's question about the naming of his favourite cattle as "they were here before me". We, each one of us, always arrive into a social world already structured, in which meaning is already sedimented, a world already named in language. We are inserted into relations of kinship and culture, into the flows and prejudices of what Gadamer (1975) calls "tradition" or Merleau-Ponty (2013) calls "sedimentation". Second, he repeats his older brother's observation that "little boys give cows bad names". This disciplining of young subjects is ubiquitous; we socialise the young into our ways of doing and being and through their engagement with others (and the cultural artefacts of the social world) children are enculturated. However, we always have the capacity for becoming what Judith Butler (1997) calls "bad subjects" and perhaps this potential is most evident in the young; each successive generation is simultaneously trapped and yet escapes the "prison house" (Jameson, 1975) of language. This is possible because language is internalised not as an inert set of "instructions" or even a set of potential meanings that must simply then be articulated anew in the appropriate circumstances. Rather, language is internalised as dialogue, enabling us to talk to ourselves and, in Vygotskian terms, to self-regulate.

Mediation: narrating action and dialogical selves

By focusing on the developmental stage of egocentric speech in young children, catching speech on its route inward, Vygotsky was able to delineate the functions of inner speech. A famous story from Vygotsky illustrates how talking to oneself enables new relations with the world and transforms thought and action. A little girl is observed solving a problem of great importance to any small child: how to obtain sweets that are beyond the reach of her short arms!

(*Stands on a stool, quietly looking, feeling along a shelf with stick*)
"On the stool." (*glances at the experimenter. Puts stick in other hand.*)

"Is that really the candy?" (*Hesitates*)

"I can get it from that other stool, stand and get it." (*Gets second stool.*)

"No, that doesn't get it. I could use the stick." (*Takes stick, knocks at the candy.*)

"It will move now." (*Knocks candy.*)

"It moved, I couldn't get it with the stool, but the, but the stick worked".

(Vygotsky, 1978, p. 25)

This story demonstrates the way in which, as Vygotsky (1999, p. 50) says, "children solve problems not just with their hands and eyes but with their speech as well". The little girl comments on her actions, plans what to do next, co-ordinates and re-organises objects and, finally, concludes with a model of successful action that might be usefully deployed in future to solve similar problems: *"I couldn't get it with the stool, but the, but the stick worked."* Language thus enables decontextualisation, the restructuring of the perceptual field, the imagining of alternatives, the possibility of memory, and the transferability of understanding to new situations.

While each successive generation is born into a pre-existing (social) world and cannot escape history or stand outside of culture, the very nature of language allows us to "slip our moorings", and contains in its constraining form, the possibility for creativity. Vygotsky's analysis emphasises the polysemous, polyvocal quality of language. The same word (or longer discursive units of sentences or texts) may have different meanings and, conversely, the same meaning can be conveyed in different words, different sentence constructions or textual forms. In *The Idea of Culture*, Eagleton outlines the ambiguous power of language to simultaneously imprison and liberate, and to constitute human life as at once natural (or material and embodied) and symbolic (or social and transcendent):

> Language helps to release us from the prison-house of our senses, at the same time as it damagingly abstracts us from them. Like Marx's capitalism then, language opens up at a stroke new possibilities of communication and new modes of exploitation.
>
> (*Eagleton, 2000, p. 97*)

His contemporary Marxist perspective resonates with Vygotsky's (e.g. 1986, 1994) earlier assertion that the peculiar qualities of human thought and action emerge through the convergence of *two* lines of development: the natural and the cultural. For both Vygotsky and Eagleton, these developmental lines are not oppositional; culture emerges from and is dependent on the natural capacity for language peculiar to humans.

> Because they move within a symbolic medium, and because they are of a certain material kind, our own bodies have the capacity to extend themselves far beyond their sensuous limits, in what we know as culture, society or technology. It is because our entry into the symbolic order – language and all it brings in its wake – puts some free play between ourselves and our determinants that we are those internally dislocated, non-self-identical creatures known as historical beings. History is what happens to an animal so constituted as to be able, within limits, to determine its own determinations. What is peculiar about a symbol-making creature is that it is of its nature to transcend itself. It is the sign which opens up that operative distance between ourselves and our material surroundings which allows us to transform them into history. Not just the sign, to be sure, but the way that our bodies are fashioned in the first place, capable of complex labour as well as the communication which must necessarily underpin it.
>
> (Eagleton, 2000, p. 97)

Eagleton beautifully captures the thrust of Vygotsky's analysis of the human capacity to use tools and signs. The opening up of this "operative distance between ourselves and our material surroundings" is possible not because of the communicative function of language but, rather, because language directed inwards splits the human subject, placing her at a distance to herself. The Vygotskian, Van der Veer (1996, p. 255), suggests that "speech is like a two-edged sword" functioning communicatively and creating particular ways of analysing and conceptualising the world, but simultaneously, directed towards the interior domain of the self. "Another way of putting it is to say that by means of words we can act upon other people and the things that surround us but that by doing so we are at the same time acting upon ourselves" (Van der Veer, 1996, p. 255). The transformation of material conditions (through the peculiarly human activity of labour) is possible because language enables us to plan, that is to regulate *our action in advance of our acting in the world* and creates the possibility for projection into the imaginary, not-yet world of possibility, the future. This is why the marvels of nature (the nest-building of birds and beavers or the intricate dance of bees) are for Vygotsky (and Marx) trumped by even the worst human architect or the clumsiest choreographer. Vygotsky declares this capacity to plan in advance to be pivotal to the development of meaningful human life, making the strong claim, "The fact that he provides himself with a tool in advance is *undoubtedly the beginning of culture*" (1999, p. 64). It is also what makes individual subjectivity or a sense of oneself as a person, possible. As Vygotsky says, children become the "subjects and objects of their own behaviour" (1978, p. 26) or in narrative terms, we become both the narrators of, and characters in, our own life stories. Vygotsky's conceptualisation of the human subject as articulated through the use of psychological signs, provides the psychological ground for contemporary theories of the self as a narrated and narrating subject. What characterises Vygotsky's subject is her use of signs to regulate her actions and herself. Vygotsky (1987, p. 285) could not put it more strongly: "The meaningful word is a microcosm of human consciousness".

Narrative psychology: storied selves

Narrative psychology picks up the story from Vygotsky, the story of the self, narrating its "self", creating connections, continuities and coherence across fragmented experiential disjunctures, disparate spaces and through time. The split consciousness of the I-me coheres both diachronically and synchronically (McAdams, 2001) in a (changing) narrative self. An extended quote from Crites (1986, p. 162) outlines this conceptualisation of narrative subjectivity, both as a theory-method for psychology and as it is enacted and articulated by ordinary people in making sense of their lives:

> [The self] is a narrative recollection of what no longer physically exists, is no longer present. In the I-me formulation, I is the narrator, me is the narrative figure in the life story. In autobiography, the writer, the I, is the story-teller. The subject of the autobiography is a narrative figure, the me, constructed from recollection.
>
> Yet this recollected self of my personal story has an immense psychic importance, My personal identity, without which I do not know who I am, is at stake in this formative application of narrative art and the more complete the story, the more integrated the self. The poignant search for roots that is such a prominent feature of our rootless age testifies to the acute unease a human being can feel without a coherent story of a personal past. ... Whether the way is rough or smooth in this respect, being a self entails having a story.

Talking to ourselves, narrating our actions (including our mental meaning-making actions) enables us to escape the immediate exigencies of the present and traverse multiple paths from this point in time, shuttling between the past and future, to re-present that which is absent or lost or not-yet, or even never-to-be, and the present. In language, we are able to turn material life into fiction, matter into meaning. As Fay (1996, p. 197) has observed, this process is not a unidirectional movement from world to mind: we simultaneously articulate these imagined realities in action, infusing the world of matter with meaning: "Our stories are enlived, and our lives are enstoried".

Memory: past–present

Like all living creatures, we live in time, inexorably moving forward, unable to turn back the clock. Who we are in the present is both the accumulation of past experiences and the effect of past events, and we can use this narrative framing to understand ourselves and the lives of others as stories with plots and characters. In the stories of our-selves, the protagonist is also the narrator, an almost omniscient narrator in that she carries the accumulated clutter of memory into each new present moment of experience. Yet, despite the fact that her memories are hers and hers alone by virtue of their embodiment in her body, the *same* body across time and place (even if it doesn't necessarily look or feel "the same"), the narrator is never fully in control of her own memories or her own story.

It is now a taken-for-granted fact that memory is not just about reproduction or recollection or accumulation of the facts of the past. Our inner stories are more than chronological records of past events and experiences. Indeed, both social histories and personal life stories are perpetually rewritten and once-central events may slip to the periphery as merely incidental or even be entirely forgotten, depending on their significance or relevance to current circumstances and present interlocutors or audiences. The wonderful novelist (and superb non-psychologist analyst of psychological life) Siri Hustvedt (2012, pp. 94–95) notes that:

> Memories are revised over time, and their meanings change as we age, something now recognised by neuroscience and referred to as the *reconsolidation* of memory. … Memory, like perception, is not passive retrieval but an active and creative process that involves the imagination. We are all always reinventing our pasts.

As Vygotsky (1978) demonstrated, through the most empirical aspects of his work, the mental processes of perception, attention and memory that we share with other animals are not only quantitatively enhanced or expanded but qualitatively *transformed* by the use of symbolic systems (most notably language), directed towards ourselves. "The very essence of human memory consists in the fact that human beings actively remember with the help of signs" (Vygotsky, 1978, p. 51). By utilising what he called the "experimental–developmental" method, the processes of attention and memory are demonstrated in their developmental trajectories. Drawing on experiments conducted by Leont'ev and Luria, Vygotsky demonstrated that older children and adults not only remember more than young children, they also remember differently (Van der Veer & Valsiner, 1991). Initially, external aides-memoires were variously (and, admittedly, somewhat anachronistically from our contemporary perspective) provided by concrete symbols such as coloured cards or other objects or stimuli. Adults presented with these tasks quickly internalised (or independently generated) mnemonic systems to facilitate and organise their engagement with these tasks whereas younger children's actions and talk is more erratic and spontaneous. Sometimes they are able to make use of external aids but arbitrary shifts in the organising system (such as switching the "meaning" of the colour of a card) made the task confusing and more difficult, indicating that the corresponding mental inhibitors and triggers of encoding and recall were still in the process of formation.

These experiments demonstrate that what is stored in human memory is not simply an impressively increasing volume of isolated facts but a systematically organised set of "invented links" (Van der Veer & Valsiner, 1991) and relationships between these experiential elements, including complex connections between both internal (personal) and external (social) memory. The intergenerational nature of human life (necessitated and facilitated by the lengthy physical dependency of human offspring) means that memory stretches beyond the individual lifespan, encoded and carried forward in multiple cultural forms. Oral histories, song and other ritual forms such as dance or practices associated with life-transitions such as birth and death, instantiate the processes of objectifying (in the sense of externalising) memory. The technology of writing extends the historical reach of memory dramatically and has transformative effects on cognitive processes and material actions. Whether we lament these effects as eroding the power (and linguistic beauty) of oral traditions as Plato did, or celebrate the creative possibilities that are released by the relinquishment of the burden of reproductive memory (see, for example, Ong, 1982), the impact of writing (first, and later, print) on intergenerational cultural life and knowledge production is undeniably significant. These earlier inventions precipitate the whirlwind exponential force of digitalisation that characterises contemporary life and promises (or threatens) the imminent advent of the so-called fourth industrial revolution.

However, despite these elaborate systems to preserve and transmit memory, remembering always inevitably and simultaneously entails the converse process of forgetting, not simply as a failure to remember or recall, but as a process that (consciously but often unconsciously) infuses and shapes memory (Brockmeier, 2002). As Ricoeur (2004, p. 21) observes: "the deficiencies stemming from forgetting ... should not be treated straight away as pathological forms, as dysfunctions, but as the shadowy underside of the bright region of memory, which binds us to what has passed before we remember it". Narratives of the past are never the "whole story", never the "whole truth and nothing but the truth" and always contain traces of that which is inarticulable, that which is not remembered or perhaps even actively forgotten for either psychological or political reasons (or both). The human capacity for remembering even ostensibly unimportant details is captured in the English saying, "An elephant never forgets". Partly of course this allusion rests on the sheer size of the elephant's brain which must surely enable it to store a great deal of information. But we all know that while size matters, it is not all that matters. The human brain is in real terms far smaller than the brain of an elephant but larger in proportion to our bodies, with a remarkable ability to *organise* rather than just store information. The idea of the brain as a "storehouse of memory" or the accumulation of one-damn-fact-after-another, has long been rejected, beginning with Piaget's constructivist account of the active developmental making of mind. Remembering entails re-membering, recreating a past than we cannot directly access. The contestations about the possibilities for "truth" or even for "knowing" at all are well documented in debates about narrative theory. It is evident that whatever our conclusions about the implications for both the practice of research or knowledge-making, and the practices of life itself, we cannot ever reverse the insight that memories are constructed, and that personal and collective histories are not inert substrata to our daily lives but are always alive and emergent in the present. This is the more pertinent quality of elephant memory for thinking about human remembering: not that they "never forget" but that they re-member what is no longer present. Elephants, like humans, are among the few species of mammals who attend to their dead in practices of mourning, covering the bodies of the dead among them with leaves and twigs, "burying" them and returning to these "graves", and gently turning over the bones of dead elephants when they encounter them on their migratory routes (see Figure 1.3).

The human past is never fully dead and buried, re-membered or restored to presence in individual life histories and collective narratives, and in cultural practices, rituals and inscribed in the built environment.

FIGURE 1.3 Elephants mourning

Reproduced by kind permission of the photographer, Clive Millar, Safari & Guide Services

Vygotsky (1978, p. 51) makes the link between the processes of individual cognitive memory and collective cultural histories:

> It has been remarked that the very essence of civilization consists of purposely building monuments so as not to forget. In both the knot and the monument we have manifestations of the most fundamental and characteristic feature distinguishing human from animal memory.

Memorials to the dead may take triumphant forms, most often in the celebration of conquests but also in the valorising of victims of conflict, those who gave their physical lives for the symbolic worlds that were once imagined futures and are now present realities. The postcolonial and post-apartheid landscape of South Africa is a highly contested symbolic space in which competing histories are articulated and fixed in memorial architecture. Bunn (1998, p. 94) notes that "South African monuments, to put it bluntly, find it almost impossible to be the bearers of collective meaning; instead they are inhabited by contradiction, because of their reluctance to imagine the idea of citizenship outside the boundaries of race". The cityscapes of South Africa are liberally dotted with statues erected in honour of colonial or apartheid "heroes", usually single male figures often on horseback. The first focal protest action of The South African "Fallist" Student Movement that began in 2015[5] was the demand for the removal of the statue of Cecil John Rhodes that stood in the most central prominent place on the campus of the University of Cape Town. While monuments may become invisible in their familiarity (Kros, 2012), the Rhodes statue became highly visible, valorising an oppressive racist colonial history and proclaiming the perpetual exclusion from and alienation of new cohorts of black students in the university. The removal of this statue symbolically initiated the ongoing project of decolonisation and triggered the subsequent country-wide protest actions focusing on multiple dimensions of alienation experienced by students on university campuses, including financial exclusions and pervasive gender-based violence. (See further discussion of decolonisation and the student movement in Chapter 5.)

Bunn (1998, p. 100) points to African memorial practices that are quite unlike the statues that seek to cement and concretise victory: "memorial performances, burial sites and ancestral presences, sacred groves and the ubiquitous stone cairns known as isivivane". Re-membering always entails loss and absence, and in memorials to the dead we attempt to substantiate this loss. At the intimate level of families, tombstones that bear the names of the dead simultaneously mark their presence and their absence, and graveyards are, in all cultures, considered places of sanctity and fear, connecting the worlds of the living and the dead. Marschall (2010, p. 41) remarks that, particularly in societies where recent history remains alive in personal memory, public memorials may be less about conquest and more about mourning those lost: "memorials as meant to evoke empathy and instil a sense of respect – both for the victims of the past and by extension for all members of the present society, as descendants of the heroes of the past". In this way memorials paradoxically inscribe absence in the present. A moving tribute to erasure and loss is the inconspicuous Bebelplatz memorial in Berlin, the empty white space sunk below ground that marks the place of the Nazi book-burning in 1933.[6] More recently, the apartheid regime of South Africa, similarly censored, banned and burned books that were considered incendiary (Dick, 2018) (see Figure 1.4).

This burning of books is a literal instance of attempted "evidentiary genocide" (Mangcu, 2011) but the desire to erase black culture, memory and history was all-pervasive in the apartheid project. Archbishop Desmond Tutu (2010, pp. 1–2) indicates the critical importance of memory for both individual and collective identity:

FIGURE 1.4 Apartheid-era book-burning
Reproduced by kind permission from the Archives of the University of the Witwatersrand

> My identity is very intimately linked to my memory. ... What I know is what I remember, and that helps to make me who I am. Nations are built through sharing experiences, memories and a history. That is why people have often tried to destroy their enemies by destroying their histories, their memories, that which gives them an identity.

The imaginative project of narrating our individual lives, making our identities, is thus entwined with the wider historical processes of collective life. In a concept that resonates with Jameson's (1982) notion of a "political unconscious", Freeman (2010) articulates how history lives on in the "narrative unconsciousness" of successive generations. Although this idea is not synonymous with the psychoanalytic unconscious, it does refer to an interior psychological domain and in that sense, it is a property of persons, constituting selves as including aspects of being that lie outside of our control, or knowing, outside of our agentic sense of who we are. Although Freeman refers to this as a "narrative" unconsciousness it is not always easily articulated and may not follow the recognisable shape or neatly analysed emplotted form. This concept is highly relevant for contexts where traumatic, conflictual political histories live on in the told (and silenced) stories of successive generations, particularly in the "hinge generation" (Hoffman, 2004) who did not themselves live through the events of political conflict but live in community with the older generation who did. Where past traumas are unspoken because they are unspeakable, they continue to haunt the present, creating a perpetual inescapable state of melancholia (Fine, 2018; Peterson, 2019a; Sharpe, 2016). In a provocative, melancholic and poetic eulogy, Christina Sharpe (2016) refers to post-slavery black life as "in the wake". She metaphorically evokes multiple allusions, oscillating between the past and the present to describe lives: (1) caught in the slipstream of the slave-ships, in disturbed choppy waters; (2) cursed by the wakefulness of insomnia, unable to recuperate, rest or dream; and (3) as watchful vigils for the dying or dead.

Interlocution: stories for others and ourselves

An individual life history is entwined with the wider historical processes of our collective life and the narrative self is never disconnected from the narratives of others, past, present and future. We tell the story of our lives to others and can only tell these stories in the words or language of others. The narrative is experience recollected and reformulated; the story worth telling (re)presents a life "worth living" and the dominant narratives of our contextual time and place will affect the content and form of what counts as worth living and telling. Scheibe (1986) suggests that stories of interest and by implication, lives worth living, are those characterised by adventurous movement rather than stasis. Bauman's (1996, p. 19) conceptualisation of identity as a "verb, albeit a strange one to be sure: it appears only in the future tense" traces the different travelling characters of pilgrims, strollers, vagabonds, tourists and players in the making of our (post)modern selves.

Scheibe (1986) suggests that sports and electronic gaming may provide alternative adventures to physical activities such as climbing mountains or swimming oceans or even the ultimate "adventure" of war but regardless of the particular form of action, it is the elements of risk (of danger or loss) and uncertainty that make for adventure. In narrative terms, these are activities worth telling; overcoming dangers, succeeding against the odds, and Scheibe argues that potential future audiences for the recollection of experience may influence the kinds of experiences we seek out in the first place. The speed and reach of sharing of experience has been exponentially accelerated by social media. However, those who have suffered the effects of centuries of colonial exploration and conquest would not frame this history in heroic or triumphant terms. Further, Mary Gergen (2001) observes that women are less likely to frame their narratives in the narrow terms of individual action, including talk of love, families and bodies in the telling of their lives. Despite the perpetual resilience of the trope of adventurer (particularly, sporting greats or celebrity icons) there is a counter-current to value diversity of experience and evaluate both lives and narratives in more capacious ways. A less-than-inspiring expression of this diversity may be the peculiar phenomenon of "reality TV" (which was of course only a precursor to social media platforms) in which the unadventurous domestic life features as an "adventurous" sphere in its own right, with audiences (admittedly, sometimes including me!) watching the cooking, gardening, renovating or parenting skills of others. An optimistic interpretation is that this genre reflects a more inclusive valuing of other domains of life beyond aggressively masculine and heteronormative activities. However, it may conversely simply reflect the increasing penetration of competitive consumerist values into the most intimate "private" spheres of family and personal life, creating homogenising improvement projects in the image of the market. We may, however, reject these dominant competitive narratives in favour of a search for alternative forms of "narrative integrity" (Freeman, 2010, p. 200) or coherence and relatedness. The making and shaping of human subjectivity thus entails questions of both "aesthetics and ethics" (Freeman, 2014, p. 9).

The critical point is that these questions cannot be answered independently; the life story is not self-contained, the "self" (or human subject) is not that which remains once we extricate the individual from the social. We know ourselves or come to be ourselves, through the stories of others, through the cultural texts that we encounter.

> In contrast to the tradition of the *cogito* and to the pretension of the subject to know itself by immediate intuition, it must be said that we understand ourselves only by the long detour of the signs of humanity deposited in cultural works. What would we know of love and hate, of moral feelings and, in general, of all that we call the *self*, if these had not been brought to language and articulated by literature? Thus what seems most contrary to subjectivity, and what structural analysis discloses as the texture of the text, is the very *medium* within which we can understand ourselves.
>
> *(Ricoeur, 1981, p. 143)*

In this view, the self is not a circumscribed entity set against or formed in opposition to the social world, rather, social and psychological realities are "interpenetrating" (Sampson, 1989, p. 4). The self becomes herself, can indeed *only* become herself, *within* traditions, in relation to historical and contemporary others. Through the internal regulative function of language, the individual subject is infused with the historical meanings of others and develops the split form of human consciousness that incorporates relational others through inner conversations, simultaneously creating resistances to and possibilities for change.

> Vygotsky's approach to inner speech is interesting precisely because, within a systematic psychological theory of mind, he describes important details of its structure and dynamics as underlying a crucial aspect of human consciousness, namely, that the latter is structured by relatedness and otherness. Instead of accounting for the unity of a unitary consciousness, he claimed that consciousness only comes in the form of the difference and borders with others, as foreign consciousness.
>
> *(Larrain & Haye, 2012, p. 4)*

Recognising these relational and historical processes in the formation and articulation of individual subjectivity raises critical questions about power, change and resistance. Which cultural traditions are valued and strengthened in the practices and language of everyday life? Which narratives of experience are worth telling and listening to? How are children and young people inducted into the "long detour of the signs of humanity deposited in cultural works"? (Ricoeur, 1981, p. 143). Education, particularly in the formal institutions of schooling, intergenerational conversations in families and, increasingly variable forms of community, including social media and other forms of global culture and media, may serve to empower and affirm particular dominant identities and subjectivities. In the context of reactionary regressive political movements across the globe, in which the Trump presidency is a florid instantiation of, rather than an extreme exception to, the general zeitgeist of the times, these forces of tradition take new menacing, mutating forms. However, without overplaying the "liquidity of modernity" (Bauman, 2000) these different domains and modalities of culture *are* increasingly heterogeneous and contradictory, offering children the material of multiple "traditions" in which to recognise and from which to construct themselves. In a more hopeful framing of the relations between the past and the future, the cracks and fissures, conflicts and synergies between multiple histories and contemporary cultural resources, may offer opportunities for resistances to alter the direction of the forward flow of these traditions.

From the possibly surprising quarter of neuropsychology, in his last lovely book before he died, *The River of Consciousness*, Oliver Sacks (2017, pp. 121–122) provides a strong argument for the linkages between history, memory, narrative and individual consciousness:

> Our only truth is narrative truth, the stories we tell each other and ourselves – the stories we continually recategorize and refine. Such subjectivity is built into the very nature of memory and follows from its basis and mechanisms in the brains we have. ... We, as human beings, are landed with memories which have fallibilities, frailties, and imperfections – but also great flexibility and creativity. ... It allows us to see and hear with other eyes and ears, to enter into other minds, to assimilate the art and science and religion of the whole culture, to enter into and contribute to the common mind, the general commonwealth of knowledge. Memory arises not only from experience but from the intercourse of many minds.

Likewise, Freeman's concept of the "narrative unconscious" (2010) suggests that culture (the stories of others' experiences) is internalised and lies deep within us rather than, as is typically suggested, in external social contexts that surround and influence persons. This is Vygotsky's cultural-historical subject. Hoffman's analysis in her book, *After such Knowledge* (2004), of the secondary transmission of trauma provides an account of how the events of history and the stories (both told and silent) of these events may come to structure our psyches. In South Africa, we often speak of "the legacy of apartheid" as referring to the continuing material effects of inequality and poverty. However, this legacy is also less material or tangible and forcefully felt in the visceral traces of racism that the segregationist system that no longer exists has left in our collective (un)consciousness.

Again, the idea that the individual is thoroughly social, that the self cannot naively be accessed outside of culture, resonates so strongly with Vygotsky's social self. Even when we are alone, there is always an audience for ourselves, an internalised social other for whom we perform, who is our interlocuter. As Fay (1996, p. 34) points out, "selves can stand outside themselves" and this means that "in an important sense a self can be other to itself". What is internalised with language is not just the contents of social talk, the cultural baggage (or capital) of history but, more importantly, *the structure of conversation*. The possibility of dialogue with one's self that enables new relations with the world through the child's "internal socialisation" or "social interaction with oneself" (Vygotsky, 1987, p. 254). This inner conversation creates a play of possibility and critical distance on our lives and our-selves.

In this process, it becomes possible to treat "oneself as another" as suggested by Ricoeur (1981), and we become simultaneously agents who act and are acted upon, narrators and protagonists, speakers and listeners, creating a social (dialogical) subjectivity in which we can only be our-selves through the incorporation of the internalised "other". In particular, our earlier remembered selves and projected future selves become subject to our present interpretation and action. Vygotsky (1997, p. 77) refers to this "dual nature of consciousness" and comments that, "the notion of a double is the picture of consciousness that comes closest to reality".

> I am conscious of myself only to the extent that I am another to myself, i.e., to the extent that I can again perceive my own reflexes as stimuli. In principle, there is no difference in mechanism whatsoever between the fact that I can repeat aloud a word spoken silently and the fact that I can repeat a word spoken by another.
>
> *(Vygotsky, 1997, p. 77)*

The possibility of dialogue with one's self enables new relations with the world, the possibility to imagine alternatives and transform the present parameters of our situation.[7] To the contemporary eye and ear, this formulation of consciousness as "doubled" is remarkably resonant with Du Bois's (1903) idea of double consciousness that was being developed at the same time across the globe from a very different position for differ-ent theoretical and political purposes. Du Bois (1903, p. 3) conceptualised this doubling of consciousness as created under conditions of oppression, entailing "a sense of always looking at one's self through the eyes of others". Paradoxically, this oppressive positioning offers those who are oppressed "second sight" and a clearer vision of the oppressor's world and being. However, it also conversely robs them of a sense of their own "true" selves and creates a psychic "twoness" of "unreconciled strivings; two warring ideals". Du Bois argued that for black people this psychic dislocation would be resolved through merging this "double self into a better and truer self". This "merging" does not imply the erasure of identities or the loss of "older selves" and, by implication, would not excise the internalised voice of the other nor reduce consciousness to a monolithic entity. Rather, when the oppressed self is not divided against itself through the internal regulation of a hostile other, a new emanci-pated consciousness enables her to fully participate as "a co-worker in the kingdom of culture" (du Bois, 1903, p. 3).

By the internalisation of language and the structuring of consciousness[8] as dialogical, culture not only forms us but is formed by us, enabling us to "create new worlds that were not there before" (Manganyi, 1973, p. x). We are both made by and makers of the world, both narrators and characters in our own life stories, subjected to histories and the subjects of present experience and future imaginings. Manganyi (1973, p. x) refers to the making of culture through these imagined possibilities and transformative actions as a "shared human necessity", definitive of rather than a superfluous variable addition to human life. This inner dialogue is "tensed" in that the split-subject both speaks and listens, taking up dual interlocutionary positions and talking to herself as both remembered and imagined characters with whom she is identified and yet differentiated. Speaking to our earlier past and future potential selves releases us from the exigencies of the immediate present and in the tension between past and future, intentional action and change become possible. Like all living creatures, we live in time, unable to turn back the clock but, unlike other creatures, we are able to imaginatively *talk* the clock backwards and forwards. Our inner stories are not woven through the simple accumulation of past events and experiences, rather they are continually reworked (sometimes consciously but mostly in less conscious ways). New patterns of significance and coherence emerge through perpetual cycles of remembering and forgetting in relation to current events and present interlocutors or audiences. While our bodies can only live forwards, our narrated inner stories are not linear, oscillating between past and future, forgetting and remembering and changing direction.

Narrative imagination and mediated futures

Even in the stories of ourselves that we might be expected to be intimately attuned to, the plot unfolds unpredictably, sometimes in line with the precipitous force of the past or our intentions, sometimes producing surprising twists that remind us that narrators have only partial control over how things will "turn out". Kierkegaard's best-known adage powerfully alerts us to the historical or retrospective quality of meaning-making: "Life is lived forwards but can only be understood backwards" (cited in Crites, 1986, p. 165). The significance of a particular event can only be identified in terms of its later effects. Good storytellers may be able to lead us to surprising and unpredictable outcomes but which nonetheless seem to have a kind of narrative inevitability or fictional truth about them. However, contrary to the explanatory aspirations of social scientists, life must continue to be "lived forwards", and may be unpredictable and often incoherent, unfolding in ways that often take us by surprise although we may all with hindsight be soothsayers.

While our bodies can only live forwards, our narrated inner stories are not linear, oscillating between past and future, forgetting and remembering and changing direction. Brockmeier (2009, p. 227), following Bruner, suggests that "narrative imagination" is definitive of human agency, generating new possibilities for action in the fusion of "the real and possible with the impossible". He argues that

> narrative is our most powerful device to 'subjunctivise' the world. It opens up the hypothetical, the possible, and the actual. It invites us to live in more than one reality, in more than one context of meaning, in more than one order of time"
>
> (Brockmeier, 2009, p. 228).

Living in more than one order of time, imaginatively entering the worlds of others, being prepared to tell and listen to stories of the past and generate storylines for imagined futures, is what makes (social and personal) change possible. This temporal movement is beautifully described in Eva Hoffman's (2009, pp. 63–64) words:

> And it is hard to imagine any human act or endeavour that does not depend on the ability to conceive the existence of time beyond the immediate moment. We could not have intentions or decide to go out of the house, or build dwellings or voyage across the sea and savannah, without some projection into the future. We could not recognise ourselves each morning as the person we were yesterday without the mind's constant reach into the past through memory. We could not even register the awareness of a fleeting moment without the perception of time's fleeting progress.

It is in this imaginative fusion of past and future horizons that we are least like our distant-cousin zebras. Each generation of zebras repeats the pattern of life of the previous generation, a pattern that is strikingly monotonous to the human eye. Zebras eat grass. They eat grass pretty much all day long, sleeping a mere 15 minutes in a 24-hour cycle. They eat grass in order to survive to eat more grass. And each generation does it just the way it was done before. Critics of theories that view human life as formed through the process of socialisation (even as complex and sophisticated a version of this as Vygotsky's sociogenesis) argue that this would imply an inevitable zebra-like repetition of history or, more accurately, an inability to create history at all, as each generation would simply reproduce the life of the previous one, clones rather than vibrant offspring. While of course in some senses we do reproduce the patterns of the past, we also escape them. A student of mine[9] sent me this picture after I had insistently reiterated in class for the umpteenth time, "We are not zebras!". This image whimsically suggests that human beings are always imaginatively, innovatively unravelling what is there in the world to remake it anew (see Figure 1.5).

The symbolic trope of the zebra, or its imaginative unravelling, represents the counterpart to the narrated, imaginative life of human beings, not just in its artistic inscriptions or the texts of literature, but as Molly Andrews (2014) alerts us in her wonderful book, in "everyday life", in the practices of learning and teaching, in magic tricks, as we age and in the child's play of climbing trees. We are not zebras! Of course this imaginative projection is not only innovative and positively transformative and entails "the insinuation of duplicity, ambiguity and suspicion into all

FIGURE 1.5 Zebra unravelling
Image sourced from www.Deviantart.com

speech, into human consciousness itself" (Cohen, 2013, p. 173). In this way, imagination is implicated not only in formulating possible futures but also, in re-presenting or making present, the past, in *making* of memories, revising and rewriting ourselves:

> A coherent life experience is not simply given, or a track laid down in the living. To the extent that a coherent identity is achievable at all, *the thing must be made*, a story-like production with many pitfalls, and it is constantly being revised, sometimes from beginning to end, from the vantage point of some new situation of the 'I' that recollects.
>
> *(Crites, 1986, p. 160, emphasis added)*

Conclusion

Vygotsky's conceptualisation of the human subject as articulated through the use of psychological signs, provides the psychological ground for contemporary theories of the self as a narrated and narrating subject. To conclude, what characterises Vygotsky's subject is her use of signs to regulate her actions and herself.

> Therefore thinking and speech are the key to understanding the nature of human consciousness. If language is as ancient as consciousness itself, if language is consciousness that exists in practice for other people and therefore for myself, then it is not only the development of thought but the development of consciousness as a whole that is connected with the development of the word. ... *The word is the most direct manifestation of the historical nature of human consciousness.*
>
> *(Vygotsky, 1987, p. 285, emphasis added)*

Both Vygotsky and narrative theory offer us a way of re-centring the human subject; however, this subject is not the naive, original locus of control, the individual disembodied mind set in opposition to the social world. The subject who carries on an inner conversation, who narrates her self into being, does so in the collective languages of culture, for a social audience, even if this audience is only herself, and she does so in time, in history. Unlike Bourdieu's (2006) fish in water, we are more like hopping frogs, amphibiously moving between possible worlds, able to be surprised by and imaginatively enchanted by the ordinary. Being storytelling animals is the most natural thing in the world but it is also simultaneously what makes it possible to alter nature, to imaginatively create new worlds and new modes of being both personally and, importantly, culturally and collectively. Paradoxically, therefore, the process of self-regulation by inner speech (Vygotsky, 1986, 1999), dialogue or conversation (Archer, 2000) inserts us into culture *and* inserts culture into us. Individual subjectivity or a sense of oneself as a person is thus formed in language which simultaneously constrains us *and* creates capacity for intentional action, through memory and imagination. The Narrative Subject is both *subjected to* the (historical) stories and meanings of others *and*, in the grammatical sense of the term, the *subject of* present and future-tensed utterances and actions.

Notes

1 An earlier version of this chapter was presented in a conference paper, "Cows, zebras and elephants: animal metaphors for thinking about narrating humans", *Narrative Matters: Narrative Knowing/Récit et Savoir*, Paris, France, 23–27 June 2014. By utilising different animals to highlight aspects of human subjectivity, I am following Vygotsky's argument that human (cognitive, social, cultural and affective) life emerges through the convergence of two lines of development: natural and social. In this way, he dismisses the ludicrous nature-nurture debate that has dominated psychology for decades and remains virulent in more serious contemporary framing of the issue such as that explored by Rutherford (2018) in *The Book of Humans*. If Vygotsky were able to offer an opinion, I think he would say that we are both like other animals and not at all like them, products of the long (pre)history of evolution *and* the faster-paced cultural revolutions of our own making. And it is these latter processes of change that most interested him and in relation to which his theory has most to offer.
2 Although stage theories have been widely critiqued (e.g. Burman, 1994/2008/ 2017) for describing and explaining psychological development as biologically determinist and progressively teleological, misrepresenting culturally normative processes as universal, these theories have in common a focus on processes of dynamic change. It is an error to consign these theories to a section of the psychology curriculum called "developmental psychology" or even "child psychology" assuming that psychic dynamism ceases once the destination of adulthood is reached. Further, while these constructivist "grand narratives" may be insufficiently fluid and flexible for some postmodern tastes, their attention to changing processes stands in contradistinction to the (still) pervasive focus on states that is adopted by statistical modelling and in the measurement of individual differences. Psychoanalysis, in particular, can be understood as a retrospective, historical or narrative project, in which development always remains incomplete and problematic, in contrast with the predictive and scientific pretensions of many disciplinary branches of psychology (Gergen & Gergen, 1986).
3 I am indebted to Ginsberg and Opper (1979) for this distinction between necessary and sufficient conditions for (cognitive) development as they outline in *Piaget's theory of intellectual development: an introduction*. This critical distinction is glossed over in the assertion of the standard objection that Piaget failed to acknowledge the importance of social interaction and cultural practices in the making of mind. Given that Piaget's early work focused very specifically on children's language and symbolic play, and he also wrote on the sociology of

childhood, it is ironic that this received view is reproduced without nuance in both introductory textbooks and in more advanced work in the field of cognitive science, and rendered almost incontestable. Piaget recognised that the social context is *necessary* or essential for children's (cognitive) development as without it no development would be possible at all. However, focusing exclusively on the social context is insufficient; a further surplus must be incorporated into a comprehensive account, a surplus of thought and action provided by the child herself.

4   Although Linda is conventionally a girl's name in English, this name is typically masculine in isiXhosa, Linda's home language. As is standard for African naming practices, the meaning of the name is still vividly accessible in the language rather than consigned to forgotten origins as is usually the case with English names. Linda literally means "wait" and may be a shortened version of a longer name such as "Lindokuhle" (waiting for the good).

5   The South African "Fallist" Student Movement is discussed in greater detail in Chapter 5. For accounts and analysis of this recent history from diverse perspectives, see, for example: Booysen, 2016; Heffernan and Nieftagodien, 2016; Langa, Ndelu, Edwin & Vilakazi, 2017; Rayner, Baldwin-Ragaven & Naidoo, 2017; Gillespie & Naidoo, 2019. For a view from Vice-chancellors, Jansen, 2017; and for opposing views, contributions by student activists themselves: Chikane, 2018; Chinguno et al., 2017; Motimele, 2019.

6   See Brockmeier (2002) for an engaging discussion of the emblematic monument to remembering and forgetting, the Bebelplatz book-burning memorial. My own attempts to find this memorial on a visit to Berlin, provoked by Brockmeier's article, initially proved futile. The glass ceiling through which one sees the empty memorial space below one's feet had been covered over by a modelling ramp for the Mercedes Benz Fashion week.

7   Lacan's (1977) mirror stage offers a way of thinking about this split subject as simultaneously enabling us to think about ourselves from the perspective of others who can see our bodies in the round. However, because this projected image is always only a two-dimensional representation, this condemns us to an inevitable sense of fragmentation and perpetual misrecognition (*méconnaissance*) in the eyes of others and in relation to the world of representation.

8   In Lacan's (1977, p. 41) extension of, rather than departure from, Freud's psychoanalytic theory, the "unconscious of the subject is the discourse of the other". Language informs not only conscious experience but also the contents of the unconscious and its very form: "The Other is (in some respect) the unconscious and the unconscious is (according to Lacan) "structured like a language. It therefore must be the case that the Other (at least in some sense) *is* language (or is *in* language, or comes out *from* or *out of* language)" (Murray, 2016, p. 147).

9   Thanks to Zehl Delport for the gift of this image.

2

THE SUBJECT OF PSYCHOLOGY

A narrative of Vygotsky and critical psychologies

Introduction

This chapter will bring Vygotsky into the narrative of psychology in the 21st century and explore explicit links to contemporary notions of subjectivity and critical ways of doing psychology: social constructionist, discursive and narrative psychologies. These fields are all extremely contentious, multiple, diverse and resistant to definition – perhaps, one could even argue, by definition! While some scholars (notably, Harré, 2000; Shotter, 2006) and many students of psychology label Vygotsky a "social constructionist" it will be argued that this retrospective historical conflation inaccurately characterises the theory in ways that conceal more radical implications for conceptual and political work in the present, and in projected social and disciplinary futures. There are evident links between the Foucauldian notion of "technologies of the self", discourses of power, and Vygotsky's concept of "self-regulation", and many contemporary critiques of Vygotsky point to the limitations of focusing on the dyadic form of mediation (Burman, 2017; Henriques, Holloway, Urwin, Venn & Walkerdine, 1984; Jovanović, 2015). The claim is that this restricted focus excludes questions of authority and power in the family and educational systems that may perpetuate and reproduce unequal societal forms and practices in the course of socialisation and "development".

However, the inverse challenge that Vygotsky presents for social constructionism and the relativist world view lies in the question of how self-regulating embodied individuals immersed in intergenerational social life nonetheless produce new, novel ideas and even emancipatory possibilities. Miller's (2011, 2014) elaboration of different orders of mediation provides an important extension of Vygotsky's notion of mediation, linking spoken instruction to the material world of cultural artefacts, and to macro-level social structures. Vygotskian theory has been inflected in particular ways in the South African context that may offer a productive challenge to ways in which he has been taken up in the USA, predominantly, in the field of CHAT (Cultural historical activity theory) and to the discursive, social constructionist turn that is more strongly represented by UK psychologists. Whereas CHAT and discursive approaches may erase or at least displace the subject (albeit in different directions), suggesting that we are in a post-human era, reading critical psychologies through Vygotsky's theory and re-reading Vygotsky retrospectively through contemporary theories offers a way to reconceptualise psychosocial realities and possibilities for change.

Social constructionism: relativist knowing and being

It is obviously beyond the scope of this chapter to offer a comprehensive overview of all the varieties of social constructionism or the related fields of discursive and/or critical psychology. In his introductions to two special issues of *Theory and Psychology*, the editor, Henrik Stam (2001, 2002), highlights the difficulties of comprehensively engaging with the multiple schisms in the field and suggests that these theoretical difficulties are complicated by, on the one hand, the conflation of social constructionism and postmodernism[1] and, on the other, a pervasive confusion of ontogenetic and epistemic considerations in the (anti)realist debate. The particular articulations of social constructionism, beyond the "weak consensus that … human psychological processes are conditional on the linguistic and cultural practices and structures of human communities" (Stam, 2002, p. 573) are contextually contingent, as the theory itself would suggest. However, beyond this "weak consensus" (and the stronger disagreements) we may yet be able to outline some key contributions, implications and limitations, particularly in relation to the discipline of psychology and to the concerns of this book with changing subjects.

In what has become a core text for many psychology curricula, Burr (1995/2003/2015) concurs that social constructionism is a highly contested terrain but provides a useful overview of key tenets. The world is not naturally given a priori but constructed through language and culture. Things that seems to be part of "nature" and, therefore, unchangeable, are historically and culturally inflected and demonstrably mutable. Our knowledge of the world, both common sense or as developed in the formal disciplines of the academy, does not re-present reality directly. The language and concepts that we use to interpret and explain experience are imposed on the world rather than derived from it, and different ways of knowing construct different worlds of experience. This conclusion typically leads to a relativist and anti-realist worldview: if "reality" can only be known through interpretive schema and the invented languages of culture or theory, it is never independent from and always relative to this meaning system.

These ways of knowing are developed and sustained in social interactions and through the formal institutional structures of society, e.g. families, education and in the economic organisation of work. Knowledge is therefore not neutral and is linked to the unequal hierarchal organisation of society. In other words, while all knowledge is relative, some knowledge is privileged and more highly valued. Bourdieu (1986) made the links between knowledge and power explicit by referring to knowledge as "cultural capital". Those who possess the dominant forms of cultural capital and are linked into powerful social networks ("social capital") are able to translate both what and who they know into socioeconomic capital. In this way, the world and the people in it are organised through these understandings that reinforce and perpetuate intergenerational unequal hierarchies and asymmetries of power.[2] Bourdieu's analysis of the "modern" capitalist system and its positioning of individual persons is a precursor to more fluid social constructionist versions of how power circulates in language and informs social worlds and subjectivity.

Multiple forms and flows of power

Class hierarchies and economic inequality remain stubbornly rigid, intransigent and globally pervasive. However, it is now clear that this structural oppression manifests in multiple ways in different geographical and historical contexts. An exclusive focus on material conditions offers limited resources for the analysis of subjectivity that is simultaneously raced, gendered and queered. Feminists and Black consciousness theorists and activists have demonstrated that although race and gender coincide with class, (the exploitation of women and black people is part and parcel of the capitalist system), the experience of being female and/or black exceeds and complicates a reductionist materialist view. Black feminists have also convincingly demonstrated that these categories are not additive (or subtractive) but "intersectional" (Crenshaw, 1991). Being black (or white) and female (or male) is a gestalt rather than sequential or alternating dimension of identity, even if some aspects become more or less salient at different times and in different contexts, in relation to different others.[3]

Hall (1996) describes this motility in identity as a process of identification and othering, connecting with, and distancing ourselves from, others. While this implies an "us" (with whom we identify) and "them" (whom we other), who is incorporated within or excluded from these designations shifts as these processes are fluid and negate conventional dualisms.

Mama (1995) argues that an exclusive focus on a single dimension of identity is inadequate to understand lived experience, particularly in the postmodern/postcolonial world.

> My own experiences as a feminist raised and educated as both African and European, as both black and white, and with intimate connections to a good many other places and peoples besides these has always made a nonsense of all these dualisms. ... I view the historically produced category of "black women" with the eyes of an insider and an outsider, seeing multiplicity and differences between and within individuals and the struggle to construct coherences and commonalities out of a potentially infinite set of possibilities.
>
> *(Mama, 1995, p. 13)*

Add into this mix, multiple lines of identity, class, sexuality, ethnicity, language, nationality, belonging to generational cohorts, living in rural or urban homes, and the intersectional possibilities proliferate. This complexity is further challenged by queer theory that rejects the notion of binaries altogether (even if along multiple intersecting lines). Queer subjectivities include many more than two genders or sexualities, and any other categories of identity can be similarly queered. The discursive and performative qualities of language mean that power circulates actively and more fluidly, positioning people in complex ways. "Poststructuralism proposes a subjectivity which is precarious, contradictory and in process, constantly being constituted in discourse each time we think or speak" (Weedon, 1997, p. 32). The socially constructed person is made, and makes herself, and is articulated in and through, these languages and discourses of power. Subjectivity is constrained but not determined by material conditions and, although multiple lines of oppressive power may coalesce, people also always possess and express the potential for creative resistances.

Psychology and discourse: disciplining and displacing the subject

The challenge of social constructionism and discursive theories to binary notions of the subject is highly pertinent to psychology. Despite the ostensible focus on a universal abstract individual, the project of psychology has always been concerned with variation and, in its popular interpretations, the uniqueness of each individual person. However, although these variations occur across a continuum, this is a spectrum with an average reference point, fitting the bell curve in which outliers are dismissed as aberrations. It could even be argued that this is the core business of the profession of psychology: the assessment and diagnosis of variation in relation to normative standards, differentiating healthy from unhealthy, and normal from abnormal ways of thinking, doing and being in the world.[4] Psychology, thus, has the effect of "inventing man" (Foucault, 1970) in its own image.[5] Although this construction of difference from the norm is construed as neutral, the "science" of psychology, particularly as exercised in its testing apparatus, is highly susceptible to misuse in support of discriminatory frameworks such as racism, sexism, hetero-sexism and transphobia in which difference is construed as deviance.

Methodologies for making the subject

The "object" of psychological enquiry has been the subject matter of philosophical or religious enquiries throughout history and ordinary people are constantly interpreting themselves and others. However, Foucault's (1970) "man" is invented and (re)made in and through the methods of science. In efforts to establish these scientific credentials, early psychologists sometimes adopted a more positivist stance than the natural scientists they sought to emulate (Danziger, 1990). In particular, the multiple variables at play in any psychological phenomenon necessitated complex experimental design to control conditions and isolate effects. Although behaviourist laboratories have shut up shop in many, if not most, places, the burgeoning quasi-medical field of neuropsychology and the new technologies of MRI and brain imaging make it possible to do what behaviourists argued was impossible: look inside people's heads. (But this does not mean that we can read their minds!) Beyond this particular sub-discipline and the walls of laboratories, it is the quantitative methods of statistics that have the greatest ongoing and pervasive influence on psychological methodologies.

Statistical procedures are presumed to be theory-free or neutral, the numbers reflecting the patterns, trends, averages and outliers in the population out there in the world. This results in a "cookbook approach" (Danziger, 1990, p. 152) to the subject of research methodology in which matters of conceptual or ethical controversy may be considered extraneous. This focus on techniques rather than content leads to what Danziger (1990,

p. 154) wittily refers to as a "methodological fetish" or "methodolatory". Einstein's delightful aphorism springs to mind: "Not all things that count can be counted, and not all things that can be counted, count."

In addition to a proliferation of research with little explanatory power, this approach works to whittle away and reduce the richness of people's lived experience and sense of themselves.

> This is not to say that quantitative methods necessarily make researchers dehumanise people, but there is a powerful tendency for the systematic fracturing and measurement of human experience to work in this way. That approach also fits with the surveillance and calibration of individuals in society outside of the laboratory.
>
> *(Parker, 2015a, p. 10)*

In the South African context both the "science" of neuropsychology and the associated fields of practice, traumatic brain injuries and forensics, and the statistical mapping of social trends, are considered high forms of cultural capital in psychology departments with the potential for cashing in on the market. Students often tell me that they "love research" in the abstract without expressing curiosity about anything in particular that they think we could know more about or know differently. Many also take on trust the apparatus and forms of professional practice, including testing, assessment, therapeutic contracts and definitions of (ab)normality. Psychology in our context is a strange mix of scientific research (predominantly quantitative in approach) and therapeutic practices that are often psychoanalytic in orientation and sometimes aligned with religious counselling and/or traditional healing practices.[6] Although ostensibly incongruous, these orientations address both the demands of the market and a pervasive romantic, nostalgic desperation for meaning and certainty. As Danziger (1990, p. 147) observes: "Quantitative psychological knowledge [is] a species of esoteric knowledge that [is] held to have profound social implications. The keepers of that knowledge were to constitute a new kind of priesthood, which was to replace the philosopher or theologian". Sanders (2010) explores the "complicity" of intellectuals (specifically in apartheid South Africa but his arguments apply now and elsewhere too) in wider processes of oppression. Knowledge generated in and legitimated by the academy has effects, "politically, socially, or in the *intimacy of mental colonization and the psychological inscription of the body*" (Sanders, 2010, p. 15, emphasis added). The discourses of psychology work at the most intimate level of people's sense of themselves and, particularly, of themselves in relation to others, positioning people (individually and collectively) on a spectrum of normality in ways that may have pernicious effects.

Qualitative methods: discursive and narrative resources

Qualitative methodologies from different paradigmatic frameworks are presented in social constructionist language, promising to avoid the ethical pitfalls of quantitative methods and, moreover, to contribute in progressive ways to emancipatory possibilities. From a phenomenological perspective, the focus would be on the ways in which people make sense of their experiences and themselves. From a more critical discursive perspective, attention shifts away from people's own (reported) meanings to how discourses of power are infused in people's talk and sense-making. Both perspectives assume the social constructionism of meaning but differ in adopting a "hermeneutics of faith or suspicion" (Josselson, 2004). Because persons and discourses are not mutually exclusive categories, research may be "bifocal" (Fine, 2018), combining attention to experiential narratives *and* social discourses and the politics of subjectivity (Livholts & Tamboukou, 2015). The project of discursive psychology might be broadly conceptualised as deconstructionist or critical and shifts attention away from the internal psychological plane:

> This movement represents a critical reflexive shift away from the search for mental paraphernalia inside each individual's head and towards a socially mediated and historically situated study of action and experience. This is an endeavour that postmodernism both encourages and sabotages.
>
> *(Parker, 2015b, p. 30)*

However, this correction to the worst errors of quantitative scientism and the rational self-contained individual by emphasising the social construction of the subject, may do little more than invert the problem. Danziger (1990, p. 195) cautions that we should not:

> now replace the naïve naturalism of the past with a simpleminded sociological reductionism. To say that psychological knowledge bears the mark of the social conditions under which it was produced is not the same as saying that it is *nothing but* a reflection of these conditions.

Switching focus from the psychic interior to the social exterior world does nothing to deconstruct the problematic binary framework in which social and psychological phenomena are construed as opposing realities. This split reality is not peculiar to psychology; social sciences such as sociology and political science are situated on the other side of the fault-line and so jumping the gap does not solve the conceptual problem. "[R]etaining dualism reproduced an equivalent but opposite set of problems for social theory, namely that the latter, in its turn, remained blind to the process of subjective change" (Henriques et al., 1984, p. 91).

Although, as will become evident, this is not a firm position, in his most social constructionist voice, Parker (2015c, p. 13) argues that psychological theories are "no more than *fictions*", implying that they are indistinguishable in truth terms from the narratives from any other source, grandmothers, journalists, artists, priests, rabbis or imams. While this may have the desired effect of questioning the false authority of methodolatry and challenging ethnocentrism, relativism taken to the extreme is self-defeating in that its own claims are likewise relative and thus indefensible (Fay, 1996). The relativist view is often further distorted in support of discourses of individual uniqueness that are pervasive both within and beyond psychology. Social *constructivism* (as opposed to constructionism) recognises that each individual person has a unique personal history that shapes her view on the world: interpretation becomes a matter of personal opinion that cannot be challenged as it is relative to the particular individual's own life which cannot be known or experienced by anyone else.[7] By asserting individual and cultural freedoms as beyond dispute, extreme relativism may serve to support the status quo, closing down debate about how things could be different in the world, with potentially regressive epistemic and reactionary political consequences.

Subjective histories and futures: the politics of people and psychology in contexts

Social constructionism coincides with and is compatible with postmodernism historically and epistemologically but the idea that culture (including language and other forms of symbolic representations and practices) shapes collective and individual life is hardly new. Migration, which is as old as human history, has always brought people into contact with others who do things differently, organise their social relationships in ways that seem strange to an outsider or, in the early anthropological vision, exotically interesting. Of course this interest in difference and otherness was (and is) very seldom expressed as innocent curiosity. The intensification of movement and conquest in the colonial project was infused with two apparently opposing but actually mutually reinforcing responses to difference: (1) as expressed in proselytising Christianity (or Islam), to convert people, to re-make "them" in "our own image"; and (2) to exploit the labour and belongings (particularly land and natural resources) of others who were considered less human. The social constructionist world view is a forceful challenge to the ethnocentric conversion narrative: all forms of cultural life are constructed in response to contextual demands, rather than given by god or nature and, therefore, equally valid. However, this strength is also its weakness as it is not necessarily as effective in countering questions of power that are most overtly articulated in the exploitative dehumanising discourses and practices that occurred (and continue to occur) in synergy with the conversion narrative.

In its most progressive articulations and most emancipatory implications, social constructionism widens our view on human life, enlarging the boundaries of what is thinkable, loosening the edges of psychological disciplinary knowledge and expanding the horizons of psychosocial subjectivities. However, Parker (2002) notes some troublesome political implications of relativism for those that are interested in going beyond interpreting the world to engaging with possibilities for changing it. First, acknowledging differences and variability in experiences and world views may splinter and diffuse the social justice agenda[8]; second, if power is all-pervasive and operates not only hegemonically but also in resistant forms of agency, this undercuts imperatives for systemic change; and third, the demand for reflexivity in the research process may recentre the subject of the researcher deflecting attention from the subjectivities and experiences of participants, leading to an unproductive tentativeness about "intervening" to change things in any way.[9]

Beyond social constructionism

The intractability of the relativist-realism debate is partly a semantic problem because the term "real" has multiple meanings: essence, truth and materiality (Burr, 1998). The first two senses of the term pose few difficulties for contemporary psychology. The view that there is a singular essential legitimate form of human life, or that there are reliable scientific methods through which to establish unquestionable truths or predictable laws about human behaviour, is no longer dominant and, in this sense, we might all be social constructionists now. Stam's (2002, p. 293) conclusion is that "most social constructionists are so in the epistemic sense, namely they are constructionist about descriptions rather than the entities that are so described". This may be a way to socially construct our cake and eat it!

However, even at the level of ontology (or the material that makes up the cake), there is still a social constructionist challenge for psychology. As Hacking (1999, p. 103) observes, "[t]here is a big difference between quarks and children". Because human life or ways of being a person in the world are culturally rather than (only) naturally formed, epistemological constructions, or ways or thinking and talking about the world, act back on this world of acting and experiencing, altering ontological (or at least experiential) realities. This is precisely the argument of social constructionism: people's experience of the world is shaped (in strong versions, determined) by discursive and cultural meanings. In Vygotsky's terms, "language-based tools 'backfire', that is, serve to influence the inner world of the subject" (Van der Veer, 1996, p. 256). Psychology is thus a rather strange discipline in which it is difficult to provide a straight answer to Hacking's question: "The social construction of what?". Surely children are different to quarks but perhaps the peculiarity of the discipline is that its rubric includes both quarks and children (and children too, include quarks!). The frequent confusion between these kinds of phenomena leads to the epistemological and political troubles that characterise the seemingly endless crises of the discipline. Hacking's "looping kind" of humanity takes embodied form and so he cautions us to always ask the question that is also the title of his book: "The social construction of what?".[10] People matter and, while they cannot be reduced to it, the matter that makes them up matters in the task of making up meaning about them.

Although he acknowledges the problematic implications of relativism, Parker remains a vocal advocate for discursive methodologies that expose the socially constructed forms of taken-for-granted realities. To avoid messy entanglements with the embodied experiences of human subjects, Parker advises that critical psychologists take texts (literally) rather than people as data. This certainly may be a possible route for some researchers: language and discourse are evocative and intriguing fields that demand rigorous enquiry. However, the claim that this is a kind of (critical) psychology is only sustainable if we link these discourses to persons. He suggests that his earlier version of discursive psychology as aligned with critical realism which he outlined in *Critical Discursive Psychology* (2002), before the "after series", was mistaken. But I think that he is mistaken about being mistaken! I agree that labels such as "critical realism" or "critical psychology" are not particularly useful and may in fact lead us down theoretical tracks to dead-end camps. But the task that Parker undertook in that earlier work (to link discursive psychology to structuralist accounts of the psychosocial world, notably those of Freud and Marx) clearly remains a central concern in his later writings. He explicitly links his critique of psychology to four theoretical strands: Marxism, feminism, Foucault, psychoanalysis, that (with the possible exception of Foucault) are antecedent structural accounts to discursive psychology, linking the realms of discourse and the material world. I do not mean to suggest that the material world (including bodies) is itself not also "socially constructed" (in the weak sense that we (humans) always attach meaning to this material world and indeed transform it). But bodies and brains, and trees and rocks are "indifferent kinds" (Hacking, 1999), indifferent to the meanings that we make of them, and different in kind to human psychic and social life.

Narrative psychology may offer a way to connect the embodied temporal processes of life with the discursive meanings that inform and derive from these experiences. Crossley (2000, p. 530) argues that the narrative approach "appreciates the linguistic and discursive structuring of 'self' and 'experience' but also maintains a sense of the essentially personal, coherent and 'real' nature of individual subjectivity". This reassertion of a (critical) subjectivity resonates with Archer's (2000) project of "resisting the dissolution of humanity" (or persons or selves). She argues that it is possible to distance oneself from both the enlightenment project of rational control and individuality *and* the postmodern dissolution of the human subject. She grounds the human subject in the embodied practices made possible by our evolution as a species and the evolution of the worlds (both natural and social) in which we live. Both Archer (2000) and Eagleton (2000) argue that prioritising discourse (or culture) over the material world of bodies and practices (or labour) creates not only theoretical but also political (or moral) problems. It is difficult to argue that ciphers or puppets can either be violated by or resist the discourses said to produce them.

Human embodiment

Decentring the human subject in favour of an exclusive focus on disembodied discourses negates the powers of nature and of the social world beyond language. This has the strange (surely unintended) consequence of prioritising[11] (in both senses of temporally antecedent and being most important) and centring the socially constructed space of words and language. For all the rhetorical flourishes of the relativist argument in the (in) famous death and furniture debate (Edwards, Ashmore & Potter, 1995), this seems little more than philosophical play. Tables may be beautiful or not, may serve as surfaces for eating feasts or for repairing broken cell phones in a workshop. Scientists and medics may argue about whether the time of death is when the heart stops or other organs fail, whether bodies kept functioning by machines or frozen in capsules are "alive" or not. There is immense cultural variation in the interpretation of the meaning of death and in the imagination of an "after-life". However, bodies still bump into tables and chairs, and anyone who has sat with the dying, or lost someone whom they love, knows that death may escape definition but overwhelms the bodies of both the dead and the living. I share Hustvedt's (2016, p. 350) observation:

> As vital as I believe language is to delineating both my experience and my perceptions and to the creation of an autobiographical narrative for my own life, which is indeed a form of fiction … I have found myself intellectually and emotionally dissatisfied with the airy postmodern subjects that seem never to put their feet on the ground.

Cromby and Nightingale's (1999) answer to their own question, "What's wrong with social constructionism?" is that it fails to address both the sources and effects of discourse in the material world, particularly in the body. While we all know that "race" is socially constructed, it is potently real, inscribed on our bodies and realised in experience. Patriarchy and capitalism similarly are clearly socially constructed, invented discourses that conceal and defend unequal distributions of power, with very real material effects. Perhaps Hacking (1999, p. 35) is right: "The metaphor of social construction once had excellent shock value, but now it has become tired".

Harré (2010) has proposed a hybrid psychology that draws together the two domains of meanings and molecules that he differentiated in his earlier work. The dual nature of psychology as a discipline is evident in that affinities with very disparate cognate disciplines may be easier to identify than unifying fields within the discipline: at one end of the spectrum, with the biological (and medical) sciences, and at the other, the arts and the meaningful practices of culture. "Hybrid psychology depends on the intuition that while brains can be assimilated into the world of persons, people cannot be assimilated into the world of cell structures and molecular processes" (Harré, 2010, p. 33). Perhaps a hybrid approach may be sensible and possible or perhaps it will prove a bridge too far as quite different methods must be used to understand these phenomena and sub-disciplines may develop in even more differentiated ways. Either way, it would be unwise for practitioners in either field to dismiss the importance of the other in understanding human life. "[T]o dismiss the neurological is to retreat to the comfort zone of familiar dualist schisms" (Cromby, Newton & Williams, 2011, p. 224). But to reduce all of psychology to this level of explanation would be equally problematic and there could be no better authority for this position than the world's most celebrated neuroscientist:

> The constructions of science or biology, may be lyrical, but are impersonal and theoretical. There is no "story" in the life of an orchid or earthworm – no *personal* story, no drama, no plight, no predicament. Therefore the art of storytelling, of narrative is not necessary for its description. But with human life, human nature, it is wholly different: there is drama, there is intentionality, at every point. Its exploration demands the seeing and telling of a story, demands a narrative structure and sensibility and science.
>
> *(Sacks, 2014, p. 527)*

Hustvedt (2016) provides a challenging and inspiring example of intrepid transdisciplinary travels, an artist delving into psychoanalysis, cognitive science and neuroscientific terrains with meticulous and rigorous attention to connections and divergences. She offers us a remarkably beautiful depiction of the peculiar synergy of bodies and discourses that make us who we are, not one thing or the other, nor one thing after the other, but embodied meaning-making creatures in the relational flows of life lived with others:

> Human beings are animals with hearts and livers and bones and brains and genitals. We yearn and lust, feel hunger and cold, are still all born from a woman's body, and we all die. These natural realities are inevitably framed and understood through the culture we live in. If each of us has a narrative, conscious and unconscious, a narrative that begins in the preverbal rhythms and patterns of our early lives, that cannot be extricated from other people, those to whom we were attached, people who were part of shaping the sensual, muscular, emotional rhythms that lie beneath what become fully articulated narratives intended to describe symbolically the arc of a singular existence, then each of us has been and is always already bound up in a world of others.
>
> *Hustvedt (2016, p. 335)*

It is a "grammar" of the body (or organism) that Harré (2010) suggests as the connecting tissue between molecules and meaning for a new hybrid psychology.[12] Bodies mutate and can be subjected to artificial manipulations of all kinds. Everyday practices constantly alter our natural bodies: shaving, dying, straightening or curling hair, make-up, perfuming and the tattooing and piercing of skin. Medical technologies enable pacemakers to do the work of bleeding hearts, some of us can move about on prosthetic limbs that are able to respond to electronic stimulation of the brain, implants can change our sexy curves and gender reassignment surgery can rename us and change our social relations in dramatic ways. Bodies are interpreted and crafted but they are pivotal in the making of meaning and exceed our control of the meaning-making process, inserting us into the material world of objects and others. The mutability of the body is not infinite: it may grow fatter or thinner, fitter or creakier, but always older, never younger. In theorising personhood from the margins of the discipline of psychology several decades ago,[13] the South African psychologist Manganyi (1973) centred the body as pivotal in the formation of human subjectivity and, hence, for our understanding of personhood and, in particular, the implications for "being-black-in-the world".

> The body is the nexus of all the fundamental relations (dialogue) which an individual person develops with others, with objects and with space and time. If the integrity of the body is violated, as it is has been in the case of black people, the other existential relationships also become distorted.
>
> *(Manganyi, 1973, p. 52)*

Embodied humanism: an African perspective in dialogue with Vygotsky

Erasmus (2017) frames her exploration of 'race' (the quintessential socially constructed category) as an engagement with "rehumaning our times" to "forge a new humanism for South Africa". Neither she nor I would claim that 'race' is any less real for being socially constructed and, thus, imagined new capacious notions of humanness may similarly be asserted as concepts worth realising. It strikes me as somewhat odd that just as some people are claiming their status as "human", the category is consigned to the post-phenomena litterbin of history. Humanism may be tainted by its colonial roots, but post-humanism seems to leave us with dirty bathwater rather than a squirming infant idea that might develop into something virile.

> For what I am calling humanism can be provisional, historically contingent, anti-essentialist (in other words, postmodern) and still be demanding. We can surely maintain a powerful engagement with the concern to avoid cruelty and pain while nevertheless recognising the contingency of that concern. Maybe then, we can recover within postmodernism the postcolonial writers' humanism – the concern for

human suffering, for the victims of the postcolonial state … while still rejecting the master narratives of modernism.

(Appiah, 1992, pp. 250–251)

Manganyi (1973) is quite clear that his treatise, *Being black in the world*, proposes distinct modes of being for black and white bodies due to our historical constitution through centuries of colonialism. His approach is not premised on the rejection of humanism but on the project of claiming it for new forms of theorising and living that may provide the threads from which to weave a critical, relational humanism.[14] The humanity that he theorises is embodied, temporal and relational. In broad paradigmatic terms, there are striking synergies with Vygotsky's theory of consciousness and aspects of the two theories are interwoven here, highlighting connections and differences between them. The dialogical structure of human life entails being in relation to, first (and foremost), one's own body as an "existential fact" and the "significance" of this fact in both sociological and psychological terms (Manganyi, 1973, p. 18). Vygotsky (1994, p. 41) similarly suggested that consciousness is a "correlative activity of the human body with itself". The body is not merely an inert substrate; rather, it "constitutes an individual's anchor in the world. It is the physical body which makes it possible for an individual to be given a name, to tell all and sundry who he is – to constitute lived space" (Manganyi, 1973, p. 52). In other words, it is only through the body that our social relationality is possible, particularly through communal networks of family, kin and geographical neighbourhoods. In Vygotskian terms, the formation of human consciousness occurs through the mediational other (parent, teacher, more capable peer) who links children into intergenerational social life. This relationality may be characterised by the mutual recognition or reciprocity implied in family interactions but Manganyi also outlines how we constitute one another in the racialised relations of "us" and "them" entwining interpersonal interactions in the fabric of political life.

In line with Vygotsky's emphasis on how the intentional meanings of historical others are inscribed in the tools and objects of culture, Manganyi outlines modes of life in which the objects of material culture create and re-create meaningful practices and constitute identity. But again, he extends Vygotsky's frame to explicitly include the effects of oppressive relations with the material world. The relational attitude and potential creative effects of engagement with cultural artefacts, performances and practices is juxtaposed with materialist consumerism that erodes the self through the insatiable desire for the acquisition of objects of culture. Finally, Manganyi theorises subjectivity as constituted in time and space, constrained by context and histories but activated and articulated in relation to anticipated futures. Each individual person "should be free to constitute his lived-space on the basis of an open appeal to time. An individual has potential. Time appeals to this potential to be realised freely. Such potential may only be realised in *freedom-in-security*" (Manganyi, 1973, p. 32, emphasis added). As elaborated in Chapter 1, the realisation of potential in Vygotskian terms is possible because the decontextualising power of language enables us to go beyond the here and now, imagining and planning for potential futures. Manganyi highlights how the oppressive conditions of colonial histories, poverty and systemic racism rob people of futures and thwart their potential: "In the absence of freedom-in-security, planning becomes existentially meaningless and the individual life becomes provisional" (Manganyi, 1973, p. 33).

Parker (2002, p. 135) argues that "a thorough-going discursive psychology is strongly 'anti-humanist' and is suspicious of the notion of a unified 'self' that lies beneath discourse". He rejects both humanism and relationality as liberal shreds of the enlightenment project rather than radical responses to questions of change, presumably because the macro-politics of socioeconomic structuring of society are occluded by interpersonal micro-level analyses. This may be the case in some neoliberal interpretations and applications but this is clearly not the relational humanity of African thought outlined above and a feminist lens reminds us that interactions between people do not take place in an apolitical sphere; the personal is always political. A critical humanist position need not imply a "unified" self nor imagine that discourse is overlaid on top of this anterior entity. On the contrary, appeals to the discursive realm to displace the grounding of experience in the body may perversely lead to a reification of language, discourse and culture that creates a new kind of orthodoxy that closes explanations in circular arguments that chase their own tails in the error of infinite regress. If meanings are inscribed in discourses (including discursive practices and objects) outside of us (which they surely are) who inscribed them there? If one is not to resort to the possibility of divine intervention, the only feasible origin of culture is in the meaningful actions of other humans living in history. This knotty problem seems to be produced by two conceptual confusions: psychological phenomena are processes rather than entities, and social discourses are not outside of and opposed to the interior subjective world.

Despite his resistance to humanism, his political commitments mean that Parker remains vehemently opposed to what he believes are the *dehumanising* effects of psychology's practices in scientific laboratories and therapeutic rooms. Although his critique of psychology continues to be infused with remnants of Marxist thought (even "after" everything), Parker relies on Foucault's more fluid notions of power, particularly disciplinary power as articulated in knowledge-making both within and beyond the academy. However, he concedes that even in this discursive scheme of things, embodied persons seem to make a (ghostly) appearance: "Foucault ... sometimes seems to call for spontaneous acts of resistance that presuppose an inner subject, or at least *a body* with some remaining untamed pleasures" (Parker, 2015c, p. 32). Our bodies may be "docile" much of the time but they remain enervated to the ways in which they are subjugated, even when resorting to uncomfortable strategies of resilience, always potentially resistant and infused with transformatory potential.

From a Vygotskian point of view, the potential for this transformation lies in the mediation of the outer social world *and* the inner psychological world, the membrane between which is a thin, permeable skin. The psychological plane of consciousness and the natural processes of perception, attention and memory are *transformed* through the cultural line development and, conversely, the domain of cultural life is imagined and enacted by embodied human persons.

> The first law of the development and structure of higher mental functions which are the basic nucleus of the personality being formed can be called the law of the *transition from direct, innate, natural forms and methods of behaviour to mediated, artificial mental functions that develop in the course of cultural development*. This transition during ontogenesis corresponds to the process of the historical development of human behaviour, a process as we know, did not consist of acquiring new natural physiological functions, but in a complex combination of elementary functions, in a perfecting of forms and methods of thinking, in the development of new methods of thinking based mainly on speech or some other system of signs.
>
> *(Vygotsky, 1998, p. 168)*

A Vygotskian narrative of mediated selves

In tune with the "turn to language" long before psychology twisted itself into this frame and before the stories of discursive or narrative psychology began, Vygotsky's theory places language at the heart of human life as the animating force of human subjectivity, joining together and entwining the natural and cultural lines of development as described above. His conceptualisation of language foreshadows both structuralism and poststructuralism or postmodernism.

In this respect the word's meaning is inexhaustible. The word acquires its sense in the phrase. The phrase itself, however, acquires its sense only in the context of the paragraph, the paragraph in the context of the book, and the book in context of the author's collected works. Ultimately, the word's real sense is determined by everything in consciousness which is related to what the word expresses. According to Paulhan, the sense of the Earth is the solar system, the sense of the solar system is the milky way … We may never know the complete sense of anything, including that of a given word. The word is an inexhaustible source of new problems. Its sense is never complete. Ultimately, the sense of a word depends on one's understanding of the world as a whole and on the internal structure of personality.

(Vygotsky, 1987, p. 276)

In this, Vygotsky seems to leapfrog straight into the heart of contemporary linguistic theory, foretelling both Chomsky's deep and surface structures *and* the developments of socio-linguistics that focus on language in use (parole) rather than as a structural system (langue) and even points to the deconstructivist emphasis on *play of difference* in a system that makes for meaning. (It is the system not associative meanings or referents that creates the possibilities for meaning.) From Vygotsky's perspective, this system of meaning-making is not idiosyncratic and can only function in social "webs of interlocution" (Taylor, 1992) where meanings are shared, providing the nexus for the "interpenetration" (Sampson, 1989, p. 4) of social and psychological life in the formation of the subject.

Stam (2002, p. 574) suggests that Vygotsky (and Mead) "made constructionism possible", in other words, that his constructivist theory of interpsychological development and the internalisation of the symbolic tool of language was antecedent to the more thoroughly *social* constructionism of the late 20th century. This may well be true but I would argue that in line with a more fluid understanding of the sociohistorical trajectories of knowledge-making, the relation is more complex and that Vygotskian theory also enables us to read social constructionism retrospectively, as if it were a later rather than earlier development. Stam (2002, p. 574) notes that, in social constructionism (and I would add, similarly, in the CHAT version of activity theory), "the internal relation of thinking and speaking has been downplayed in favour of an external relation between speakers". In Vygotsky's conceptualisation, consciousness is not evacuated into the social world but transformed through the convergence of the natural and cultural lines of development.

A narrative take on Vygotsky's self-regulating inner conversation extends our sense of what it means to be the subject and object of our own behaviour; the stories that we tell ourselves not only regulate our actions in the world, but generate the contours of our being, our selves, our subjectivity. This formulation of the self in language has elsewhere led to a view that there is no subject, no psychological reality, only language that construes our experience "as if" there were a self.[15] I have argued that it is fallacious to conclude that the subject is a mere artefact of language and that this conclusion is premised on a separation of the realities that Vygotsky's theory brings together: the world of language and meaning is part of the natural world, part of our species-specific embodiment: "when Vygotsky speaks of a uniquely human psychology defined by higher mental processes, he shifts the traditional boundaries of psychology and, in effect, initiates a discipline or domain of enquiry that lies at the interface between nature and culture" (Miller, 1989, p. 11).

This conceptualisation of subjectivity as both embodied and symbolic is commensurate with Archer's (2000) position outlined earlier in which she rejects the notion of a rational locus of control in the enlightenment subject but simultaneously refuses a full postmodern erasure of the subject. Her version of human subjectivity emerges in the embodied practices made possible by our evolution as a species and the evolution of the worlds (both natural and social) in which we live. From a narrative perspective, Freeman (1993, p. 70) likewise suggests that the while we may make our-selves and our worlds in language, these imaginative constructions are no less "real" for that: "yes, self and world *are* fundamentally products of the imagination. But no, they are not *merely* imaginary, in the sense of being essentially fictional creations".

The Vygotskian notion of mediation typically refers to face-to-face interaction between adults and children. The younger generation is inducted into the world by parents, teachers or older children, (Vygotsky's, (1978) "more capable peers"). Ways of doing and being are transmitted partly through demonstration and imitation but, most importantly, through verbal instruction that directs and guides the child's attention and action. This is the full force of the process of mediation: the child (or learner or initiate) does not act independently (or spontaneously in Piaget's terms) on the basis of her own understanding or grasp of the situation but, rather, acts under regulation, *on the basis of the other's understanding*. Vygotsky's famous law of sociogenesis proposes that cultural development occurs first, interpersonally and then intrapersonally. Self-regulation therefore originates in social interaction and it is the language of the other that becomes the inner voice of private speech. In addition to talk that has didactic or at least overtly directive or instructive purposes in reference to immediate daily life, *all* cultures are storytelling cultures. Canonised narratives (such as fables or fairy tales) are passed down by word of mouth, carrying meanings and values from the past. But narratives are also generated spontaneously in the context of everyday life to capture and communicate the ordinary shared events and experiences of "what happened at school" or "who did what to whom". Children's worlds are full of stories: sometimes fun, sometimes scary, always meaningful!

The processes of change in individual lives are most evident in children's development as they grow up and take on adult roles in the social world. From a range of perspectives, (including trajectories of empirical and theoretical work initiated by Piaget and Freud) developmental psychology has mapped the stages of ontogenetic development as unfolding towards adulthood within a social context that is assumed to be relatively stable. The adults in children's worlds model the social roles into which each successive generation will grow. In these formulations, developmental psychology is ahistorical and apolitical, occluding both the agentic actions of persons and the structural effects of society that pre-exist each life. By contrast, individual lives are lived in time, growing up and growing old (with narrative beginnings, middles and ends) in the flows of changing social patterns and collective histories. The making of a personal identity in the recollected memory of experience is not neatly contained within the passage of the individual life but is linked to the historical passage of time, the histories of others who have lived before us in time, and communicated through intergenerational conversation and shared life experiences.

Orders of mediation

Miller (2011) proposes that Vygotskian theory implies two additional inter-related orders of mediation or ways in which the child's world is shaped by intergenerational history: the second order of mediation is instantiated in cultural tools, and the third, in the social structures and institutions by which society is organised. (Both of these orders of mediation are engaged with or implicit in Manganyi's theorisation of relational being outlined above.) To illustrate these orders of mediation and how they work together, I will use the example of a hammer.[16] The hammer's function is inscribed in its design: it is *for* banging. Any small child who picks up a hammer quickly discovers this and parents are equally quick to contain the possible consequences, "Hammers are for hitting nails not people!". And hammers are ordinarily not for children but for adults, and while the toolboxes of many households may contain a hammer, it (and various technological advances on its original design) is also a standard tool of the trade for builders of houses and skyscrapers and all kinds of physical structures in between. But the hammer in the hands of one person is only one part of the collective action necessary to make the exceptional built environment of human settlements and, particularly, cities. The use of this tool (and others), designed to be held and wielded by an individual human hand, is co-ordinated or regulated at the social level in collective patterns of action, subsumed as one small cog in the functioning of national and global economies. The young child who learns how to use a toy hammer to slam shaped objects into their respective holes or the slightly older child who assists a parent to hang a picture with a "real" hammer, is learning about her own physical world and hand–eye co-ordination, about actions and consequences, about objects and people. But she is also simultaneously being introduced to the wider mediated world of tool use and the social structures of labour.

In much the same way as the hammer concretely exemplifies these orders of mediation, narrative functions at multiple levels to transmit intergenerational knowledge and modes of being. In the telling of and listening to stories, perhaps in culturally prescribed settings such as fireside oral histories or bed-time story reading, the voices of adults in dyads or larger communal conversations carry the meanings of history, typically as instructions for the regulation of behaviour and social interactions. However, Valsiner & van der Veer (2014) emphasise that mediation is not solely dependent on the physical presence of another person (or her voice) as each child must construct her understanding for herself. The meanings of the absent "other" are however not entirely absent. The second order of *narrative* mediation is the inscription of meaning in cultural texts, most obviously through the technology of writing in books but also in other forms and modalities such as film, media, dance, art and music. The making of these cultural artefacts entails technological know-how and symbolic or artistic skill and expertise, but can be "used" with relatively little explicit verbal instruction. These narrative objects are open to "anyone who can read" (Ricoeur, 1981, p. 192) and can be appropriated by each generation of new audiences in the making of personal and collective meanings for living their lives. The processes of generating and engaging with these cultural objects or narrative artefacts occur within a third order of mediation, which we might think of as the discourses that circulate in society and constitute the social structures that organise and regulate social life. The transmission and internalisation of these discourses of how the world works may be formalised in the disciplinary traditions of knowledge in educational institutions, serving to frame and legitimate certain cultural artefacts rather than others (second order mediation) and transmit these forms of knowledge through expert instruction (first order mediation). This transmission of knowledge (art and science) is enabling in that each generation does not have to reinvent wheels or hammers, or theories of relativity, afresh. This is the way in which culture is not only transmitted but also created and re-created, changing across time and place as new subjects articulate its form and content in new contextual conditions. However, these discourses may not provide incontrovertibly positive resources for all people. In much the same way that the social structures that organise collective tool use may be inequitable and exploitative, discourses or grand narratives may serve to reinscribe and validate various forms of inequitably distributed power such as class, race or gender, rendering the mediated world "natural" and inevitable. Small children may learn that hammers are "boys' toys" laying the foundations for later life in which particular gendered, raced and classed bodies are the ones who are expected to hammer things into existence under the instruction of others. Construction sites become buildings that are then inhabited and enacted in socially sanctioned and culturally accepted ways. In the home, each family enacts or resists gendered patterns in kitchens and the relaxing spaces of lounges and bedrooms, and over dining-room table talk. Economic power buys occupation of the corner office or the penthouse suite, reflecting social status. In most countries, and certainly in South Africa, growing homelessness and the failure to provide low-cost housing reflects not a lack of physical resources or limited tools or skilled labour but the highly unequal socioeconomic structure of society and the political priorities of those in power. Questions of what is built where, why, by whom and for whom entail many more possibilities and dangers than the initial question solved by the invention of the hammer: how to intensify the strength of the human hand to act on and create shelter from the natural world.

In summary, mediation is effected by the simultaneous articulation of these different orders: (1) interpersonal social interactions in which language plays a crucial communicative role; (2) the sociohistorical trajectory of the development of the tools (artefacts) of culture that transforms the natural world (in Marx's sense of "labour"); and (3) the consequent structural formations of society (or relations of production in Marxist language) that regulate social interactions and organise tool use. However, we do not only internalise the discourses of society and enact the roles or take up the positions that social structures prescribe for us; our actions are not completely constrained by the design of the tools that we use nor are our-selves solely informed by the cultural texts available to us; we do not always listen to our mothers or our own internalised voices! People also generate these very narratives, make these tools, form and transform the complex social networks that we call "society".

Conclusion

For those interested in change, the three orders of Vygotskian mediation suggest various entry points for theory and activism: in dialogical exchange, in the creative construction of new objects of knowledge and practice, and in resistance to and reconstruction of institutional social formations. Although the impetus for radical change may appear to lie in subversive texts or the circulation of discourses in the virtual world, or in mass movements that take to the streets, these actions can only be effected by human agency: "culture cannot creep into the system from the bottom up but must march in at the top and annex the system of self-regulation" (Miller, 1989, p. 9). In other words, no change to social structures or to the lived experiences or subjectivity of individual persons can happen without animating agents who imagine, plan and act in the world. What makes this possible, despite the powerful discursive effects to which we are subjected (and subjugated), is that the subject is an embodied, dialogical, narrating person in whose mouth and mind new versions of herself and the world may be made in the old stuff of language. Discourses may float in the ether but dominant and counter-narratives are told and lived by embodied persons in relationship with one another, living and breathing, talking and acting in time. The language of Vygotsky's subject is inside her head and for this reason she has a say in what happens to her and what she does in the world.

Notes

1 Appiah (1992) highlights a similar problematic conflation of postmodernism and postcolonialism that complicates engagement with these ideas even further, particularly in geographically and intellectually colonised territories, such as the field of psychology in South Africa.
2 Although the social constructionist argument includes the natural sciences, this is a larger, contentious debate and I have, therefore, confined my argument to disciplines that focus on psychological and/or social life as the central concerns of this text.
3 The recognition that there are multiple ways to be a person in the world leads to questions of authority in speaking and writing about these realities; who gets to say what about whom? Appiah's (1992, 2005, 2006, 2018) opus of work on identity troubles the boundaries of identification and othering

(Hall, 1996). Fay (1996) explores whether "one has to be one to know one" and in his exemplary expression of the classic form of academic argument, concludes yes and no. These issues are obviously imperative for psychologists who are explicitly engaged in the business of making knowledge about other people. This debate far exceeds the bounds of this text; however, I will attempt some further engagement with this conundrum in Chapters 5 and 6. In the context of the South African Student Movement and in the context of South African society that is unambiguously *not* postrace, the answer to Fay's question is, for many people, an unambiguous: yes!

4 Psychoanalytic theory is an important exception to this binary frame in that the same unconscious processes that constitute the developing psyche in functional, socially adaptive ways may also cause psychic distress in later life and require unravelling through therapy. Typically, rather than this serving to normalise psychological troubles or shifting attention to the conditions of society that may contribute towards this psychological dis-ease, the implication is to render all of us in need of therapeutic intervention. Conversely, in its articulation of the connections between psychological and social troubles, the Frankfurt school (including psychologists such as Adorno, Erich Fromm and Wilhelm Reich) located both the origins and solutions to these troubles at the societal rather than individual level. The contemporary field of Marxist psychology that emerges from this intellectual tradition is typically (and perhaps surprisingly for outsiders) strongly associated with psychoanalysis, linking the social and unconscious domains of human life. Instantiating this theoretical interface, the second Marxism and psychology conference held in Mexico in 2012 provided an international forum for some of the key debates. (For a helpful overview of this event that serves as introduction to the problems and possibilities of conjoining these theoretical fields, see Painter, 2012.)

5 Appiah (1992) outlines the parallel "invention of Africa" that served the colonial imaginary well in extending and establishing the reach of industrialisation and subsequently global capitalism. Many have argued that these processes were symbiotic: the invention of the ostensibly universal "man" of psychology and the social sciences simultaneously entailed the invention of the sub-human "other".

6 In South Africa, the training of professional psychotherapists happens in academic psychology departments. I am aware that this is not the case in the UK and this sometimes means that the "psychology" at which the critique of Parker (and others) is levelled is a somewhat more narrowly defined discipline. In particular, although cognitive behavioural therapy (CBT) and other approaches proliferate, the psychoanalytic orientation is a dominant rather than marginal framework for practice and (neo)Freudian theory is an integral part of any psychology curriculum in South Africa.

7 This meaning of constructivism distorts the origins of the term in a very different psychological tradition. In Piagetian (and Vygotskian) theory "constructivism" means something antithetical to this sense of solipsistic individuality, describing species-specific universal mental processes, shared by all people, regardless of time or place, that construct human intelligence.

8 The argument that emancipatory politics requires a unified focus was entailed in what is now referred to as the two-stage political process in South Africa in which the first and primary project was to deracialise society and, in particular, for black South Africans to take control of formal political and institutional structures. The second phase of liberation would then address questions of

socio-economic inequality and other dimensions of oppression such as gender. Current conditions of gross inequality and widespread gender-based, homophobic and transphobic violence provide an empirical challenge to the effectiveness of this strategy, and the agenda of new political movements such as the Student Movement is increasingly articulated in intersectional terms.

9 See the discussion of these dynamics of power in the educational process in Chapter 6, and the caution from bell hooks (1994) that teachers who are too cautious about their own power in classrooms may inadvertently disempower their students.

10 The medical procedure of an "awake craniotomy" provides a dramatic demonstration of the neural processes of the talking, meaning-making subject. *The Guardian* (23 December 2018) reported that at a public hospital, Inkosi Albert Luthuli, in Durban, South Africa, surgeons operated to remove a tumour on the brain of jazz guitarist, Musa Manzini. Not only was he conscious during the operation and able to talk to the surgeons but he played his guitar while supine on the operating table so that they could carefully monitor the effects of their excisions. The physical precision of the surgeons' hands and instruments in combination with the talking music-making person ensured that after they closed the flap of skin over his brain, it was not just his body but his person, Musa Manzini, the musician, that was restored to wholeness.

11 Archer (2000) highlights the double meaning of "priority": temporally prior or antecedent, and of importance or significance. She argues for the priority of *practice*, in both senses, in the perennial agency-structure debate.

12 The evolutionary psychologist Plotkin, (1994), frames the relation between the instincts of the human body and intelligence (or, in Vygotsky's terms, the natural and cultural lines of development) as a "nested hierarchy". In contrast to the oppositional Cartesian split, it is the body and its instinctual functioning that makes mind possible.

13 Manganyi's context is not incidental in his development of a complex psychology in which the body is so central long before the currently fashionable notion of embodiment and the turn to affect. In his 2016 memoire, *Becoming a black psychologist under Apartheid*, he describes how he was barred from the established sites for supervised internships on the grounds of his race. Under apartheid, it would have been unthinkable for a black intern psychologist to attend to white clients and no psychological services were provided for black people. Instead, he was assigned to work in a neurology ward in a public hospital. By virtue of his black body, Manganyi was turned away from conventional psychological practices to focus on the brain and somatic processes of psychic life. In this way, his thinking is informed by, on the one hand, the politics of discursive constructions of the raced body and, on the other, by a focus on the substratum of natural physical processes through which minds work.

14 See the discussion of "ubuntu" in Chapter 3 for further discussion of this African conceptualisation of dialogical, relational subjectivity.

15 Harré's (1998) "self" is a grammatical fiction, a way of talking about something that doesn't exist, imposing a unity on three disconnected versions of the self as (1) a collection of traits; (2) others' constructions of me (I can only be an object in the gaze of the other); and (3) a curiously ahistorical locus for viewing the world.

16 Miller wonderfully illustrates these orders of mediation using the example of a pair of scissors (see 2011, pp. 397–404). The hammer is a less than original

example for explaining the qualities of human action, having been extensively elaborated on by Heidegger in his formulation of the processes of human "being". Heidegger's hammer is simultaneously "ready-to-hand", a material, functional object that elicits and facilitates particular kinds of practical action, and "present-at-hand", composed of and constituted by a totality of referential meanings that locate both makers and users in relation to the object in a field of action (Cerbone, 1999).

Conceptual tools from the south

Changing the subject of psychology

3

UBUNTU

Reconceptualising personhood

Introduction

Current debates in South Africa (that have resonances elsewhere) about the decolonisation of the academy, in general, and psychology, in particular, are framed in terms of demands for the indigenous genesis of knowledge-making and the relevance of such knowledge to the concerns and needs of the contemporary social world in which we live, learn and teach, and work. Resistance to economic and political colonisation is rightly coupled with resistance to the totalising effects of knowledge developed elsewhere for different purposes that is asserted as universally explanatory. The project of developing new (even if not entirely novel) bodies of knowledge and forms of practice is, however, complicated by the necessity of using the very disciplinary tools of the established theoretical canon that is the target of critique. In this way, both the content and form of disciplines are perpetuated, reshaped only minimally by the inflections and accents of new voices, or by extension or limitation in empirical application to new contexts. This is not to suggest that there is nothing to be gained by these incremental adjustments, particularly in relation to the learning and teaching of psychology for new cohorts of students. It is, however, unlikely that this process will lead to a Khunian-type paradigm shift or enable the construction of a decolonised or "Africa(n) centred" (Ratele, 2017) psychology. These more radical possibilities are currently being creatively and contentiously explored by a number of contemporary South African scholars, at least partly as a reaction to the demands of the South African

Student Movement (#MustFall) that gained momentum in 2015 and often in public dialogue in the media (see discussion of these developments in the third section of the book, particularly in Chapter 5). This political and intellectual project is in motion and offers new possible horizons for knowledge-making, curriculum and pedagogy.

Chapters 1 and 2 have provided a broad reframing of the human subject and the discipline of psychology in Vygotskian and narrative terms. In this chapter, I adopt a more specifically focused approach by utilising a core theoretical concept from (South) African philosophical thought, "ubuntu", to rethink the subject of psychological enquiry by placing it in dialogue with Vygotskian theory. As is being argued throughout this book, although Vygotskian theory is widely utilised in educational applications, it is not centrally deployed in delineating the subject of psychology. Similarly, while the ethical implications of ubuntu are well known and clearly important, the concept offers a broader theoretical contribution that generally remains unrecognised. Ubuntu (Umuntu ngumuntu ngabantu[1]) literally means that a person becomes a person *through* others. This idea of individual persons being relationally constituted resonates very clearly with Vygotsky's notion of sociogenesis and theories of relational or dialogical selves (e.g. Bertau, 2014; Hermans, 2001). The chapter will draw together these perspectives suggesting remarkable synergies between ancient African philosophy and a theory of psychology developed in the early decades of the Soviet Union, offering resources through which to reframe what is understood as "psychological" in the Western tradition. I suggest that both Vygotskian theory and the African concept of "ubuntu" provoke and enable more fundamental revisions of our disciplinary parameters, potently reconceptualising the subject, or the ontological phenomenon under investigation. In a nutshell, the synergy between these approaches lies in a reformulation of the relations between individual and social realities, or the psychological and political domains of experience and epistemology, offering possibilities for the required paradigmatic shift.

Psychology and apartheid: service, resistance and the aftermath

The colonising effects of particular strands of psychological theory and practice have been particularly pernicious in the South African context; I think here of psychometrics and related practices of measurement, classification and diagnosis. The history of IQ testing is implicated in racist (and sexist) ideologies worldwide but very overtly so in the South African context in which the science of psychology was expressly coupled with religious discourses to legitimise the discriminatory and segregationist system of apartheid.[2] In the clinical domain, assessment is similarly framed by dichotomous constructions of (ab)normality that can be identified by diagnostic categories to inform individual treatment. The complicity of clinical psychologists in the implementation of apartheid and other authoritarian systems, particularly in contexts of conflict or war, is well recognised. For example, psychologists with official backing from the APA (American Psychological Association) participated in devising and implementing interrogation and torture tactics such as those utilised in the American Abu Ghraib prison particularly post September 9/11 (see for example, Riesen, 2015). In South Africa, psychologists administered electric-shock conversion therapy for gay white men in the apartheid-era defence force (see for example, Kaplan, 2001) and often worked alongside medical doctors in the assessment of political detainees, effectively legitimating torture and both physically and psychologically abusive interrogation techniques. The complicity of the medical profession was dramatically exposed in the death in detention of Stephen Bantu Biko in 1977; medical doctors Lang and Tucker had examined the detainee shortly before his death and failed to provide medical care or register any objection to the clear evidence of systematic physical torture. Active intervention could have saved Biko's life. The extent of, particularly physical, abusive interrogation practices was documented in a dossier compiled by Dr Wendy Orr in the late 1980s and the complicity of medical professionals was also further corroborated in a subsequent study by NAMDA (National Medical and Dental Association) (Dowdall, 1991). Perhaps the most chilling complicity of the medical profession is personified in the medic Wouter Basson who led the apartheid state's project for the development and use of chemical weapons (earning him the label "Dr Death") .

Psychologists may have been less explicitly implicated than their medical counterparts in the implementation of torture and abuse of human rights under detention and beyond in the brutal policing and military control of townships and everyday life for black South Africans. But the profession's complicity was inexcusably manifest in

> bland inattention to the human and psychological effects of the oppressive social engineering experiment of apartheid, and in the face of evidence of torture. ... Attempts to raise these issues at congresses of the Psychological Association of South Africa [SAPA] raised heated arguments, walk-outs by sections of the audience and charges that certain members were attempting to intrude politics into what should be a professional forum.
>
> *(Dowdall, 1991, p. 53)*

In 1961, a break-away "whites only" organisation, the Psychological Institute of the Republic of South Africa (PIRSA), was formed, evidence that a broadly anti-racist stance (at least in relation to membership) had prevailed within the existing professional body.[3]

There were always some pockets of more radical (although incomplete) resistance to the disciplinary effects of the discipline within the academy and by extension, in applied practice. The theories and techniques of clinical psychology were harnessed to provide therapeutic interventions and support to the victims of apartheid, particularly to survivors of brutal state violence or to families of detained or murdered activists. The formation and programmes of action of OASSSA (Organisation for Appropriate Social Services in South Africa) (Dowdall, 1991; Hayes, 1986; Vogelman, 1987) provide a notable example of these resistant practices. The organisation began in 1983, establishing regional branches and holding four national conferences (1986–1989) in various locations across the country on the campuses of the University of the Witwatersrand (1986 and 1989) the University of the Western Cape (1987), the (then) University of Natal (1988). Particularly through OASSSA's Emergency Services Group in collaboration with activist groups such as DESCOM (Detainees' Support Committee) and NAMDA (National Medical and Dental Association) psychologists (alongside social workers and other healthcare practitioners) used their training in the service of social justice goals with an expressly political agenda (Vogelman, 1987). "OASSSA became the social conscience for psychology" (Hayes, 2000, p. 336). More ambitiously, there were some who thought that OASSSA might contribute to the formation of "A social science of liberation" (Webster, 1986, p. 38) or provide a forum for the development of theories of and alternative practices for "intervening with the political psyche" (Hayes, 1986, p. 44).

While OASSSA may have been (necessarily) primarily practice orientated in response to the psychological and social damage of the inhumane system of apartheid, the context did also provoke an emerging tradition of critical theoretical psychology. Chabani Manganyi's seminal text, *Being black in the world*, published in 1973 by Ravan Press, provided a complex engagement with the processes of psychic life in our raced context. However, as is clear in his recently published autobiographical reflections, at the time and throughout the decade of the 1980s, he was consigned to work on the margins of his chosen field, severely limiting the impact of these ideas on the discipline. Often drawing on the work of critical psychology in the West (as discussed in Chapter 2 of this book) a small but significant group of South African psychologists were engaged in thinking about the (ir)relevance of their discipline for their context. The South African journal PINS (whose agenda is reflected in its title: *Psychology in Society*) was launched in 1983 and published much of this work. Other practices of knowledge construction from outside of the discipline of psychology during this period such as the literary works of Es'kia Mphahlele and Njabulo Ndebele and, of course, Steve Biko's conceptualisation of "black consciousness", have been retrospectively recognised as not only of cultural and political value but also having *psychological* import.

However, it is interesting that these theoretical developments were (and, to a large extent, still are) parallel to, and relatively marginal to, the practice of psychology. In the mode that Ratele (2017) calls "psychology *in* Africa", the priority was to extend therapeutic understandings and practices of care to the most vulnerable in society, in this case, to those oppressed by colonial history and victimised by the apartheid state apparatus. In other words, the recognition that psychological trauma may have sociopolitical rather than individual or biological roots, does not necessarily dislodge or challenge essentialist conceptualisations of psychological life. Many such interventions were quite conventionally framed in psychoanalytic or therapeutic terms to ameliorate "damage" done to individuals and find ways to recuperate mental health in social conditions that did not seem amenable to change anytime soon. While this was extremely important in both psychological and political terms, as Hayes (2000, p. 337) self-critically reflects, "OASSSA's successes were primarily located in the sphere of practice, and yet failed to transform the conventional understandings of the causes of social and personal problems". As we know with the clarity of political hindsight, OASSSA was operating in the dying days of a repressive regime, soon to collapse and give rise to the phoenix of the "new" South Africa. The question of what the "post" landscape of apartheid means is as contested as all other phenomena labelled "post" and had particular implications for the evolving practices of psychology with an agenda primarily framed negatively in terms of apartheid as an inhumane system or, more generally, as anti-racist. The discipline was now confronted with new challenges of praxis but these were now mostly aligned with the new political order. However, again, rather than an articulation of a forward vision of alternatives, many progressive psychologists were initially engaged in a retrospective project to resolve and "heal" the psychic traumas of the past through an adaptation of Freud's "talking cure" in the form of the national Truth and Reconciliation Commission. The TRC focused our collective attention on the past on the assumption that the dual imperatives of truth and reconciliation would provide the basis for healing and nation-building.

The particular framing of the process of nation-building as entailing uncovering "truths" that would provide closure for victims and amnesty or the possibility of forgiveness for perpetrators has most often been linked to the Christian practice of confession, the association re-inscribed by the proceedings being presided over by the Archbishop of the Anglican Church, Desmond Tutu.[4] However, there are also resonances with African philosophical principles and political practices that predate colonialism and have a continuous, mutable vitality both through and post the colonial era. Peterson (2019a) traces the first mention of ubuntu to two decades before the British colonial conquest of the Zulu nation and expressly links the notion to kinship structures, age-cohorts and communal relationships to land. He also outlines multiple social and poetic forms (such as the practices of lobola or creative orature in celebrating clan relationships or performing proverbial "truths") of this communal life that strengthened both hierarchical and more horizontal connections between people or served reparative and reconciliatory purposes when these connections were ruptured or damaged in some way.

This history confirms indigenous notions of justice that resonate with and inform the more overtly religious manifestations of the TRC framework or, perhaps, offers us a conceptual route for understanding the particular African inflections of Christianity that underpin the unique path taken by South Africa. In the synergy between these worldviews, justice is premised on dialogical exchange and consensus decision-making, and is achieved through reparation (or possibly reconciliation) rather than (solely) by punitive consequences. Both Tutu (1999) and Gobodo-Madikizela (2016), who served as commissioners, have made these links explicit in their writings about the TRC.

The ethics of ubuntu

The concept of "ubuntu" has been widely taken up in philosophical (and/or spiritual or religious) considerations of ethics (e.g. Metz, 2007, 2011; Peterson, 2012, 2016) and deployed particularly for anti-racist and other humanist political agendas (e.g. Tutu, 1999, 2004). In the worldview of ubuntu, our well-being is inextricably connected to that of others and the needs of individual selves are subject to communal responsibilities of care. In its current formulation, it is widely utilised quite loosely in the national narrative of South Africa to create a sense of an "imagined community" (Anderson, 1983), sometimes functioning productively to enlarge our circles of care across race and other lines of difference such as gender, sexuality or linguistic identities.[5]

In order to develop the concept and explore its value in psychological theory, I will utilise a working definition provided by Desmond Tutu in 1999:

> Ubuntu is very difficult to render into a Western language. It speaks of the very essence of being human. When we want to give high praise to someone we say, "Yo, unobuntu"; "Hey, he or she has ubuntu." This means they are generous, hospitable, friendly, caring and compassionate. They share what they have. It also means my humanity is caught up, is inextricably bound up, in theirs. We belong in a bundle of life.
>
> *(Tutu, 1999, pp. 34–35)*

Ramose (2015, p. 69) similarly claims that

> botho/hunhu/Ubuntu is not readily translated into humanism ... [rather, it is] opposed to any ism including humanism for this tends to suggest a condition of finality, a closedness or a kind of absolute either incapable of or resistant to any further movement.

In contrast to this idea of a categorical or taxonomic definition, he argues that ubuntu is more process than product, better translated as "humanness": "a condition of being and the state of becoming, of openness or ceaseless unfolding" (Ramose, 2015, p. 69).

Whenever a term or word is difficult to translate from the source language into the target language or languages, this is indicative of different conceptual roots, suggesting alternative systems of meaning or a different worldview. This presents us with both difficulties and opportunities, requiring and enabling a process of "negotiating" meaning (Eco, 2004), doing conceptual *work*. The concept of ubuntu is typically asserted as a kind of antidote to the "individualism" (for which read "selfishness") of Western systems of both thought and social organisation. Interdependence and mutuality replace the enlightenment subject: "the single individual is incomplete without the other" (Ramose, 2015, p. 70). In this formulation, "ubuntu" offers an ethical alternative that is communal or collective, stressing the preservation or restoration of relationships between people as essential to our humanity. Where these relations are strained or damaged or even ostensibly destroyed beyond repair, rather than punitive justice, "ubuntu" both requires *and makes possible* "the healing of breaches, the redressing of imbalances, the restoration of broken relationships" (Tutu, 1999, p. 5). These relationships extend to include the "dead-yet-alive", linking the day-to-day practices and face-to-face encounters to the present-absence of the ancestral community. Mphahlele (2002, p. 154) offers a similar perspective on the spiritual dimensions of ubuntu:

> African humanism was originally a religious state of mind producing moral action; attachment to the soil; social relationships; the art of healing; the sense of community and its welfare; and a sense of organic unity or oneness in the universe in which man is the principal participant, and which is the process permeated by the Supreme Being.

As has already been observed above, this formulation of an African cosmology predates colonialism (Peterson, 2019a) and this long history alerts us to the problematics of assimilating this worldview to later Christian templates. In particular, the central emphasis on an ethical relation between humanity and the earth was alien to early colonising morality and remains antithetical to contemporary dominant philosophical paradigms and the global political engagements of late capitalism. This organic sense of human life in tune with the natural order resonates with Nkrumah's (1998) notion of consciencism which emphasises balance, motion and wholeness. From this perspective, in addition to its evident economic value, land becomes more than simply the material ground for communal living or solely of economic value (without negating this), and takes on symbolic significance in the processes and interactive practices of social relationships. From the agonised position of exile, Mphahlele (2002, p. 340) speaks of the importance of place in the making of selves and the experience of belonging: "geographical place, which, however brutal, will never let you go. The very memory of it gives you identity". Ubuntu as a system of ethical human relationality (or the breach or disruption of these empathic relations) has personal, geographical and cosmological significance.

Ubuntu: justice, reconciliation and forgiveness

Drawing on this philosophical (spiritual) tradition and blending it with notions of both confession and forgiveness in Christian thought, the South African TRC adopted this approach to justice: truth as a basis for reconciliation and forgiveness rather than judgement or punishment. Muruthi (2006) suggests that ubuntu is an approach to conflict resolution or peace-making, to be exercised in sustaining, developing or reconstructing cohesion and community. Ubuntu offers a way of "managing disputes in a way that preserves the integrity and fabric of society" (Muruthi, 2006, p. 25). Nadubera (2005, p. 2) similarly suggests that ubuntu is a proto-legal concept to be deployed in dispute resolution through "conscious application" where harmonious relations between people have been disrupted. And, although Metz (2011) is primarily interested to elaborate an ethics based on the concept of ubuntu, he too has explicitly linked the concept to legal frameworks and practices of justice.

But, in addition to this public collective notion, ubuntu is also understood as a quality of individual persons, an admirable character trait that one may possess more or less of, a normative value or attitude that guides ethical choices and ways of acting in the world. The enactment of ubuntu entails acts of altruism, "kindness" or generosity towards others in need but the effects of these actions are reflexive, as much about the actor as about the other or others with whom one identifies, or with whom one acts in solidarity. Rather than a transaction between individuals or a transfer from one person to another, ubuntu is *reciprocal* or relationally developed, and individual well-being or psychological health is dependent on the well-being and health of others. Metz frames this "sharing" in a more reciprocal way:

> The favoured moral theory is that actions are right, or confer *Ubuntu* (humanness) on a person, insofar as they prize communal relationships, ones in which people identify with each other, or share a way of life, and exhibit solidarity toward *one another*, or care about *each other's* quality of life.
>
> *(Metz, 2011, p. 559, emphasis added)*

In Metz's analysis, ubuntu is more than an impersonal proto-legal concept and he goes so far as to associate it with friendship or filial affection. In a similar move beyond the legal obligations of citizenship or encoded systems of ethics that govern societal formations and practices, Sanders (2002) suggests a more generous interpretation, linking the concept to "hospitality" extended to strangers who are neither kin nor friends but maybe angels in disguise! Philips and Taylor (2009) provide a provocative exploratory history of the concept of kindness and argue for the revitalisation of what has come to be taken as an irrational, weak and ineffectual mode for interacting with others. Mark Freeman's (2014) text, *The priority of the Other*, explores the conditions and possibilities for prioritising others over the self in both aesthetic (or hermeneutic) and ethical terms. In Freeman's framework, the "other" that demands priority is anything that is outside of the self, variably identified as the sensuous stimuli of experience, a task or project to be undertaken or to be done, or cultural objects such as texts or performances to which we surrender ourselves. However, the primary force of the other that requires our attention is in the face (Levinas, 1963) of an-other person who calls on us to recognise ourselves in them.

These (filial, kind, ex-centric or empathic) relationships between the self and others are affective and embodied rather than abstract or conceptual. It could be argued that African kinship systems and communal modes of life foster and strengthen these relational bonds of ubuntu and confirm the reciprocal dignity of persons (Peterson, 2012, forthcoming). Conversely, that colonial and capitalist modes of life destroy social relations, reducing people to an isolated individualistic existence. As Philips and Taylor (2009, p. 6) observe: "Independence and self-reliance are now the great aspirations; 'mutual belonging' is feared and unspoken; it has become one of the great taboos of our society".

There is some Afrocentric literature that goes beyond this to suggest that only Africans (with varying associative meanings of place/culture/race) are both deserving of, and capable of, "ubuntu". Gade's (2013) review of the concept demonstrates a wide range of opinion on this that predominantly seems to hinge on the contested concept of personhood. Only persons (rather than animals) may be characterised by ubuntu but some persons may lose ubuntu (and by extension, their status as human) through immoral actions or ruptures in social relationships, including relations with the ancestral community. Gobodo-Madikizela (2013, p. 493) cites a fellow TRC commissioner, Bongani Finca: "That sense of community is what makes you who you are, and if that community becomes broken, then you yourselves also become broken".

Perhaps the historical injustices of colonialism mean that white people or those who live in the global north (who are necessarily, by definition, settlers rather than *of* Africa, or hostile outsiders) are inevitably severed from this communal harmony with others and with the land. This seems to be the unexplicated assumption underpinning a position such as that expressed by Mkhize (2004) and others that there is a distinctive "African personality ... grounded on the assumptions of a common African worldview and the Africentric paradigm" (Nwoye, 2015, p. 97). The place of the continent of Africa is asserted as inextricably linked to this worldview, culture and the particularities of personality (or personhood). However, similar[6] relational concepts exist in other indigenous languages and cultures, such as in the holistic worldviews of Native American, or of other first-nation or Aboriginal peoples from, literally, opposite ends of the earth (the Sami of northern Lapland and the Australian Aborigines or Maori of New Zealand). These cultural and conceptual commonalities likely reflect similarities in (precolonial) relationships to nature and in the practices of human community. To illustrate, the Filipino notion of "kapwa" provides a particularly beautiful example of this synergy across very different and distant contexts. Translation into English is fraught but the convoluted attempts below suggest that without the necessity of a mediated detour through this mutually alien language, translation between Filipino and African languages might be less challenging:

> Filipino-English dictionaries generally give the words "both" and "fellow-being" as translations of kapwa. ... It should be noted however, one word that comes to mind is the English word "others". However, the Filipino word kapwa is very different from the English word "others". In Filipino, kapwa is the unity of the "self" and "others". The English "others" is actually used in opposition to the "self" and implies the recognition of the self as a separate identity. In contrast, kapwa is a recognition of shared identity, an inner self shared with others.
>
> *(Enriques, 1992, p. 52)*

It is also worth noting that the idea of a distinctive "African personality" may have less than progressive origins and applications. Manganyi (1973) and Mama (1995) both report racist caricatures of the "African personality" or the "African mind" in colonial records. As Böhmke & Tlali (2008, pp. 144–145) note, this idea of an essential African was very commensurate with apartheid ideology and deployed, "[f]irst in order to justify the inferiority of Africans and, second, to enable the control and modification of African behaviour". Ratele (2017, p. 320) also highlights that conversely constructing Africans as "exceptional" and as defined by morally superior cultural resources may uncritically conceal "prevalent and injurious African cultural practices".[7]

In as much as face-to-face relations or a "shared way of life" may serve to knit people together, they may also serve to exclude people with whom one does *not* share either a way of life or a geographical communal space. Tutu and Ramose (as examples of this perspective) explicitly claim the force of the concept of ubuntu lies in its universal scope, as defining of humanity, and of continuing critical relevance in less personal and more diverse social formations. Gobodo-Madikizela (2009, 2012, 2013, 2016) similarly emphasises the importance of mutual recognition and empathic imagination and suggests that this was the purpose and power of the TRC process. Various and multiple criticisms of the TRC have been extensively documented (e.g. Abe, 2014; Mamdani, 2002, 2009; Mangcu, 2003; Meintjies, 2013; Ntsebeza, 2005; Peterson, 2012; Ramphele, 2008) and are increasingly prevalent not only in academic circles but also in the popular press and on social media, as we live forward in the aftermath of that historic moment. The analytic, political and psychosocial shortcomings of the process include: (1) the reduction of the long history of colonial oppression to the specific short history of apartheid; (2) the focus on individual acts of interpersonal violence to the exclusion of more systemic practices of violence such as the dispossession of people from their land, exploitative labour practices and the abusive effects on the poor through the discriminatory provision of basic services such as health and education[8]; (3) the extremely limited provision of material compensation afforded to victims was little more than a token; and (4) an over-emphasis on reconciliation rather than truth (and justice).

However, despite these limitations, Gobodo-Madikizela (2016, p. 10) argues that

> [t]he TRC transformed the silence of trauma – the wordless speech of trauma – and restored victims' sense of agency by providing an environment in which victims were able to break their silence in front of a national audience. Being recognized leads to the experience of healthy subjectivity.

In addition to the transformative power of recognition by providing a national audience for the traumatic narratives of victims, the TRC also afforded perpetrators a "context within which a new perpetrator subjectivity unfolds, one that seeks integration of the uncomfortable reality within the self at a deeper internal level" (Gobodo-Madikizela, 2016, p. 12). Mirroring the transformative effects for victims who experienced recognition, confronting the effects of their past actions, particularly when this confrontation happens in an encounter with victims or their surviving family members, perpetrators may experience remorse, a feeling that entails "recognition of the pain that the perpetrator's actions have caused the victim. It is, in other words, an expression of the perpetrator's *empathic response* to the victim's pain" (Gobodo-Madikizela, 2016, p. 12, emphasis added).

In this approach, ubuntu has the potential to extend and widen our networks of belonging and concern beyond those who are "like us", whom we know and love, suggesting a need to think about ethics (or ubuntu) in a "world of strangers". The Ghanaian philosopher Kwame Anthony Appiah (2005, 2006) offers us a nuanced application of Benedict Anderson's (1983) concept of nationhood as an "imagined" rather than actual community in the African context, to explore the inclusionary effects beyond the "natural" bonds of kinship and neighbourliness to an abstract impersonal category while simultaneously erecting boundaries of exclusion.

> [N]ationalism … exhorts quite a loftily abstract level of allegiance – a vast, encompassing project that extends far beyond ourselves and our families. (For Ghanaians of my father's generation, national feeling was a hard-won achievement, one enabled by political principle and dispassion: though it did not supplant the special obligations one had with respect to one's *ethnie*, matriclan, and family, it did, in some sense, demote them.) … Nations, if they aren't universal enough for the universalist, certainly aren't local enough for the localist.
>
> *(Appiah, 2005, p. 239)*

Through the capacity for imaginative empathic thought (Gobodo-Madikizela, 2009, 2012, 2013, 2016; Peterson, 2012; Philips & Taylor, 2009) and acts of compassion towards or in solidarity with others, and through enlarging the scope of inclusion of others to whom we are connected and accountable, the individual's own ubuntu or humanness is expanded, strengthened, deepened or grown. The inverse effect when we fail to exercise ubuntu when the situation demands it or, more abstractly, fail to recognise the humanity of the other, is that our own humanity is eroded and emaciated. In the post-conflict society of the German Democratic Republic, the political psychologist Molly Andrews conducted narrative interviews with activists immediately after the Berlin Wall was dismantled and again 20 years later. Countering the idea that forgiveness is the task and burden of victims, one of her participants, Katja Havemann, made the following poignant and profound statement about the Stasi who had spied on, harassed and tortured anti-state activists: "They still can't forgive us *[for] what they did to us*. … We are the living guilty conscience. … We're still alive, we experienced it all. We are also still witnesses" (Andrews, 2018, p. 2, emphasis added). Being confronted by one's own lack of ethical action (or worse) in the eyes of those whom we (or our ancestors) oppressed and treated inhumanely makes it difficult for the perpetrator to forgive him/herself and, in a move that mirrors the classic psychoanalytic defence mechanisms of displacement and projection, displaces this guilt and projects the lack of forgiveness onto the victims whose presence sears the "living guilty conscience".

There are thus dehumanising effects for the perpetrator who dehumanises the other. As Mphahlela (2002, p. 151) expresses it: "When you commit a wrong against others you are hurting *yourself, your own soul*". And, again, this idea resonates beyond the continent with the Filipino framework:

"Without kapwa ones ceases to be Filipino. One also ceases to be human" (Enriquez, 1992, p. 76).

In this inversion of the ethical impetus of ubuntu, we find the seeds of a more comprehensive conceptualisation of personhood: the best *and worst* of what we might become is formed through relations with others. Muruthi (2006, p. 26) suggests that the concept of ubuntu is a response to two different questions: "What does it mean to be human? What is – or ought to be – the nature of human relations?" While the second is a critical question not only for theoretical ethics but also for all of us interested in a more equitable world and for the ethical practice of psychology, the first is a (possibly even, *the*) properly psychological question. And the answer that ubuntu provides us with is that humanity is defined relationally, not only when these relations are positive and humane, but inevitably and inextricably. The dialectical process of our relations with each other consists of morphing syntheses of good and bad, beauty and terror, competition and collaboration. Our actions towards others impact not only on their lives but on ours too; selves are formed relationally, reciprocally and reflexively. From this perspective then, the subject of psychology is not the "individual" because as Tutu, without elaborating on his meaning, somewhat enigmatically states, "the solitary individual is a contradiction in terms" (1999, p. 22). The implications for psychology is that our unit of analysis cannot be the abstract individual, even where we explicitly recognise the influences of the cultural, historical and political contexts within which such individuals live. The concept of ubuntu challenges this dichotomous framing and provokes us to rethink personhood.

Vygotskian theory: relational consciousness

Mirroring the argument I have just developed about "ubuntu" I would like to suggest that the conceptual force of Vygotsky's theory is to be found in his unique analysis of the relations between individual minds and social relations or societal formations. Although Vygotsky's name is as well known as Freud's or Piaget's, the impact of his theory has been far less pervasive both within and beyond the discipline of psychology. The "zone of proximal development" serves as the touchstone of the theory, instantiating Vygotsky's argument that the potential of mind develops *in society*, in relation with others.

The world is mediated for human children, who encounter the world and its objects *through others* or through the understanding of others. In this way, each successive generation can (and cannot but) build on and develop the culture and knowledge of the previous generation whose lives overlap with and accompany them in their engagement with the present. The extended temporal zones of human development in shared intergenerational life provide the scope for education or the optimistic, progressive future-orientated zone of proximal development (ZPD). In Vygotsky's famous law of sociogenesis:

> [E]very function in the cultural development of the child appears on the stage twice, in two forms – at first as social, then as psychological; at first as a form of cooperation between people, as a group, an intermental category, then as a means of individual behaviour, as an intramental category. This is the law for the construction of all higher mental functions.
>
> *(Vygotsky, 1998, p. 169)*

While these claims are widely recognised as "true" they have been reduced to little more than truisms. It is hardly contentious to suggest that children are socialised or "learn from others" and this formulation is seamlessly assimilated to reductionist behaviourist social learning theory. Turning the developmental sequence described here by Vygotsky as *first* between people (*interpsychological*) and *then* inside the child (*intrapsychological*) on its head, the burgeoning field of "activity theory" empties heads and disperses their contents into the social world of tools and collective action. In much the same way that ubuntu has been deployed in critique of "individualism", these neo-Vygotskians (e.g. Cole, 1995; Daniels, 2001; Daniels, Cole & Wertsch, 2007; Wertsch, 1998, 2007)[9] conflate individual mental processes with individualism (bad) and collective activity with social collaboration (good). In the process, they miss the radical conceptual force of Vygotsky's perspective. It is a moot point that culture (or "the social") influences psychological life and it is also quite evident that because people live in social groups, they are able to exert exponential control over the natural environment through tool design and use in collective action. There is nothing distinctively Vygotskian about these claims.

The contribution of Vygotsky lies in the way that the theory fundamentally alters the dichotomous framing of individual psychological life and the social, cultural, political and historical world. It is not simply that the individual person's meaningful experience of the objects and landscape of the world is filtered through the understandings of others; rather, her personhood is formed through interactions with others. Meaning (or thought) occurs first between people and is subsequently *internalised* providing the very substance for the construction of individual personhood. The child becomes herself, through others. And doesn't that sound familiar!

Miller's (2011, p. 197) explication of Vygotsky emphasises his conception of the "social self"[10] and the inextricable links between the processes of psychological and social life that are formed in and through language:

> [T]he thinker or person engaged in the drama is not "social" because she is compelled, or constrained, or encouraged, or enabled to act in conformity with some external "social" or "cultural" or "historical" force. Such forces may exist and certainly other people exist with whom we communicate and interact. But in verbal thinking, the social other is not out there but is part of the *social interaction with oneself.* ... This concept of the person as a social individual, a person who is socialized not from the outside but from within, a person for whom the other is also me, my-self, a person who does not live in opposition to society but who by living constitutes society, culture, and history, stands at the very core of all his [Vygotsky's] thinking and serves to unify the various strands of his theory. Social activity may *originate* in interaction with others but it *culminates* in an inner dialogue.

As outlined in Chapter 1, from a Vygotskian perspective, the process of development is one of increasing individuation rather than the reverse but this "individual" is formed in and through the shared medium of language that moves inward from the social terrain of communication to enable "[s]ocial interaction with oneself" (Vygotsky, 1987, p. 274). The internalisation of language means that the psychic interior is permeated by, and never severed from, shared social system of meanings.

> Speech for oneself has its source in a differentiation of an initially social speech function, a differentiation of speech for others. Thus, the central tendency of the child's development is not a gradual socialisation introduced from the outside, but a gradual *individualisation* that emerges on the foundation of the child's internal socialisation.
>
> *(Vygotsky, 1987, p. 259, emphasis added)*

In this way, we develop a social (dialogical) subjectivity in which we can only be ourselves through the incorporation of the internalised "other", in which it becomes possible to treat "oneself as another" as suggested by Ricoeur (1992). Vygotsky (1997, p. 77) refers to this as the "dual nature of consciousness" and comments that, "the notion of a double is the picture of consciousness that comes closest to reality". Self-regulation may be seen as constraining possibilities for innovative thought and action due to the internalisation of the regulatory language of social prescripts and prohibitions, whereby we police ourselves through what Foucault (1988) terms the "technologies of the self". In Du Bois' (1903) theory of race and psychic life, the concept of "double consciousness" entails a damaging fracturing of the self. (See Chapter 1.) Manganyi (1973) likewise refers to two schemas for the body, individual and sociological, that may be congruent (for white subjects) or conflictual (for black subjects). This splitting is thus a form of psychic damage inflicted on marginalised subjects (by race or other dimensions of identity such as gender or sexuality) who are denied wholeness or singularity.

However, while marginalised subjects may experience a dislocation between the internalised other and the "true self", Vygotsky's theory of human development suggests that dual consciousness or the splitting of the self (as both the I who acts and the me who is observed and regulated) is a defining feature of human psychological life.[11] The capacity for self-regulation that produces the anxieties and dislocations that Du Bois describes above, simultaneously creates the psychic distance from current realities (including one's experience of one's self in the world) to enable resistance, in which the "two warring ideals" may be overcome, effecting change in the self and possibly in the world. We are never entirely subsumed either by the regulatory other (as an external social interlocutor or as the internalised self-regulator) nor by the exigencies of the present material world. Du Bois recognises this contradictory quality of the "double consciousness" in his articulation of the "second sight" afforded to raced (or otherwise marginalised) subjects who, unlike those in dominant or privileged positions, always have access to more than a single (ignorant) perspective on the world.

In other words, the splitting of the self and the capacity for self-regulation is simultaneously the means by which we can dialogically become distinctly ourselves, agentic and creative actors in the world. Without the internalisation of the other, without the internalisation of the language and meanings of intergenerational life, the individual child would not develop recognisably human forms of life, would not be *individuated*. Ratele (2017, p. 325) asks: "Is it possible then to conceive of subjects as primarily part of *others*, as some cultures are wont to do?"

Paradoxically, we can only become individual persons capable of independent ethical choices and agentic actions to change present (inherited) conditions and shape different futures, through our interdependent relationships with others. These others through whom we become ourselves offer us the resources of culture not as dead relics of knowledge but as living traditions within whose tides each subsequent generation, if they are not to drown, must learn to swim or surf. "[H]uman life presupposes a specific social nature and a process by which children grow into the intellectual life of those around them" (Vygotsky, 1978, p. 88). Contrary to conceptions of personhood as individual subjectivity, culture provides "the very *medium* within which we can understand ourselves" (Ricoeur, 1981, p. 143). These historical legacies, the cultural air that we breathe or the tides of tradition that we ride are not unequivocally positive or good; on the contrary, much of what we inherit is, at best, only partial understanding or erroneous and, at worst, violent, traumatic and damaging. However, we cannot escape being implicated in these histories, they are the stuff from which we make ourselves.

Although this process of individuation, of becoming ourselves is developmentally delineated in Vygotsky's theory, this does not imply culmination in adult identity as a final, fixed form. While the process of becoming ourselves may be more evidently active as children grow up in the socialising domains of the family and education, the self remains a process rather than a product, perpetually encountering the world through others and engaged in a flow of internal conversation. In the words of Margaret Archer (2003, p. 193):

> As human beings, we all know that we live a rich inner life: that we are in continuous communion with ourselves and that we engage in a continual running commentary with the events going on around us. We are aware of how our inner lives monitor our responses to external situations in which we find ourselves and indeed modify some of the circumstances to which we willingly expose ourselves, be these natural, practical or social.

The dialogical structure and narrative flow of psychological life that are constituted by and, in turn, constitute the social interactions of communal life, produces a form of psychic power that defines human agency. The notion of individual uniqueness or the idea of a particular individual personality in opposition to the social (or cultural or political) world is very firmly entrenched in the discipline of psychology and more widely in the post-industrial world. But it is a static misconception that conceals both oppressive conditions and possibilities for individual and social change.

> Vygotsky's conception of a person as a social individual is one of the major contributions of cultural-historical psychology to our understanding of what it means to be human; a human be-ing. Although social activity may *originate* in interaction with others, it

culminates in an inner dialogue that is the expression of conscious awareness or self-consciousness. … Herein lies the key that unlocks some of the intractable theoretical problems in psychology, and beyond that are often formulated as unbridgeable oppositions between mind, on the one hand, and body, matter, environment, and society on the fingers of the other hand. Underlying these oppositions is an inner-outer or inside-outside dialectic that stubbornly resists the collapse of one pole into the other, despite vigorous attempts to accord primacy to one or the other.

(Miller, 2014, pp. 43–44)

The conventional split between psychological (or private) life and the political public world is challenged by this alternative framework that enables me to think of my-self as an-other and conversely, the other as my-self. Therein lie both theoretical and political (or ethical) implications and provocations for new forms of psychological praxis.

In conclusion: rethinking personhood

Psychological life cannot be understood through attempts to isolate individuals as natural bounded entities from social life but neither will we make much progress by attempts to negate the interiority of human life to focus solely on social life or collective practices. Vygotsky's law of sociogenesis and the concept of ubuntu both emphasise the formation of personhood *through others*. But neither framework of thinking erases individuality or interiority.[12] While ubuntu offers a distinctly African perspective on psychological life, I have argued that it does not define a peculiarly African psyche but rather, is a productive reconceptualisation of psychological life, of all *human* psychological life. My argument is thus in line with Ratele's (2017, p. 316) objective to delineate a psychology that is "not provincial or essentialised" and to "produce Africa(n) centred knowledge that is at home in Africa *as well as within global psychology*" (emphasis added).

In this way, the concept of ubuntu offers a radical shift in theorisation, and possibilities for resistance and renewal in developing the discipline. I have argued that this reconceptualisation resonates with Vygotskian theory which emphasises the internalised other that creates a "double consciousness" or the capacity to treat "one's self as another" (Ricoeur, 1992). This splitting of the "self" enables the converse empathic construction of the "other as self" in relations of ubuntu. The self is thus, by definition, a "social self" formed in language, in relation with others. Culture, history and the social world do not form an external backdrop to personhood but infuse the inner world of the self, are the very stuff of which we are made, through which we narrate our individual and collective identities, connecting the present to the past and future, and ourselves to imagined others in different places and times.

From both perspectives, what is suggested is not the evacuation of the psychological into the social, or the erasure of interior subjectivity. Rather, these conceptual resources articulate the movement of the social within, enlarging the scope of what is termed psychological and reframing possibilities for understanding what it means to be human, and the dynamics of both individual and social change. In place of the "individual psyche" in opposition to the "collective communal social world" we have a psychosocial phenomenon that is relational, reciprocal and reflexive – a *dialectical* process of being and becoming rather than an inert entity. This rethinking of personhood has important implications for both the theory and practice of psychology.

Notes

1 The term "ubuntu" and this definition, "Umuntu ngumuntu ngabantu" (or sometimes "Ngabany' abantu" – more literally, *other* people), are in the Zulu language but the concept exists in almost all indigenous South African languages and also beyond in sub-Saharan Africa. The seSotho term "Botho" is also commonly utilised in official contexts in South Africa and defined as "motho ke motho ka batho".

2 In the domain of education, resistant practices include attempts at translation (of tests into indigenous languages or at least from American into South African English) and attention to the cultural relevance of test items. The pointlessness of this project is explored in greater detail in Chapter 5 of this book. For now, suffice it to say that this kind of surface level tinkering does nothing at all to shift the underlying premise of the approach: that psychological life (in this instance, cognitive processes or intelligence) is a quantifiable substance that is differentially and normally distributed among people, producing universal standards by means of which to categorise individuals.

3 For more detailed discussions of the history of psychology in South Africa, see Long, 2016; van Ommen & Painter, 2008. Sanders (2002) offers a rich history of psychological questions about "race" and humanity addressed by Afrikaans intellectuals within, but mainly without, the discipline of psychology in the formation of the apartheid state.

4 The Anglican church in South Africa is also referred to as the "Church of England" and represents a particular form of Christianity that retains the important emphasis on confession that is typical of Catholicism. These traditions of confession, forgiveness and reconciliation resonate with both the TRC and the African concept of ubuntu. However, as noted by sociological theories (particularly, Weber) about the processes industrialisation, there are other protestant traditions that underpin the highly individualised units of labour required by capitalist formations of society. Foucault (1988) has linked these forms of work and social organisation to the "confessional" form of therapeutic practice. These disparate

discursive strands were likely all influential in the constitution and experience of the TRC, and continue to inform analysis of this crucial historical process.

5 However, the notion of "ubuntu" may be misused to distract attention from failing state provision in a severely asymmetrical society by insisting on some inherently African sensibility of "community" that will ensure social cohesion and care for those most marginalised. The democratic order has struggled to deliver adequate basic services (such as housing, water, sanitation, electricity, security, health and educational facilities) to large numbers of South Africans. These failures of the state cannot be absolved by an appeal to noble African values of communal reciprocity and responsibility.

6 Noting these similarities does not imply homogeneity. On the contrary, the notion of holism incorporates widely diverse interpretations and practices across time and place. However, the linkages between these modes of life and meaning-making are useful to displace the dominant formulation of these questions in terms of oppositions between Africa and "the West".

7 Although he does not elaborate on what these "injurious" practices might be, we may legitimately extrapolate from Ratele's scholarship on African masculinities that culture is gendered and differentially rather than homogenously experienced.

8 The Apartheid Archives project established at the University of the Witwatersrand was an attempt to engage with ordinary people in the narration of everyday life experiences under apartheid and to engage these realities from a psychosocial perspective (see Stevens, Duncan & Hook, 2013). This project has continuities with, but more importantly discontinuities from, the collection of narrative testimony in the TRC. It is noteworthy that the project was initiated only in 2008, more than a decade after the TRC process had been completed, reflecting a kind of hiatus in both political and theoretical work that was sadly characteristic of many fields of (academic) life in the initial post-apartheid period. (For example, see Chapter 5 for a discussion of how political and intellectual energies were deflected and lulled in higher education in South Africa during this period.)

9 See Yasnitsky (2012) for a critique of activity theory framed as a "revisionist revolution" in Vygotskian studies. Miller (2011) provides a detailed analysis of Vygotsky's texts in support of his scathing critique of activity theory, including a particularly incisive dismantling of Wertsch's explanation of mediation as a form of distributed cognition. In a much earlier critique, Miller (1989, p. 5) suggests that activity theory involves an "inside-out transformation of Vygotsky into a social learning theorist".

10 For an extended discussion of Vygostky's "person as a social individual", see (Miller, 2014, pp. 40–44).

11 William James (1962, p. 189) similarly conceptualised the self as consisting of an "I" and a "me", "being as it were duplex, partly known and partly knower, partly object and partly subject".

12 In another disciplinary context, Njabulo Ndebele (1986) alerted us to the ways in which protest literature (and other forms of art) while speaking critically to oppressive political conditions, inadvertently re-inscribed colonial perspectives that focused on Africa as an arena of spectacular action, flattening the interiority of African subjectivity.

4

(MIS)UNDERSTANDINGS AND ACTIVE IGNORANCE

Introduction

This chapter creates a conceptual dialogue between ideas taken from the disciplines of psychology and sociology to explore the ways in which we make knowledge about the world and, yet, simultaneously and almost more vigorously, actively defend our ignorance. In similar vein to the focused conceptual exploration of ubuntu in Chapter 3, this chapter utilises a particular key concept, in this case, a concept that is conventionally associated with cognitive psychology and may be productively articulated in Vygotskian language: (mis)understanding. However, by connecting this psychological theorisation of the process of "changing minds" to the problematics of power and political change, the chapter extends the conceptualisation of human subjectivity provided in Chapter 1 and challenges the content and form of the discipline of psychology as explored in Chapter 2. Two South African theorists provide the conceptual touchstones for the exploration of this issue: (1) Ronald Miller's idea (2011, p. 407) of mis-understanding as a kind of "absolute understanding"; and (2) Melissa Steyn's idea (2012, p. 11) of an "ignorance contract". I bring these two theories into dialogue with one another out of both theoretical and practical interest. My sense of the limits of the boundaries of psychology is partly informed by my own learning history that has entailed many detours and diversions off the beaten disciplinary track and, partly, informed by the particular conceptions and historical trajectory of psychology in the South African context. As described in Chapter 2, the curriculum for undergraduate studies reproduces the "standard" divisions of the North/ Western textbook (personality, development, social and cognitive psychology including all the classic experimental studies and grand narrative theories) while the postgraduate curriculum is predominantly conceptualised as professional training focused on therapeutic interventions in response to individual problems formulated in the binary terms of (ab)normality. Neither of these formulations (which are of course mutually reinforcing) has proved particularly useful to me theoretically, practically or politically in the domains in which I work. But then again, simply abandoning the disciplinary ship for alternatives in philosophy, sociology or literary discursive theory is not a viable option for me either in relation to the questions that matter to me and which are central to the concerns of this book: How is learning possible? How does change happen? Or, even more importantly, what prevents learning or blocks change?

A dialogical exchange between these two specific theoretical resources extends our thinking through these questions. Miller offers a particular articulation of Vygotskian theory and Steyn interprets and applies the "*Racial Contract*" of Charles Mills (1997) to the South African context. My version of their ideas may not entirely coincide with theirs and, further, the synergies that I find between their positions may not be recognised by either Steyn or Miller independently. This is another way of saying any mis-understandings are mine entirely! The specificities of the South African context are most certainly relevant to the development of their individual positions and to my employment of their arguments; in particular, the challenges of learning-teaching in higher education in a highly unequal and racialised terrain; and, more broadly, the problematics of understanding one another across lines of difference in post-apartheid[1] society. But the provocations of this particular context may have something pertinent to offer for all of those who are engaged in knowledge production and, indeed, in the tricky business of education or in the development of intergenerational narratives or intercultural dialogues about the world as it is and as we would like it to be. The past may not predict the future, but the present is never entirely severed from the past, more continuous with it than we would like to imagine. The dual shocks of the UK Brexit and the US Trump presidency are only eruptions along global fault-lines that have long been present, submerged not too far below the surface. While current global movements and migrations are accelerated across physical, cultural and technoscapes (Appadurai, 1990), it is clear that far from the (digital and terrestrial) game being played on increasingly level playing fields, the terrain traversed remains rocky and extremely uneven. As is well established in classical social psychology (most famously in Sherif's Robbers Cave experiment), increased contact between groups of people does not inevitably lead to increased understanding. Conversely, when the context of interaction is unequal, contact may increase conflict and deepen misunderstanding. I will primarily use the South African context to explore these issues because it is my context, and because it is an intense crucible of historical and contemporary global conflicts.

Mis-understanding, understanding and not understanding

As a departure point for his argument, Miller (2011) uses Vygotsky's (1987, p. 182) concept of "conscious awareness", a composite term that captures the distinction between "knowing *of*" or the *awareness* derived from experience, and "knowing *about*" or the meaning that we attach to our experiences. This distinction is very clear in the different meanings or conceptions that children and adults attach to the same situation or experience as demonstrated by both Piagetian and Vygotskian theories of cognitive development. Using the distinction between awareness (of-ness) and consciousness (about-ness), Miller distinguishes between different kinds of understanding (or knowing). The term "innocence" refers to the absence of any awareness or consciousness of something. But the term "ignorance", unlike innocence, refers to a kind of knowing and *non*-knowing. We cannot ignore (be ignorant of) something we know nothing about. The act of ignoring involves excluding certain experiences or shutting down our awareness of the situations we wish to ignore. Ignorance, then, is a state of consciousness in which awareness is limited and produces gaps in our knowing or what we could refer to as *non*-understanding. Although we may choose to ignore (to be ignorant of) certain things or situations, a state of ignorance may also be thrust upon us; chosen for us by powerful others such as parents or teachers or media informed by state or business interests, or it may simply be a function of age such that our experience is limited or distorted in ways that, although we may know *about* something, our understanding remains incomplete as non-understanding. Here the analogy is with the term non-entity that does not refer to a not-entity or nothingness but to a limited or restricted kind of entity.

Unlike ignorance that derives from a failure or absence of awareness, there is another kind of lack of, or limited, or distorted understanding that Miller calls *not*-understanding. In this case, it is consciousness or the about-ness of our experiences, the meanings we attach to our awareness, that are problematic. The radically different ways we can understand, conceptualise or rationalise our lived experience is well captured in the

Marxist concept of "false consciousness" as opposed to a conscientised class consciousness[2]: the same "facts of the matter" are understood in radically different ways. Not-understanding, then, is a problem of consciousness (of meaning or conceptualisation) rather than awareness. Hearing people speaking an unfamiliar language captures this sense of not understanding very clearly; we are aware of the sounds and are even aware that these sounds are meaningful to those happily conversing in Zulu or Swahili or Spanish, but do not understand their meaning. Similarly, we may have an awareness that domains of knowledge exist although we cannot ourselves participate in these fields as we do not understand their particular forms, techniques and conceptual language. This kind of general surface knowing that something exists is of course typical in the internet information age and puts a new spin on the old adage "a little knowledge is a bad thing". I myself have this clear sense of "not-understanding" the concept of imaginary numbers despite my scientist partner repeatedly explaining it to me. I can follow the English words that come out of his mouth and even reproduce the explanation fairly accurately in a way that sounds quite sensible but, nonetheless, I know that I don't really "get it". In cases such as these, we know that we do not know, that we do "not understand"! The condition of "not-understanding" entails awareness but without the attachment of meaning or understanding to the experience. We may have a sense that there is a domain of meaningful action and thinking belonging to others but for us, this remains a blurred, out-of-focus field. This kind of not understanding is of course very typical in classrooms where we are busy learning to know about something that is not yet known and are doing so deliberately. But as teachers, we also know that if students can tell us what it is that they do not understand, the problem is half-solved, and the more precisely they can put their finger on what is "not understood", the easier our task becomes.

A far greater problem confronts us when students do not know that they do not understand and may even be very certain of their understanding but it is simply, from our perspective, wrong! Miller argues that this absolute form of not understanding or "misunderstanding" occurs when we inappropriately impose an "aboutness" or meaning on an event or task. And in this sense, misunderstanding is a form of "absolute understanding" (Miller, 2011, p. 407).

> The paradoxical nature of misunderstanding is that it is experienced as understanding. To misunderstand a situation is to attach an incorrect aboutness to the awareness of a situation that produces a kind of perseveration of experience in which consciousness and awareness are locked together. In this sense, misunderstanding is a condition of

misplaced consciousness. Consequently, misunderstanding cannot be experienced as such but only as understanding. Misunderstanding can only be recognized by another person and what the other person recognizes is confusion; a joining together of an *awareness* and an *aboutness* that do not belong together, at least from the perspective of the other person. Because misunderstanding is experienced as understanding, it presents a formidable barrier to learning.

(Miller, 2011, p. 407)

Although we may pay lip service to the notion that no learner approaches a task with an "empty head" we often implicitly reframe this as a "half-full" head which simply requires topping up. Conversely, in some academic circles, there is a growing timidity among teachers who are (perhaps in many cases not without reason) less certain than they once were of their pedagogical authority. This may lead to uncritical validation of what learners already know in some misguided expression of solidarity or, at best, the provision of favourable conditions for learning to occur without teaching, through exploratory trial and error. Neither of these responses will lead to what Vygotsky (1978, p. 89) called "good learning, in advance of development". Miller (2011) alerts us to the problematics of a zone of proximal development in which that which is already known may be an obstacle rather than a building block to facilitate new learning. In Piagetian terms, "schemes of assimilation rush to apply" (Pascual-Leone, pers. comm, 2018) and the act of understanding always entails the active imposition of pre-understandings. Miller refers to the preoperational child's failure to conserve[3] as an example of misunderstanding, where the child attaches or imposes a particular form of meaning on the task (assimilates to the scheme of the level of the water as the sole indicator of volume) that cannot be dislodged either by providing new meanings (explaining what the task is about) or by increased awareness through repeated experiences of the task.

The phenomenon of misunderstanding (experienced by the learner as understanding) may be of particular pertinence in instances where different learning histories coalesce, or where the pre-judgements of tradition (Gadamer, 1975) may be inappropriate for new problems or situations, resulting in what Ortega (1960, cited in Miller, 2011) refers to as "blindness", a metaphorical reference to the literal blind spots that are subsumed in an apparently complete field of vision. In Siri Hustvedt's (2012, p. 138) collection of essays entitled *Thinking, Looking and Living*, she references the substantial body of research on what is termed "change blindness", the phenomenon of simply not seeing changes that are made to images or film sequences. Having viewed something once, our frame of reference means that we see what we expect to see rather than what is before our very eyes. Perhaps the most well-known example is the "Invisible Gorilla" experiment conducted by Simons and Chabris (1999) in which a person in a gorilla suit walks through a basketball game. Despite this very unusual disruption to the scene, more than half the viewers, who had been instructed to count the number of passes between the players, fail to register the "gorilla's" presence – they simply do not see it! This mode of attending exclusively to that which is expected may work very well for repetitive, routine situations. Freeman (2014, p. 11) refers to this mode as "'ordinary oblivion', the condition of our being caught up, mindlessly, in the frantic movement of our lives" and implies this may even be a necessary and functional response in the face of too much information and stimulation. However, this inattention to detail, or failing to register that which is unexpected or novel in a given situation, is less effective for dealing with dynamic scenarios. In the same way that our attention may be directed towards some elements of the perceptual field and away from others, our thinking or knowing may be similarly constrained to exclude significant facts or even chains of argument that do not fit with what we already know. The blind spots in the rear-view mirrors of cars or the degeneration of peripheral vision are so dangerous for a driver precisely because her field of vision appears complete and she does not know that there are spots that she cannot see. So, too, such ignorant blind spots in our knowledge are not experienced as absences or lacunae; rather, they are concealed and our understanding seems comprehensive and coherent.

Miller articulates a theoretical and pedagogical response to the cognitive obstacles in teaching and learning that cannot be solved by incremental developmental accretion or simply supplying additional new information. In this context, the task of the teacher is to change the definition of the situation, to create a new way of seeing what it is about, to teach for *un*learning. Critically, this will entail a reframing of the situation for the learner, creating conditions in which the application of what is already known is disrupted rather than reinforced.[4]

> [P]erforming these [familiar or known] actions may serve to entrench the existing understanding that must be overcome if new understanding is to be achieved and in this way pre-understanding may serve to block and hinder the acquisition of new understanding. Hence, the necessity on the part of the learner for a moment of surrender or letting go in order for the learning-teaching process to succeed. For the teacher, this means that instead of trying to

"teach" new understanding, helping the learner to shed inappropriate pre-understanding may be more productive.

(Miller, 2011, p. 378)

In her remarkable autobiography, Tara Westover (2018) recounts the extraordinary journey that she undertook to earn herself the title of her book, "educated". Growing up in rural America and denied regular schooling by a father who was a religious fanatic (and surely also by Westover's own assessment, psychologically disturbed) when she finally began to participate in the world of books and theoretical knowledge, she became consciously aware of her "mis-understandings" and changing knowledge. Most learners simply take these changes for granted as they acquire new understandings about the world, forgetting previous (mis) understandings or covering over gaps in their knowledge in new apparently seamless ways of thinking. A dramatic example of this changing subjectivity is captured in Westover's recognition that history is an interpretive human endeavour:

> I knew what it was to have a misconception corrected – a misconception of such magnitude that shifting it shifted the world. Now I needed to come to terms with *how the great gatekeepers of history had come to terms with their own ignorance and partiality.* I thought if I could accept that what they had written was not absolute but was the result of a biased process of conversation and revision, maybe I could reconcile myself with the fact that the history most people agreed upon was not the history I had been taught … from the ashes of their dispute I could construct a world to live in. In knowing the ground was not ground at all, I hoped I could stand on it.
>
> *(Westover, 2018, p. 275, emphasis added)*

In her characteristic capaciousness of thought, she imagines that respected scholars might, in the ways that she has, have to deal with retrospectively recognising their "own ignorance and partiality". This imaginative sense of how thinking and knowledge develops not only for individuals but for communities of practice leads Westover not into fashionable cynicism or sceptical despair but into the practice of constructing possible grounds for new and different understanding that are always incomplete and open to further developments and insights. The question of mis-understanding is, however, importantly not confined to classrooms or to the domains of textual and disciplinary knowledge and she is in the process not just of understanding the world differently but of becoming a different person.

As Miller (2011, p. 380) says, "understanding is not simply an adjunct or product of our cognitive equipment that can be acquired or refined but is an essential aspect of our being". And so we now turn to a second theoretical thread for thinking about the production and maintenance of ignorance in the social world and in our relations with one another.

Ignorance, innocence and forgetting

Steyn's explicit focus is on knowledge of the apartheid past and particular forms of ignorance entailed by racism or other forms of sociopolitical oppression. Her engagement with the question of ignorance mirrors Miller's concept of mis-understanding as a kind of presence rather than absence. She argues that the ways in which we remember and, importantly, *forget* our social history in a conflictual society like South Africa entails collective practices of communication that actively construct and maintain "an implicit agreement to misrepresent the world" (Steyn, 2012, p. 11). This is not ignorance in the ordinary sense of not-knowing; rather it is an active assertion of ignorance, whereby what *is* known is taken as complete, certain and sufficient, shutting down our attention or closing down any question or demand to think further or differently about things. Protest-ations about "not-knowing" are simultaneously claims of innocence or a defence in mitigation of judgement. As I have already argued from Miller, ignorance and innocence are not synonymous; rather they are quite different forms of "not knowing".

Although authoritarian systems of government exercise their power by means of overt brutal force, they also critically rely on what Foucault (1979) termed "docile subjects" who will regulate their own actions and those of others in society. The apartheid state created these internalised mechanisms of control by the aggressive assertions of racist ideology and the repression of different ways of knowing the world and one another. Ignorance was actively generated not only through the absence of information or knowledge but also through the active circulation and per-petuation of myths and taboos about forbidden crossings of race boundaries through the institutions of religion, education and highly controlled media. In addition, the physical architecture of "apart-heid" (literally translated as apart-ness) entailed the separation and segregation by race in all spheres of life, including where we lived and through the control of, particularly black people's, movements and possibilities for work. Apartheid, therefore, created the conditions for ignorance both in the sense of "about-ness" (by the propagation of a particular racist version of the world and of unquestion-able differences between "us" and "them") but also, crucially, by preventing shared experiences or "awareness of" realities across boundaries of race and culture. Apartheid was quite deliberately and systemically designed to control all contact, conversation and possibilities for "knowing" one another. However, despite the powerful machinations of the state, Steyn convincingly argues that ignorance of racist oppression under apartheid was an active, deliberate process of "not wanting to know":

> Not to know or not to know enough, you have to turn aside, you have resolutely to ignore the signals of distress that come our way. In these circumstances the plea of lack of knowledge is uncompelling. It treats as an involuntary state what is in fact a choice.
>
> *(Geras, 1998, p. 35, cited in Steyn, 2012, p. 12)*

Mark Freeman (2014, pp. 68–69) distinguishes what he terms "willed ignorance" from the "ordinary oblivion" described above, and notes that this is "a much more purposeful and pernicious form of not-seeing, geared precisely toward shutting out whatever harsh realities we might encounter". Of course, this ignorance or refusal to know was (and is) as Appiah (2006, p. xviii) says, the "privilege of the powerful" – black South Africans lived under no such illusions. Although the mis-understandings and active ignorance discussed here might seem to be about the "facts" of history, this knowledge (or ignorance) of the past produces the grounds for knowing ourselves and others in the present and is particularly relevant to the intergenerational transmission of what is typically referred to as the apartheid "legacy" (which is more like the inheritance of debt than family china!):

> Increasingly some white South Africans claim that they did not know what was happening during apartheid, that it was not their generation that was responsible for apartheid; but that of their parents; and even that it was not as bad for black people under apartheid as it is for white South Africans in post-apartheid South Africa.
>
> *(Steyn, 2012, p. 8)*

Gobodo-Madikizela (2012), one of the commissioners of the Truth and Reconciliation Commission, has written about her experiences of using the testimonies of the TRC to provoke her white South African students to acknowledge their complicity in our racist past and recognise the continuing benefits of their subject positioning. In many cases, this entails recollecting or remembering events of everyday life that seemed ordinary or self-evident at the time, and recognising the ways in which we enacted oppression in the everyday acts of using "whites only" buses, benches, toilets, schools and, very often, particularly in the relationships and exchanges between young white children and adult black workers in our homes.[5] This confrontation with "new" facts about the past and recognition of personal complicity and implication in the asymmetrical power relations of society produces what Gobodo-Madikizela terms an "empathic unsettlement".

In tracing the development of his theory through his autobiography, Erikson (1970, p. 756) speaks of experiencing a "conceptual as well as a philosophical shudder" on hearing the world referred to as the "outer-psychoanalytic outerworld". In this phrase the usual antithesis between the external social world and the deeply interior psyche is disrupted, causing Erikson's frame of understanding to shift dramatically. James Baldwin observed an audience enraptured by speakers at a rally of the Nation of Islam: "the people looked toward them with a kind of intelligent hope on their faces – not as though they were being consoled or drugged but as though they were being jolted" (1993, p. 49). This displacement of what is taken-for-granted creates a shifting of the epistemic frame that is viscerally experienced. In Miller's terms, this (un)learning process entails attaching new meanings to past events, recognising earlier experiences (such as the events and experiences of an apartheid childhood) for what they were *about*.

The task of remaking the meanings of the past is complicated even further by the inter-generational "inheritance" of children born or growing up post-apartheid (in other words, who have not known first-hand, have no experiential awareness of, apartheid, even as young children). This is South Africa's "hinge generation" that Eva Hoffman (2004) has written so insightfully and eloquently about in relation to the Holocaust. The positioning of these young South Africans in the present is not severed from history. The past is present, encountered or (not) known, first and foremost, through their parents who may: (1) be silent about the past; (2) continue to actively assert racist mis-understandings of the world; or (3) make pleas of "not knowing" and, therefore, claims of "innocence". James Baldwin (1993, p. 6) "identifies white ignorance as an 'appalling achievement' that has as a core element that one should not care to know: 'It is the innocence which constitutes the crime'". For those advantaged by the inequalities of the past (all white South Africans), this "innocence" is positively asserted as an exoneration of complicity and in defence of intergenerational privilege. From this defensive position, neither the past nor the present can be understood differently or from the perspective of the other. Achebe (1988, p. 491) powerfully captures the effects of privilege as blunting the imagination by spreading "a thick layer of adipose tissue over our sensitivity".

Languages of (mis)understanding our-selves and others

Despite the destruction of the overt racialised oppression of the past and the current absence of state mechanisms of racialised control (even the converse, legislated constitutional equality), the contours of separateness remain in the tacit, taken-for-granted understandings that we have of how the world works and of racialised others. Many South Africans continue to lack awareness of one another's (racialised) realities and to assert their ignorance as innocence and their mis-understandings as absolute knowledge or certainty. The role of language in this regard is not incidental. No one can dispute the centrality of language in the Soweto uprising of 1976 in which black school learners took to the streets to protest the introduction of Afrikaans as the sole medium of instruction at school. Ironically what this did (both at the time and in popular imagination thereafter) was to eclipse the colonising power of English, situating it as a liberatory language in opposition to Afrikaans. More recently, this pro-English/anti-Afrikaans position has been articulated within the Student Movement of 2015/2016, at the University of Stellenbosch where the retention of Afrikaans as the medium of instruction (albeit with the inclusion of English translation facilities and some dual medium courses) has been interpreted as a means to bolster a racist enclave of whites-only education. The *Luister* (2015) documentary made by student activists utilises the injunction to "Listen!" to articulate the ways in which the language of Afrikaans and the institutional language policy create barriers to understanding both within and outside of classrooms.

Most South Africans are of course multilingual but, despite now two generations of post-apartheid schooling, the majority of white South Africans remain unable to speak an indigenous African language, and English remains the language of power, education and access to work and all that flows from these ostensibly meritocratic systems of the democratic state. Language hierarchies act in concert with the alignment of race and class, through the institutional mechanisms of education and the market economy. Neville Alexander's (2003, 2004, 2011, 2012, 2013) oeuvre on the critical relations between language and education, and, hence, between language and knowledge, work and class, is pivotal to thinking about the constraints and possibilities for such conversations between South Africans. Aligned with other projects of decolonisation (wa Thiong'o, 1986) and emancipatory education (Freire, 1972, 1973), Alexander (2004) argues that mother-tongue (or as he more accurately terms it, first language) instruction is imperative, particularly (but not solely) in the foundation phase of schooling. Alexander's argument is framed pedagogically: the cognitive demands in learning both skills (such as reading and writing) and content (such as life sciences) are exponentially increased if learning in an unfamiliar language which is in itself still a subject of learning. But Alexander's emphasis on mother tongue for education is more than narrowly pedagogical, extending to epistemological questions of cultural and social capital (Bourdieu, 1986), and to considerations of human worth, and both collective and individual identity.

The role of language is pivotal to the process of transmitting culture, the taken-for-granted meanings and patterns of life established by previous generations, joining the natural parameters of physical life in producing the contours of social life as simply the "way things are" in the world. In much the same way that the natural world and its constraints are experienced as part of our unthinking bodies (we breathe and walk without attending at all to the qualities of air and gravity that make these actions possible), language functions to naturalise the social world and enables us to live, breathe and walk among others without consciously attending to the specifics of that world.

Language (and by extension, culture and the law) is imposed from the outside. In Derrida's (1998, pp. 39–40) terms this process is most starkly evident in the imposition of the language and culture of the colonial other which creates a monolingualism that is also inevitably monolithic and oppressive:

> First and foremost, the monolingualism of the other would be that sovereignty, that law originating from elsewhere, certainly, but also primarily the very language of the Law. And the Law as Language. Its experience would be ostensibly autonomous, because I have to speak this law and appropriate it in order to understand it as if I was giving it to myself, but it remains necessarily heteronomous, for such is, at bottom, the essence of any law. The madness of the law places its possibility lastingly [à demeure] inside the dwelling of this auto-heteronomy.
>
> The monolingualism imposed by the other operates by relying upon that foundation, here, through a sovereignty whose essence is always colonial, which tends, repressively and irrepressibly, to reduce language to the One, that is, to the hegemony of the homogeneous. This can be verified everywhere, everywhere this homo-hegemony remains at work in the culture, effacing the folds and flattening the text.

The project of decolonisation (in all domains of cultural life but in South Africa most immediately and pressingly currently expressed in relation to higher education) might be understood as resistance to this "flattening" of the complex warp and weft of the textures of social life, against the thinning of histories into a single line, against the idea that a single language might incorporate all legitimate meaning. The limitations of monolingualism are both epistemic and political. Our ways of knowing (and not knowing or (mis)understanding) are "confined within the boundaries of our language and we can only step out of it by stepping into another language" (Van der Veer, 1996, p. 249). In the South African context, this stepping out of the dominant language of English and into other indigenous African languages in both schooling and higher education is long overdue and both the local and global academy is impoverished by our failure to respond to this imperative.[6] In addition to our knowledge losses, monolingualism re-inscribes and reproduces inequalities and racial and ethnic segregation. Those who are dominant (speak the dominant language, have access to dominant intellectual and other forms of capital) have particular vested interests in "not knowing" about the lives of others and asserting their ignorance as knowledge. In claims that seem to me perhaps only slightly exaggerated, Skutnabb-Kangas (1998, 2002) has vociferously and repeatedly argued that monolingualism threatens world peace and destroys the diversity of knowledge resources in ways that may ultimately be not only devastating for humanity but potentially fatal for the planet. Sanders (2010, p. 50) observes that repairing broken social justice depends on "one's preparedness to be heard to speak in languages one does not know … one cannot speak in a language one does not understand. … But we must all do the impossible".

Narrative imagination and conversation

Appiah (2006) proposes "conversation" as both the metaphorical and literal "solution" to the central question of this text: how is learning or change possible? The very minimal condition for such generative exchange is that we speak the same language. We must have *some* shared meaning if we are to find points of difference or otherness in these meanings. Further, Appiah alerts us to the interpretive work entailed in dialogical exchange if it is to have the power to create shifts in understandings. "[I]t is conversation, not mere conversion, that we should seek; we must be open to the prospect of gaining insight from our interlocutors" (2006, p. 264). Learning in this way from others entails more than accumulating new facts or bits of information from them; rather, it entails relinquishing our position to imagine the world from another's point of view, gaining a new sense of what things are *about*. This form of imagination is arguably best triggered by narrative, by stories of experience rather than rational argument aimed at convincing the listener. As Bruner (1986) argued, narrative has the power to "subjunctivise" experience, dislodging us from the here-and-now and suggesting possibilities, creating "what-if" worlds.

Reading novels or "true" stories, watching film-narratives or engaging with narratives in multiple visual or aural modalities provides us with moments or pockets of time in which we can "lose" our-selves (Ricoeur, 1981) and become part of other lives and worlds. From a Vygotskian perspective, Valsiner (2015, p. 94) similarly asserts the power of literature and the performing arts to release and enhance "development", affording these imaginative fictions the extraordinary role of *leading* our 'real' lives, creating futures and (re)directing action:

> Such fictional characters are synthetic – they are invented by the authors, yet they carry with them their believability as if they were real. Likewise, in real human development we create fictions – images of our future as rich or poor, married or divorced, honored or despised. We live our lives forward – imagining the pleasures of becoming adult and the wisdom or misery of becoming old. We even invent elaborate images of what happens once we stop living – hell, heaven and purgatory can be imagined but not visited. In sum – the human psyche is a perpetual constructor of the imagined world that leads our real living. The focus is on synthesis of new forms of feeling, thinking and acting.

If fictive narratives have such extraordinary power, the telling of "real" stories in conversation with one another may similarly work to release our imagination *if* we open ourselves to participate in the everyday stories of another's life. Molly Andrews' (2014) book *Narrative Imagination and Everyday Life* explores the imbrication of imagination in ordinary, everyday life. Rather than polar opposites, she argues, the imagined and the "real" operate in the same embodied domain of meaning-making. Ricoeur (1978, p. 143) suggests that the productive potential of language to release new possibilities of meaning lies in the stereoscopic or simultaneous split-reference to the world as it is and as it might be imagined through the "capacity of metaphor to provide untranslatable information and … yield some true insight about reality". This process of imaginative meaning-making happens by keeping multiple meanings in tension with one another to "produce new kinds by assimilation and to produce them not above the differences, as in the concept, but *in spite of and through* the differences" (Ricoeur, 1978, pp. 148–149, emphasis added). This involves first a "semantic impertinence" (1978, p. 145) or discordance between the "real" and imaginative domains which is then resolved in a "semantic innovation, thanks to which a new pertinence, a new congruence, is established" (1978, p. 146). Ricoeur suggests that these imaginative insights offer new exploratory trajectories of understanding before they come to be sedimented in concepts that require abstraction from experience and the consolidation or resolution of differences rather than allowing them to remain actively in play. Hermans (2001, p. 250) suggests that this capacity for imagination enables us "to construe another person or being as a position that I can occupy".

Individual life histories offer us ways of imagining the world of others across time and place and provide multiple cultural and social resources for the making of ourselves and our own understandings in our present contexts. In many ways, this is the attraction of narrative psychology: making the political, personal and restoring what the cultural psychologist Shweder (1991) so aptly describes as "the stuff" of life that seems evacuated from much of psychological (and social science) theory. However, the place and time from which the story is told, to whom it is told and for what purpose, are themselves subject to change. In particular, reading the past from the perspective of the present is fraught by the entanglement of personal lives in the historical fabric of conflict and how we understand our collective trajectory. To illustrate this, I offer my father's story, not his story but my story of him and not even really that but rather a shifting story of my reading of one aspect of his life and the ways in which it is threaded into my own. The photograph below is of my father (the little blond boy in the centre of the image) in his first school and has been a feature of my office for the past 15 years (see Figure 4.1).

I had heard stories from my father of his early schooling in a single classroom where multiple grades were taught in the same space by a single teacher who moved from one end of the room to the other, switching levels and subjects as she did so. Although this sounds chaotic and impossibly challenging to my adult (teacher's) ear, in my father's account it sounded fun and creative, and seemed the likely reason that he was able to skip the third grade, having picked up two years in one by jumping between groups with the teacher. I received this picture from my aunt after my father's death and was mesmerised by this image of a rural school. My fascination was partly because it concretised the tales I had heard of my father's exceptional intellect as a child and re-inscribed my notion of him as a role model: he was the first in his family to go to university and became a highly successful engineer. But the present

FIGURE 4.1 My father's first school
Family photograph, author's own

context of my work and life was the main reason that this picture rather than any other in the photo album leapt out at me. I was working with optimism and enthusiasm on an alternative selection programme for university admissions, aimed at identifying and developing the potential of black students, many of whom came from schools that looked very like that of my father, a small single-room classroom, pit latrine toilets and rough, grassless grounds that were weeded and hoed by the children themselves.[7] The image of my father's humble beginnings resonated with my confidence that the potential of these first-generation students would be recognised and that they would go on to succeed both at university and beyond in the world of work. And indeed they did. The picture served to remind and encourage me (and students with whom I shared the story) that education can lead to dramatic social mobility.

However, this reading of the image naively (ignorantly, not innocently) conflates historical time zones and with this, critical differences between my father's story, mine and the narratives of first-generation black students in the South African academy. The image is startling *because* the children in the picture are white[8]: no white children of either my generation or subsequent generations went to schools that looked like this. And, indeed, often students are puzzled about the picture and take a while to identify it *as a school*, sadly not because no such schools currently exist in post-apartheid South Africa but because the children in the image are white. And so the image speaks not only of the power of education but also of the effectiveness of the elaborate affirmative action programme of apartheid that provided the supportive context for my father to do what he did, and that made it possible for me in the next generation to become the first woman in my family to go to university and the first (including the boys) to continue with postgraduate study. The desire to follow in my father's footsteps and become an engineer was simply part of who I was as a young child and through my high school years. But I made a last minute switch to literature (simply because I loved to read) and psychology (about which I had no idea at all!). I am always grateful that I had the freedom to make this choice simply on the grounds of what interested me most. But this "choice" was of course inflected by my subject positioning in terms of race, class and gender. I knew from a very young age that I wanted my father's life rather than my mother's (who was, like the mothers of all my school friends, a "stay-at-home mom"). I was never dissuaded by my parents, teachers or anyone else from pursuing the (still) male-dominated career of engineering and was one of only a small minority of learners in my all-white, all-girl high school to take the requisite subjects of mathematics and physical science that would make that future possible. However, my relinquishment of this dream was also not met with any sanction, partly because of the pervasive sexism of the social milieu: no one (probably even including me although I didn't articulate this) really imagined that I would work for life rather than for a brief period before "getting married, having children and settling down". This may seem unthinkable for readers in the "West" where at that time (the early 1980s) the second wave of feminism had long since crested, but this is an effect of race and class in the colonised world and, particularly, in apartheid South Africa. I always feel that my brother who followed me to university a decade later was paradoxically disadvantaged by being a boy: he did the practical thing, studying commerce to become a banker, rather than literature although he too loved to read and went further than me in that he was a writer of poetry. Of course black girls (or boys) did not imagine futures for themselves in which they would not have to work for a living; neither could they luxuriously choose to study what they loved rather than what would deliver the best possibilities for earning a living. And the students that I teach now are all (regardless of race, class or gender) much more deliberate and conscious about the links between their studies and possibilities for work in an increasingly precarious world.

This re-reading of family history does not entirely negate the role of individual agency (including acting on idiosyncratic penchants for some things rather than others) nor the critical importance of learning and teaching, but it does situate these generational family shifts in the political contexts that produced historical privilege first for my father and then for me. While these moves were happening, the parents and grandparents of the current first-generation black students, continued to attend schools like my father's rural one-room classroom, probably in many instances, without the agile, innovative teacher. And so the picture remains in my office speaking to me of the energy, passion and hope to be found in learning and teaching *but* also demanding that I acknowledge my privilege and angering me that race, class and gender are still key determinants of possible futures for so many.

The transformative power (both for individuals and social collectives) of narrative lies in how individual stories are imaginatively connected to the stories of others across time and place, and articulated with theoretical networks of knowledge. The dynamic exchange of conversation entails something qualitatively different to the attendance of a live performance, even one in which the positions as teller and listener, performer and audience, shift. Recognising the full humanity of others entails being willing to look one another in the eye, to recognise one another (Taylor, 1994) and may entail negating something of oneself, recognising both aspects of our own identities that have been secured through inhumane and unjust histories, and recognising the gaps and lacunae in our understanding. In Levinas's famous formulation, "Consciousness is put into question by a face" (1963, p. 352). The face of the other's humanity has the potential for changing understandings and subjectivities in the "*in-between* of creative and unexpected possibilities that emerge when we open ourselves up to an otherness that is not of our own making" (Baerveldt, 2014, p. 545). Embracing such a position of vulnerability and openness may be discomforting, disruptive and unsettling, even psychically dynamic. "Black people, mainly, look down or look up but do not look at each other, not at you, and white people, mainly, look away" (Baldwin, 1962/ 1993, p. 30). While ignorance may constrain our individual and collective growth and potential for change, knowledge (of the other) may be considered risky, dangerous and threatening.

"Ignorance thus provides an important 'insulating medium' for the reproduction of a hierarchical racial order, both a consequence and cause of non-relationality, of living past each other" (Steyn, 2012, p. 21). The current repetitive reassertion of past ignorances in the present is, therefore, a way of "avoiding the truth" or avoiding our past selves, or for the younger generation, the pasts of those we love, that have delivered unjust privilege and benefits that continue in the present. For young white

South Africans, the intense shame of confronting these truths bolsters the psychic defence of ignorance. Beyond the litany of historical acts of racist violence themselves, Baldwin identifies this refusal to know, to see or to understand as the crime for "for which neither I [he] nor time nor history will ever forgive them, that they have destroyed and are destroying hundreds of thousands of lives and *do not know it and do not want to know it*" (Baldwin, 1993, p. 5, emphasis added).

Gobodo-Madikizela (2009, 2012, 2013) articulates a more fully psycho-analytic account of both the "forgetting" of painful traumatic memory, and the assertion of racist knowledge and ignorance, as psychic defences of the coherence of the subject.[9] She suggests that what is needed are "provocations to empathy" (2013, p. 221) or a kind of imaginative triggering that may circumvent the hermetically sealed self that is asserted as a knowing subject. The demand for changing the story, remaking memories and confronting live histories in the present may be risky and destabilising for subjects whose stories of them-selves include "narrative smoothing" (Spence, 1986) conceal-ing lacunae and disjunctures that enable us to "shore up" our identities against change (Crites, 1986, p. 165). By contrast, we are called on to enter into new forms of exchange that entail "the kind of intimacy, the kind of involvement with other people that we both fear and crave" (Philips & Taylor, 2009, p. 112). They further argue that this ambivalence reflects our psychological vulnerability; in the classic psychoanalytic formulation, it is our resistance to these conversations and exchanges that paradoxically reveals our desire for such intimacy. Likewise, Gobodo-Madikizela (2013, p. 221) argues that "[t]here is an intrapsychic dynamic at work in the provocation of empathy, particularly in relation to the pivotal turn to perspective taking and gaining an integrated view of both the self and the other. In essence, it is gaining new consciousness – seeing things anew".

Conclusion

Engaging with intransigent forms of knowing, misunderstanding and active ignorance is critical to the knowledge production project of the academy and beyond, to the (im)possibilities for knowing one another across boundar-ies of difference and other-ness. By using these conceptual tools for analysis, it becomes evident that the ways in which we misunderstand one another are not susceptible to change through reasoned persuasion or to correction by the supply of new information.

> Being ignorant is therefore quite a complex state of being. In large
> measure, the issue is how much we care to know about each other's

lives, past and present and where we recognise the limits of our legitimate claims to knowledge of each other to end. Choices around ignorance, to know or not to know, are deeply implicated in choices to take or evade responsibility in relation to others (Smithson, 2008). We do not, in fact, want all the knowledge we potentially could have because there are costs to having knowledge and shared intercultural and interracial meaning, a consideration which has not often been recognised.

(Steyn, 2012, p. 22)

The task confronting activists and educators alike is, therefore, to create possibilities for un-learning, for dismantling and deconstructing ways of knowing that effectively defend our ignorance and prevent new forms of both knowing and being in the world. This will entail:

1. Reframing educational tasks to dislodge mis-understandings. In this view, the zone of proximal development is not about scaffolding[10] and extending current knowledge but enabling learners to *experience* something new;
2. Hearing silenced versions of the world, and developing what Steyn (2015) calls "critical diversity literacy", the ability to read and interpret and imagine across difference;
3. Engaging in conversations with new and different interlocutors because our ignorances vary along lines of difference.

In Vygotskian terms, the construction of new understanding for one's self entails the ability to self-regulate in new ways by means of an internal dialogue. But as Miller (2011, p. 406) notes "before we talk to ourselves in the course of our inner conversations and in order to do so, we first must talk to others without whom our humanity remains only a possibility and our souls a singular impossibility". The challenge is thus to create moments for conversation between people that disrupt the powerful and affirm those less powerful; that broaden the spectrum of knowing in ways that are both destabilising and generative. Through such encounters, the internal conversation becomes plurivocal and contrapuntal (Said, 1993) including varied voices with the potential to challenge ignorance and misunderstanding masquerading as the coherence of innocence and understanding.

In narrative terms, what we are engaged in is generating new storylines. This entails not only imaginative projective futures but also imaginative empathic pasts, retold, re-appropriated in ways that will enable us to understand the present in less ignorant or purportedly innocent ways. Relinquishing our dual-role as author and protagonist in our own narratives to become less central characters (perhaps versions of ourselves that we have resisted or repressed) in the stories of others may enable us to build new versions of our-selves. Striving to overcome lacunae in our understanding of the world, ourselves and others, entails not only the accumulation of more understanding but the simultaneous unravelling of misunderstandings. Ethical ways of living and relating to one another are not to be found in a state of innocence claimed on the basis of ignorance or forgetting. Rather, recognising our culpability and entanglement with one another beyond the current moment enables us to imaginatively stretch backwards into "if only" pasts and forwards into the "what if" futures (Andrews, 2014) of ourselves and others.

Notes

1   As with other phenomena such as conflict, colonialism, modernity, structuralism typically now designated "post", the post-Apartheid era comes chronologically after but articulates a continuing living aftermath rather than a break with the apartheid past.

2   This designation of some forms of consciousness as "false" is much debated in Marxist analysis. A "class in itself" may have consciousness of societal conditions but may not yet have attained the mobilising perspective of being a "class *for* itself". This does not, however, mean that people's ideas about social realities are false.

3   For readers who are not psychologists, the classic conservation experiments enabled Piaget to demonstrate the qualitatively different cognitive schemes and operations that are applied by children at different stages of development in making sense of the world. Two containers of the same shape and size are filled to the same level with liquid. Once the child is satisfied that there is the same amount of liquid in both containers, liquid from one is poured (in full view of the child) into a differently shaped container (e.g. shorter but wider) such that the level of the liquid in the new container is now different. Despite having watched this action, the preoperational child is now convinced that the liquid volumes are no longer identical because they do not appear to be the same. This task makes it evident that understanding is informed only partly by perceptual cues. Active mental operations enable the older concrete operational child (and all adults) to conserve the volume of the liquid across the physical transformation: identity ("it is the same water, nothing has been added or taken away"); reversibility ("if the water was poured back into the original container, the levels would be the same"); compensation ("if one takes both height and width into account, rather than only one or the other, the volume is the same").

4   The pedagogical import of these ideas is more extensively explored in Chapters 5 and 6, including implications for the projects of transformation and decolonisation in higher education.

5 See, for example, Tamara Shefer's (2012) work on the emotional labour of black nannies in the upbringing of white children and the significant position that they occupy in the symbolic psychic landscape in the recollected narratives of these children once adults. The work of sociologists Jacklyn Cock (*Maids and Madams*, 1980) and more recently, Shireen Ally (2009) demonstrate the articulations between the public and private spheres and the ways in which the domestic labour of black women underpins the life of (almost entirely, white even in post-apartheid society) middle-class, nuclear families.

6 See further discussion of the issue of linguistic and cultural capital in higher education in Chapters 5 and 6.

7 See Chapter 5 for a discussion of the access programme Teach-Test-Teach at the then University of Natal.

8 Despite the fact that the picture definitely predates (my estimation is circa 1943/1944) the formal legislation of apartheid, segregation of children in schools was obviously already in force, with only white children in my father's first school despite it being situated in the majority-black rural Eastern Cape. The location of this school would have been very close to the Matatiele school, King Edward High school, which is currently still segregating learners (although ostensibly by language) into different racially homogenous classes (Govender, 2019). The 2019 academic year has begun with media exposés of this case and a similar case in another part of the country in the small town of Schweizer-Reneke, where Grade R learners were seated at different tables according to race (Shange, 2019). These shocking cases make evident how pervasive race-thinking and raced inequalities remain in an ostensibly democratic education system.

9 See Kaminer & Eagle (2010) for an overview of the historical roots and present-day manifestations of traumatic stress in (post-)apartheid South Africa. They articulate strong linkages with the well-established literature on Post Traumatic Stress Disorder (PTSD) but also explore the local particularities of the South African context and suggest possibilities for (psychoanalytic) therapeutic practice and other forms of community-based interventions.

10 This notion of scaffolding has been popularised as a Vygotskian concept, even as the central pedagogical approach to employ in the zone of proximal development. Although Vygotsky did use this metaphor, it was popularised by Bruner in an article entitled, *The role of tutoring in problem solving* (Wood, Bruner & Ross, 1976). This source elaborates a building block approach to learning that presumes a shared framework of understanding, describing learning as shadowing the regular and inevitable path of development. In this paradigm, education provides temporary structures or frames into which the developing intellect may grow. Although this approach may accelerate development, producing what Vygotsky (1978, p. 89) called "good learning … in advance of development", it is addressed to a situation in which the future shape of the structure is commensurate with the foundations. This chapter explores countersituations in which these conditions do not pertain, in which the foundations and framework are themselves subject to question, interrogation and unlearning.

SECTION 3

Intergenerational subjects in changing worlds

5

THE QUESTION OF POTENTIAL

A narrative of Vygotsky in action, then and now

Introduction

This third and final section of the book will present accounts of applications of Vygotskian and narrative psychology in the South African context, both within and beyond the academy, across three time zones: under apartheid and in the early transition to democracy (Chapter 5), in the first decade of the new millennium (Chapter 6) and finally, in Chapter 7, into the present and projected future. However, these zones of praxis are not compartmentalised nor linearly sequential and, as much as the past provides explanatory lines for thinking and practice in the present, the present vantage point provides for imaginatively reworking and reinterpreting history. These three chapters will therefore oscillate between past and present, weaving together retrospective and prospective imaginaries. Chapter 5 focuses specifically on the possibilities for individual and collective change through learning and teaching in higher education in the final decade of the 20th century in the context of South Africa's changing political landscape. However, this earlier period of change will also be explicitly linked to and rethought through the present historical moment, particularly in relation to contemporary politics of higher education.

In the inscription of culture in textual and other material objects and symbolic processes, including language, the sociohistorical meanings of previous generations remain alive within us, in our formation as narrative subjects. This is the conundrum that must be confronted in any attempt to theorise the individual processes of learning and change, the possibilities for transforming knowledge production, and the wider collective processes of sociopolitical transformation. The intergenerational quality of human life means that the present never escapes the past but it is simultaneously infused with imagined futures and the narrative arc stretches in both directions: historical traditions weigh heavily on and constrain the shape of present-day knowledge and practices, but the possibilities of yet-to-be future worlds that belong to the younger generation have a simultaneous loosening and enabling effect. Education is focused on this pivotal moment between past and future: university educators are engaged in the task of continuing and developing disciplinary traditions and the induction of a new generation of scholars who will be able to carry forward existing lines of enquiry *and* disrupt them, sometimes even rejecting them entirely to go elsewhere. The world beyond university walls in which graduates will live and work creates obligations to pressing present and future imperatives that inform the aspirations of students (and their families) in the educational space. In more generous political terms, education is also seen as a means to transform the sociopolitical landscape, creating a future that can transform relations to the past, somehow the remarkable dragon that sets its own tail on fire. The university is therefore a peculiar blend of sedimented tradition and youthful energies and future dreams. It is, in Vygotsky's most famous and widely used concept, a zone of potential development.

I will explore this idea of potential by focusing on two historical moments in South African higher education: first, the late 1980s/early 1990s when the cracks in the dominant edifice of apartheid opened up space for innovation and creativity, typically on the margins of the academy; and second, the present unfolding context, after the student uprising of 2015–2016. It is not coincidental that there is a generational gap between these two historical moments. The students of today are the children of the students of the 1980s and 1990s, the "hinge generation" (Hoffman, 2004) whose parents lived through apartheid and walked into a democratic future into which their children were born. Despite remarkable gains, current demands for free, decolonised education highlight the limitations and failures of the democratic regime in the higher education sector and beyond. In particular, changes in the racial demographics of participation rates may be cause for celebration but do not negate the perpetuation of socioeconomic inequalities in the meritocratic order. The potential of the past has been, at best, only partly realised and new zones of potential are opening up, provocatively challenging us all, especially educators, to imagine new modes of acting, thinking and being. The present project for the future entails decolonising the discipline of psychology, and the subject of psychology, the "mind" (Ngũgĩ wa Thiong'o, 1986) or, more generally, human subjectivity.

A wormhole narrative connecting past and present

In the dying decade of apartheid, historically white universities in South Africa began to incrementally open access for black students. This tentative movement happened in the context of highly unequal racialised schooling, requiring innovation to effect fair and accurate assessment of applicants, and creating an impetus for curriculum transformation. However, the disruptive potential of the political and pedagogical energies of this period were interrupted by the transition to the democratic order which effected a "normalisation" of mainstream practices in education and multiple other sectors where NGOs, civil society and researchers and practitioners were at work on the margins, imagining futures that now seemed to have arrived.[1] This produced a hiatus in which these energies were predominantly invested in national and institutional projects with the expectation that we were progressing towards the non-racial, non-sexist egalitarian society promised by the Mandela miracle and enshrined in our constitution. From the standpoint of the present, that moment often seems more mirage than miracle.

Nostalgia may delude us into thinking that before subsequent errors and mis-steps, there was an ethical political impetus or even an alternative world which might be recovered. From this perspective, all the fault-lines of the present may be traced to earlier failures that are patently obvious in the glare of hindsight. This is a dominant narrative among today's younger generation who blame their parents, teachers and political leaders for "selling out", confident that they would have done things differently. But, imagining ourselves back into that earlier context can only be done from the vantage point of the present where the consequences of those earlier actions and failures are already in play, already unravelling in new unpredictable ways. Time travelling through the wormhole between now and then cannot recover the past nor remake the present afresh through erasing it but the juxtaposition of these time zones may provide us with ways to imagine alternative futures. Past actions did not deliver a perfect present and the critique of the younger generation incisively nails ways in which we faltered and failed, particularly in ensuring the redistribution of land and other economic resources that would enable a more egalitarian social structure. However, this ostensible clarity is not all-encompassing and there are new blind spots in our retrospective vision.

The demands of the present are both continuous with and distinct from those that the older generation had to confront. In addition to the changing dynamics of our own local history, the global context has shifted dramatically. The tentacles of global capital are now far more powerful and flexible than the monolithic multinationals of the past. Climate change is a real and present threat to the future of humanity and reactionary politics and violent "othering" are mutating and exploding. The impact of these global dynamics on higher education is enormous. The ether connects us to one another across multiple borders and boundaries in liberating ways, altering the practices and possibilities of research, education and the world of work. But global connectivity is also homogenising and bureaucratising higher education, loosening traditions and tightening links to the market. The coming fourth industrial revolution promises (or threatens, depending on your perspective) to further accelerate these changes in unpredictable ways. It is therefore equally erroneous to argue that "nothing has changed" as it is to argue that "everything has changed" and harnessing history in present struggles will entail far more than retrospective pronouncements about what "should have" or "could have" been done. "Articulating the past historically does not mean recognising it 'the way it really was'. It means appropriating a memory as it flashes up in a moment of danger" (Benjamin, 1940, p. 391).

In the storm of history, each generation is compelled to meet the demands of their time but future visions may be animated by critical engagement with the past. By oscillating back and forth, we can "reconstitute the conceptual object from a point of view located in the present in such a way that the history produced is one which has calculated effects concerning present strategies for action" (Henriques, Holloway, Urwin, Venn & Walkerdine, 1984, p. 100). We are challenged to engage in what Foucault referred to as a "thoughtful presentism" which "constructs the past in order to illuminate the conditionality – not the inevitability – of the present" (Long, 2016, p. 220). In this way, without collapsing into either teleological optimism or cynical pessimism, we may be able to follow the trajectory of the mythical Ghanaian Sankofa bird, flying forward while looking backwards to gather the wisdoms of the past. Benjamin (1940, p. 392) enjoins us to "brush history against the grain [because] ... what we call progress is *this* storm".

Counting transformation then and now: what counts?

To evoke Einstein's observation once again, "Not everything that counts can be counted, and not everything that can be counted counts", the question of transformation in South Africa (which definitely counts) is a process that is routinely reduced to counting. This counting is suspect in two senses: first, it inevitably relies on the spurious apartheid categories of race and, in the process, re-inscribes them; and second, numbers tell only a partial story about what is or is not being substantively transformed, in particular, about whether society and its institutions are becoming less racist, more democratic and more economically egalitarian.[2] Nevertheless, if counting cannot tell us everything, it does tell us something rather than nothing. The first thing the numbers can tell us is that South Africa's Gini coefficient has increased rather than decreased and we have the egregious distinction of vying with Brazil for the most unequal society in the world. Statistics about "race" must be read in conjunction with this key indicator of the skewed distribution of public goods such as (higher) education and, in turn, employment opportunities and concomitant remuneration.

White privilege is clear in student participation rates in higher education. In 1993 on the brink of democracy, 69.7% of white school leavers continued into some form of higher education whereas only 12.1% of Black (African) and 13% of "Coloured" (mixed race) did so. Some 47% of the total student body were white and 40% African, most of whom would have been first generation students. Some 76% of academic staff were white (Soudien, 2008). Some shifts in these patterns are notable in national Department of Higher Education 2016 statistics: black students are now in the majority (71.9% African, 6.3% Coloured and 5.2% Indian) with white students constituting only 15.6% of the total cohort. These figures are beginning to approximate but do not yet completely reflect, national demographics that were, according to the 2011 census, 76.4% Black (African); 8.9% Coloured, 2.5% Indian and 9.1% White. However, these countrywide statistics mask differences between institutions, disciplines and levels of participation. For example, although it is less accelerated than in the student body, there has also been a shift in the demographic profile of academics over the same period, with 52% now black and 48% white, but this conceals the fact that less than 30% of academics are black at several universities: Stellenbosch (23%), University of the Free State (26%), University of Pretoria (26%) and Rhodes (29%) (DHET, 2018).[3] Soudien (2008) notes that the participation of black students in historically white institutions entails complex and ambivalent dynamics of aspiration (to gain access to and succeed in academically prestigious institutions) and alienation (from the culture and traditions of whiteness). These complex dynamics underpin the uneven, incomplete, unfolding processes of transformation and decolonisation.

Schooling: race and class in South Africa today

The conditions of inequality that characterised apartheid schooling have been well documented (e.g. Alexander, 2003, 2013; Kallaway, 2002) and do not require rehearsing here. However, these inequalities are not consigned to our shameful past, and are perpetuated (and even intensified) in the present. The distribution of resources such as the basic infrastructure of classrooms, furniture, water, electricity, (let alone technologies of computers and internet connectivity), learning materials and, critically, effective teachers, remains unequal. While there are no fee-paying schools to ensure that every child has access to the constitutional right of education, 90% of schools have no libraries, 42% of classes are overcrowded and there is a backlog of infrastructure projects to the tune of R153 billion (Vally, 2015). It is shocking, but perhaps in this context unsurprising, that 80% of Grade 4 learners are functionally illiterate (Farber, 2017). At the other end of the spectrum, increasing privatisation (including through effectively privatising public schools through charging top-up fees) means that inequalities are being entrenched and extended.

This uneven landscape is contoured by the multiple divisions of race, language, rural-urban dimensions, class and gender. Two narratives poignantly illustrate what can only be termed abusive neglect by the state of children's rights to education. In 2012 Limpopo schools had still not received textbooks from the department of education by July, the middle of the academic year which in South Africa begins in January. Chisholm's (2013) analysis identifies a range of distal contextual factors, including the economic downturn in the South African economy in the immediately preceding years in the aftermath of the global banking crisis of 2008, and fractious politics within the governing ANC at both at national and provincial levels. In this context, specific acts of maladministration and corrupt behaviour and sheer inefficiency by both government and private service providers (such as the warehousing company where the textbooks languished and the transport company) led to what is now referred to in common parlance as the "Limpopo textbook saga". It was only resolved by legal pressure brought to bear by the public interest group Section 27 who successfully argued through the courts that failure to deliver these textbooks was a violation of children's constitutional rights to education. In 2014, Michael Komape, a 6-year-old child in first grade, died after falling into a pit latrine and drowning in faeces at his school in rural Limpopo.[4] The department of education responded to litigation brought on behalf of the child's family by denying that his death was caused by "wrongful, unlawful and negligent conduct" by the state and its employees at the school and claimed that the "incident can best be described as an accident" (Govender, 2017). The callousness of this response is enervated in Michael's father's experience: "This is painful and I can't stop thinking about it. The government does not care about us. Our child died like a dog." This sickening and tragic story raises questions not only about the physical safety and hygiene of children in school but also critical questions of human dignity.

It is important to note that these conditions are not typical of all schools in South Africa and are, therefore, not simply an inevitable result of limited financial and human resources. Schooling is officially "open" and compulsory for all children but the provision of schooling remains racialised, gendered and, with increasing privatisation at the upper end of the spectrum, highly unequal. Even where basic infrastructure is in place and where teaching and learning is happening with diligent seriousness by both learners and teachers on a daily basis, access to and success in education is complicated and convoluted at every level, increasingly so, the higher up the educational rungs one climbs. Bourdieu & Waquant (1992) have provided us with an insightful analysis of how ostensibly democratic educational systems, (even where inequalities are more disguised than those just described) exercise "selectedness", reproducing unequal social structures across generations.

Testing people in testing times

Education (particularly higher education in the intellectual traditions of other times and places) promises to deliver social mobility for individuals and developmental progress for societies in which increasing numbers of people are able to access such educational opportunities. Although the myth of meritocracy has been robustly debunked (e.g. Piketty, 2015), it remains resiliently alive in popular narratives of individual aspirational futures and, in the context of unequal schooling, the question of who gets access to the limited places at institutions of higher education, particularly universities, is a matter of both accuracy (predictive of success) and fairness (in an unfair context). In designing tests for selection, two different kinds of errors are possible: the test may exclude those who would have succeeded had they been admitted for study, or select those who fail (Miller & Bradbury, 1999). The first error is "hidden", wasted human potential that is consigned to the margins of the system, whereas the second is highly visible in student performance and institutional throughput rates. Because of this, the demand for accuracy takes precedence in the construction of tests and selection decisions.

The notion that mental states and processes, particularly that thing that we call "intelligence", can be accurately measured is what spawned and sustains the field of psychometry. The history of psychometrics, particularly IQ testing, is implicated in racist (and sexist) ideologies worldwide (Rose, 1976) with particularly pernicious colonising effects in Africa (Mama, 1995). In apartheid South Africa, the science of psychology was expressly coupled with religious discourses to legitimise the discriminatory and segregationist system of apartheid (see, for example, Foxcroft & Davies, 2008; Kessi & Kiguwa, 2015; Manganyi, 1973; Sanders, 2010). The bias of psychometric tests is typically understood primarily as a function of culture and language (e.g. Laher & Cockcroft, 2017) rather than addressing more systemic structural and ideological effects or questioning the testing framework itself. In the past couple of decades, there have been attempts at translation of tests into indigenous languages, or at least from American into South African English, as the independent development of tests is generally considered too expensive, time-consuming and entailing multiple problems in relation to standardisation (Laher & Cockcroft, 2017). Attention has also been paid to the cultural relevance of test items (Foxcroft & Davies, 2008; Laher & Cockcroft, 2014) and to the cultural nuances of interaction in contexts of implementation especially, for example, in rural communities, and to combining psychometric testing with a range of qualitative assessments (Laher & Cockcroft, 2017). Despite its suspect history both within and beyond South Africa's borders, psychometry is a well-established professional field in South Africa and the prevailing view seems to be that it can be rehabilitated and utilised in more appropriate and progressive ways, articulating a version of "psychology *in* Africa" (Ratele, 2017). The continuing central positioning of the field is evident in the launch this year (2019) of the *African Journal of Psychological Assessment*, affiliated to PsySSA (The Psychological Society of South Africa).[5]

In addition to practices and developments in the field of psychometrics, a number of broader alternative testing protocols have been developed, particularly in relation to student selection for higher education. When white institutions began to admit small cohorts of black students in the late 1980s/early 1990s, it was well recognised that school results were a problematic basis for selection, inevitably reflecting unequal racialised schooling and learning histories. The task was to find or develop alternative tests. The project was driven by a unit at the University of Cape Town which is now named CETAP (Centre for Educational Testing for Access and Placement). Through many iterations a number of tests (focused primarily on the core competencies of maths and English) were developed and utilised by almost all universities across the country. The focus of test development in the 1980s was to provide an alternative to the unreliable matriculation scores with the hope that these tests would widen access for talented students despite poor school results (Yeld, 2007). The AARP (Alternative admissions research project) tests were widely implemented across the country and utilised for selection and placement, particularly in specialist elite fields such as medicine. At around the same time as previously white institutions were opening their doors to black students, the racially segregated schooling system was amalgamated and a new, single examination system was instituted. The AARP tests were subjected to a new round of design and development to become the NBT (National benchmark tests) that are still being utilised by many institutions today. The NBT assessments claim to fulfil a dual purpose: first, assessing individual students' core competencies on a standardised test would enable informed decisions about the admission and placement of these students, and second, providing a "benchmark" against which to evaluate the reliability of the standards of the school leaving examination (Yeld, 2007). There were also claims that the bands of performance in these test results could inform university teaching and curriculum responsiveness (Cliff, 2015).

However, despite recognising the significance of the teaching and learning processes that precede and follow assessment, these approaches are generally aligned with the underlying premise of the psychometric approach. Psychological life (in this instance, cognitive processes or intelligence) is viewed as a quantifiable substance that is differentially and normally distributed among people, producing universal standards by means of which to categorise individuals. Where these tests are utilised for selection (like the SATs in the USA) they function in parallel with the assessment of academic merit through the schooling system, creating yet another hurdle for learners already disadvantaged by this unequal system. In the current context, where there is a substantial cohort of black learners in private and semi-privatised "good" public schools (i.e. previously white suburban schools) and pockets of good teachers and learners in township and rural schools, it is not at all clear that these assessment techniques are more predictively reliable than matriculation scores. Individual opportunities for past learning are still radically unequal and racially skewed *but* if our concerns are not with the poor, rural or marginalised mass of young people, there are sufficient numbers of black students who qualify for admission to transform the demographic profile of institutions. More radical changes will entail engagement with questions of epistemological access (Morrow, 2009) and success, and the articulation of decolonising pedagogy and curricula.

A retrospective narrative of potential: Vygotsky in action

In contrast to the quest for a test that is able to "by-pass educational background and experience, and also that is uncontaminated by socio-economic factors" (Miller, 1992, p. 99), the assessment of potential entails engaging in ways that are "designed to alter performance and not preserve it" (Miller, 1992, p. 101).[6] In the late 1980s, the alternative selection pro-gramme, Teach-Test-Teach was launched at the then University of Natal under the directorship of Hanlie Griesel, collaborating with academics across multiple disciplines in the faculty of Humanities. Anita Craig and Ronald Miller in the department of psychology provided the overarching theoretical framing for the project and pedagogical training for academics and student-tutors.[7] These were heady times in which I cut my intellectual teeth in the best mix of research, teaching and what is now referred to as "community engagement". Students were recruited through networks of NGOs and community-based projects (some of which were front organisations for the underground liberation movement) and invited to participate in an intensive two-week on-campus programme taught by a team including senior professors (in the first few years of the project) or as numbers grew, in workshops taught by academic tutors in multiple community sites.[8]

The name of the project encapsulates the idea that any test needs to be embedded in cycles of teaching that aim to alter performance. This approach is premised on the "fundamental assumption ... that education provides learning opportunities that alter the very abilities that are assumed or treated as fixed in the construction of psychometric/edumetric tests" (Griesel, n.d., in Bradbury, 2000, p. 310). Vygotsky's concept of the zone of proximal development was central to the design, develop-ment and implementation of the programme, providing a prospective orientation to the potential for future learning rather than a retrospective description of past learning as consolidated in current knowledge and abil-ities. It is uncontentious to suggest that young people leaving school and entering higher education are yet to fulfil their potential as adults in the world. However, we most often think of the development of this future potential person as continuous with the past and present, a more mature, better version of the same self. The educational terrain is likewise seen as a homogenous plane in which increasing levels of difficulty extend beyond but are continuous with earlier simpler levels of thinking and acting. How-ever, in conditions of disjuncture between previous learning and future opportunities, between earlier selves and new possible identities, potential is as elusive as the South African rainbow. "By definition, potential cannot be measured and can only be identified once realised. Any attempt to identify academic potential must translate into an attempt to provoke individuals to realise abilities that are not manifest in their previous academic performance" (Griesel, n.d., in Bradbury, 2000, p. 309). From this perspective, the task therefore becomes a matter of teaching rather than testing, creating possibilities for new learning beyond what is already known or developed through prior learning, and provoking movement and change in the zone of proximal development.

The TTT programme aimed at creating these zones for learning that anticipated the demands of university study rather than building on previous knowledge and experience developed at school. The matriculation scores of TTT students were way below the minimum requirements for university entry and therefore all that could be derived from these scores was the unhelpful recognition that apartheid education had deliberately underprepared black learners for higher education (and the associated professions or kinds of work undertaken by graduates). These provocations for learning were carefully designed in the form of lectures, tutorials and, very importantly, textual materials[9] and tasks, introducing core concepts and the modes of thinking, reading and writing typical of the Humanities disciplines.[10] The assessment of potential entails two important departures from the usual principles of testing. First, the focus is on movement or change across two or more points in time, in contrast to static measures or psychological constructs in which time is irrelevant and should have no effect. As Vygotsky (1978) argued, a performance score may conceal very different intellectual capacities. It is uncontentious to observe that a "clever" child may perform poorly on a test because she was feeling ill on the day or because the room was uncomfortably hot or cold making it hard to concentrate. Vygotsky argued that in a similar way, the same performance score may have different roots. Excellent teaching and support may enable one learner to perform at her very best whereas another learner, without similar learning opportunities and support, may obtain the same score. What she has been able to achieve under less than optimal conditions is not a reflection of what her "best" performance may potentially be. In this approach the actual score is less significant than how much a learner is able to benefit from teaching and the shifts she makes from her original starting point even if this is an extremely low base and even if the final score is not in "objective" terms particularly impressive. The zone of learning may entail transitions, approximations and hesitant incomplete movements back and forth (Valsiner & van der Veer, 2014) in which actions prefigure possibilities for the future. This was an important strut in our argument that future potential excellence could not be predicted by selecting only those who were top performers at school – and this transformational argument had to be made repeatedly with university gatekeepers. Second, "peaks in performance" (Feuerstein, Rand & Hoffman, 1979, p. 34) were treated as indicators of potential. The conventional approach is to discount performance that is inconsistent, treat it as an anomaly and flatten its effects in an average score. If we are less interested in an accurate assessment of consolidated independent performance and more interested in potential for future learning, any "peak" achievement indicates what the learner is capable of and what will become possible in a more sustained way in the future. "The phenomena of *emergence*, *becoming*, and *transformation* become the objects of investigation in developmental science" (Valsiner & van der Veer, 2014, p. 151).

Curriculum innovation: teaching and learning

The research agenda of the TTT programme was to develop alternative selection procedures that would meet the dual imperatives of equity and excellence, but the focus on potential shifts attention away from the products of learning as reflected in test scores towards the processes of teaching and learning, both before and after testing, rather than on the products of testing. The ZPD extends in front of the point of entry into university study where each new student is inserted into traditions of knowledge. The long trajectory of these traditions are instantiated in the "fossilised" (Vygotsky, 1978) products of knowledge and in the taken-for-granted processes and practices of academia. The effect of this is to conceal the ways in which all knowledge is actively constructed by people in communities of practice. This is the "hidden curriculum" (Illich, 1971) of all higher education: students are expected to become active makers of their own knowledge through an engagement with the heavy weight of disciplinary knowledge that appears fully formed, concealing its own historical construction.

In the unequal terrain of South African schooling, then and now, students' preparation for university study is extremely variable. In the language of academic development in the apartheid era, students from disadvantaged socioeconomic and schooling backgrounds were (deliberately) underprepared in a range of ways and it was incumbent upon the university to teach and support these students by supplying that which should have been taught at school but had not.[11] The focus was on supplying missing content and developing skills such as English language competency, computer skills, study skills, academic literacy and writing skills. Bridging units (particularly in science and engineering) or foundation courses were designed and often compulsory for students entering the university via alternative selection programmes, even where students (unlike TTT students) met requirements for direct entry. These academic development programmes were often premised on a "deficit model" failing to recognise that in many respects, it was universities and academics rather than students who were underprepared. It is certainly true that universities and academics were ill-equipped (and in many cases, resistant) to engage with these new cohorts of students and, in the context of decolonising curricula and pedagogies, there is ample evidence that this remains the case. However, there is also no denying that many first-generation students who embarked on university study in the late 1980s/early 1990s needed and benefitted from these interventions as imperfect as they were and, in cases of best practice, this experimental educational work had a disruptive impact on established curricula and pedagogies.

The majority of the first TTT entrants were required to register for an extended curriculum, taking a reduced load of courses and attending supplementary tutorials and workshops taught by the TTT team. Our approach was not primarily skills based, attempting rather to create a ZPD that would create the architecture for constructivist independent knowledge-making. Our assumption was that, rather than being underprepared, students were *over*prepared (Bradbury & Miller, 2011), full of assumptions about knowledge and study that may have served them well in the school system but were inappropriate for university study, particularly in the humanities. For example, reliance on the authority of teachers and texts, a view that (scientific) knowledge is indisputable and stable and must simply be acquired and reproduced. These misunderstandings may block new approaches to thinking and knowing (see the discussion in Chapter 4) and may often actually be reinforced by the ostensible demands of university study where lectures are delivered by experts and the sheer volume of reading implies that everything that needs to be known is already there, inert chunks of information to be retrieved, reassembled and reproduced. These epistemic assumptions cannot be shifted through the accumulation of more information and "concepts can't be taught by drill ... [What is required are] different orchestrations" (Shotter, 2006, p. 25), new shapes and structures for the activities of knowledge-making. The construction of this zone of learning cannot be left to chance or to the spontaneous activities of learners themselves.[12] The zone of proximal development always entails an asymmetrical relationship (Van der Veer & Valsiner, 1991) in which the teacher or "more capable peer" orchestrates or choreographs the moves. To provoke new possibilities for learning entails deliberate mediation "controlling, directing, channelling" (Shotter, 2006, p. 28) or "framing, filtering, scheduling" (Feuerstein, Rand, Hoffman & Miller, 1980, p. 16) the actions of learners in the ZPD, enabling them to act on the basis of another's understanding rather than their own.

In a context where the relation between school and university learning was discontinuous, Craig (1992) argued for a strategy of "defamiliarisation" rather than building on previous knowledge and ways of doing things which might serve to block new and different modes of knowledge construction. (See discussion in Chapter 4.) She applied a matrix of thinking about the range of familiar-unfamiliar aspects of university tasks in terms of content and form demands. Although it might seem that the most difficult tasks would be those which are unfamiliar in both content and form, these tasks may present exceptional opportunities for learning in that prior knowledge and ways of doing things cannot be relied upon, opening up a productive and receptive space for new learning. By contrast, tasks that seem familiar because the content domain is linked to school knowledge (e.g. literature) or culturally familiar worlds (e.g. theology or politics) may create difficulties because this familiarity masks unfamiliar forms of engagement.

In the context of today's decolonisation debates, defamiliarisation smacks of alienation or "epistemic violence" (Teo, 2010). However, Žižek (2005, p. 70) suggests that intellectual pursuits always entail moments of "foreignness" and suggests that "philosophy [and I am suggesting that we interpret this broadly to mean the domain of theoretical disciplines] ... was from the very beginning not the discourse of those who feel the certainty of being at home". There may be joy and delight in this estrangement from the familiar, releasing possibilities for remaking the "normal". But for the unsettling process to be productive rather than alienating, it must entail respect for what students bring into classrooms, particularly, including resources from outside of school classrooms, in the longer histories of African life, language and meaning-making that have always co-existed with and resisted colonial attempts to contain and homogenise modalities of knowledge construction. The creation of this kind of ZPD does not erase asymmetrical relationships with respect to knowledge but requires an affirming faith in students' potential to engage with difficult and complex ideas, to challenge these ideas and to go beyond what it is that we already know. In our current context, it is very clear that the notions of "under-/over-preparedness" that we worked with in the context of apartheid schooling continue to manifest in similar ways but have also mutated in relation to the changing national and global scapes of knowledge and education. These mutations include more complex intersections between race and class, and new, much more powerful challenges to the academy's complicity in the colonising and oppressive effects of education, and *our under-/over-preparedness* to meet the learning-teaching demands of our students and respond to the changing imperatives of our local and global worlds. The content and form of the academy is being unsettled but, as Maldonado-Torres (2016, p. 11) recognises, not "everything produced by Western modernity is a colonial artefact that cannot but promote colonialism". In this context, academics have a dual accountability, towards the knowledge and traditions of the past of which we are human carriers, and towards our students and their future horizons which lie beyond what we can see from our vantage point.

> [E]ducators here stand in relation to the young as representatives of a world for which they must take responsibility although they themselves did not make it, and even though they may, secretly or openly, wish it were other than it is.
>
> *(Arendt, 1961, p. 189)*

Interdisciplinarity and epistemological access

In the early 1990s there were a number of interdisciplinary courses developed by colleagues across the Humanities faculty at the University of Natal to create a core foundation programme for students, for example, *Language, text and context* and *Individual, state and society*. This conceptualisation of the curriculum beyond disciplinary boundaries entailed many promising vibrant conversations and battles between academics who, in attempting to reconceptualise the terrain for students, had to confront their own commitments to practices, forms and canons of knowledge. The political impetus for these disruptions of the status quo within the academy was lost as the war was apparently won in the democratisation of the state. The most hopeful interpretation of current conditions is that the renewed imperatives of decolonisation may revitalise and reanimate these debates.

The first of these interdisciplinary experiments was the credit-bearing course, *The development and production of knowledge*, offered first only to cohorts of TTT students and then more widely to students in the faculty of humanities. The primary vehicle for the organisation of the course was provided by Bronowski's (1973) *The Ascent of Man*. By tracing the roots and routes of knowledge, he exposes the constructed and changing nature of knowledge. It was for me, as well as for the students, a remarkable eye-opening journey, revealing the awe-inspiring ways in which people throughout history and in places far-flung from our standard reference point of the colonial English-speaking centre had, through action and thought, *made* the world that we encounter. However, the film and text declares its celebratory progressive narrative and patriarchal bias in its very name. From our position in the present, this narrative of human history is patently partial and inaccurate and, for many contemporary readers, this text should be destined for burning or at the very least, consigned to a dusty dungeon where its "epistemic violence" can do no harm. Subjecting the enlightenment project to what Charles Mills (2013) calls "black illumination" reveals its entanglement with colonialism and exploitation. I do not propose that the text should be dusted off for new cohorts of South African students to read but in reflecting on the course now, I do think there may be something to be rescued from the fire. First, the fact that the authority of a text can shift so dramatically across time is itself an indicator of how knowledge "develops". The text is fixed but its meanings are not and new readers can create divergent or even diametrically opposed trains of thought through encountering an author's ideas. In this sense, I have great faith in creativity as a "normal human act ... not entailing some kind of herculean effort to shrug off the discursive constraints of others" (Chomsky, 2006a, p. 18). Second, the best of enlightenment scepticism entails the rejection of authority (religious or scientific) in favour of a constructivist epistemology. This orientation is essential if students are to become critical, active knowledge producers themselves rather than passive recipients of revealed or discovered truths. Third, although Bronowski valorises science, he does so by emphasising that it is a *human practice* and refuses to dichotomise technological and cultural forms, suggesting productive interdisciplinary possibilities. In response to today's geopolitical problems, antinomy between science and humanities is an intellectual indulgence we cannot afford. Finally, this version of human history is both temporally and spatially wide-ranging but nonetheless excludes more than half the world.[13] This should provoke us to constantly subject existing cannons to critical evaluation and to extend our attentions elsewhere to articulate alternative histories and ways of knowing. Histories that have been hidden or muted need to be articulated in present debates. In the current context of the South African Student Movement, resistance to science as a "Western" knowledge form erases the African origins of mathematics in ancient Egypt and negates the Hindu-Arabic invention of our contemporary numerical system. The canons of our disciplines and our colonial reference points centre Oxford and Cambridge rather than the oldest universities of India or the ancient libraries of Timbuktu.[14] New generations of scholars are immersed in the paradoxical effects of education which is often a vehicle for the transmission of particular forms of power. But in the way in which it is constituted, in the ways in which the disciplines are structured to interrogate meaning, it has within it the potential for disrupting social, cultural and economic orthodoxy. This capacity is underpinned by its constituent elements. It is the one institution that rehearses the practices and modalities for the deconstruction of knowledges that authorise the disciplines – but also the methodologies for the reconstruction of self and community.

(Soudien, 2012a, p. 31)

The form and content of psychology

In the second phase of curriculum development in the mid-1990s, as the numbers of first-generation black students increased, attention shifted from innovations at the margins to mainstream discipline-based courses at the then University of Natal. In psychology, we created an entirely new first year programme that departed from the standard (usually American) textbook format that was then (and now) in operation (Bradbury, 1995). The course was primarily focused on developing epistemic and metacognitive engagement with the form demands of the discipline and the mode of delivery reflected these concerns with active deep engagement. The number of lectures were reduced, displacing the conventional transmission mode of instruction in favour of interactive tutorials modelling the form of academic argument and extended workshop sessions that actively engaged students in reading and writing. The assessment of students' work was based on the analysis of task demands and the kinds of questions that drive our enquiry in the humanities: factual, relational and conceptual (Bradbury, 2000; Bradbury & Miller, 2011; Miller, Bradbury & Lemmon, 2000; Miller, Bradbury & Pedley, 1998). This focus on kinds of questions was not designed to prepare students for tests and examinations but rather to engage them in the defining form of intellectual engagement. The knowledge that we encounter at any given moment, particularly when it takes authoritative textual shape, in "black and white" appears in the form of answers concealing the questioning process that produced them. As Gadamer (1975, p. 333) says the "logic of the human sciences is … a logic of the question" and, for students to become part of this tradition, this form needs to be made explicit.

However, the selection of content was also an important consideration in the course design. In place of the accumulative empirical (and mostly empiricist) body of psychological knowledge, the skeleton for the course was provided by key theoretical frameworks of the 20th century, e.g.

Darwin, Freud, Piaget and Marx. Each of these theories contribute to an epistemological framing of psychological knowledge: evolutionary theory provides a framework for thinking about life as part of the natural world and simultaneously disrupts notions of the natural world as stable and permanent; Piaget accounts for human thought as actively *constructed* in contrast to the passivity of both sides of the nature-nurture debate; psychoanalysis disrupts normative notions of rationality, and (sometimes distorted) ideas of the unconscious are pervasive in multiple disciplines and in common sense discourse; Marxist theory connects human consciousness to action in the transformation of nature through labour, and to the social world through the structuring of relations to material resources and others. These grand narratives represent a particular view of the history of ideas, locate the sources of psychological and social theory in the global north but are asserted as universal explanatory frameworks. In retrospect it is remarkable and shocking to me that theories closer to home did not form part of this core curriculum. Biko's (1978) theory of black consciousness and Manganyi's (1973) theory of "being-black-in-the-world" are obvious glaring omissions. Together with feminist and queer methodologies, these theories provide more capacious ways of understanding personhood. An intersectional approach would provide an orientation to the core psychological concepts of identity and subjectivity that reconceptualises the relation between selves and the social world. Notwithstanding these serious limitations to our earlier curriculum innovations, the approach disrupted the canon of psychology and displaced the tyranny of the textbook. A contemporary appropriation of this reframing offers more radical possibilities for decolonising psychology than the substitution of an American textbook with one written by South Africans that simply reproduces the same flattened flood of information – all of which is in any case available at the touch of a Google button!

Race, class and access in South African universities today

Education, particularly university education, promises class mobility for individuals but simultaneously reproduces and maintains the status quo: "the university, and in a general way, all teaching systems, which appear simply to disseminate knowledge, are made to maintain a certain social class in power; and to exclude the instruments of power of another social class" (Foucault, 2006, p. 40). In post-apartheid South Africa this tension in the purposes and prospects of higher education is exaggerated where many black students are first-generation entrants into the system. By overturning the racially segregated education system of the past, the framework of neoliberal equality of opportunity is created. However, "[i]n moving towards the meritocratic ideal, we imagined that we'd moved beyond the old encrustations of inherited hierarchies ... that's not the real story." (Appiah, 2018, p. 141). The racialised inequalities of apartheid were highly visible because they were inscribed in the legal framework of all state institutions and in the architecture of space and everyday life. By contrast, contemporary South Africa has attempted, like neoliberal democracies elsewhere, to conceal structural inequalities in discourses of merit and opportunity. Structural racism and the generational perpetuation of socioeconomic inequality may be partially submerged but are not erased. The #Student Movement is a significant rupture of the thin social veneer of post-apartheid society in which a new generation of students has recognised that the "pursuit of a purely individual, a merely psychological, project of salvation" is futile and that the "only effective liberation from such constraint begins with the recognition that there is nothing that is not social and historical – indeed, that everything is 'in the last analysis' political" (Jameson, 1982, p. 20). The politics of the movement are fluid and unfinished but articulations of the two primary intersecting dimensions of race and class demonstrate both continuities and disjunctures with the apartheid past.

Student battles over (academic and financial) exclusion have been a permanent feature of higher education in post-apartheid South Africa running in parallel with increased access and inclusion.[15] However, for two decades these battles were often silenced, partly because students who were excluded are no longer students, returned through failure to spaces outside of the academy and rendered invisible, and partly because the primary fields of these battles were the historically black institutions with less prominence in the social and political imaginary of the "new" South Africa. In 2015, the Rhodes statue on the prestigious campus of the University of Cape Town (UCT) became the initial lightning rod that signalled a new historical storm. The toppling of the Rhodes statue was a crucial symbolic event that opened the way for the prolonged waves of protest action across the country throughout 2015 and 2016. #FeesMustFall exposed the financial precarity of the vast majority of students, disrupting the complacency of institutions who pointed to changing racial demographics in the student body as signs of their transformation, and forcing the state to acknowledge its responsibility by announcing first, zero increases in fees at the end of 2015 and expanding the national student loan fund (NSFAS) for the poorest students, followed by the announcement in 2017 of free higher education for the poor and the so-called missing middle.[16] The Student Movement has castigated government and the middle-class South African public for responding only when these protests erupted in the elite institutions of UCT and the University of the Witwatersrand (Wits). Critics of the Student Movement have highlighted the middle-class status of many student leaders and argued that their protests are driven by individual entitlement and ambition rather than a radical transformational agenda (see, for example, Long, 2018 and, particularly, Jansen, 2017). However, this critique seems to oversimply the intersections of race and class particularly for this generation of young South Africans. There is a clear logic for how and why the Student Movement emerged at this time in our history and in these particular locations. Although these prestigious universities have welcomed the children of the emerging black middle class, they have failed to recognise that these students do not come from families where their intergenerational resources provide a safety net for students in the form of securities for loans, and by absorbing accommodation and travel costs. Khunou (2015) highlights the complex and contradictory dimensions of the black middle class and the unusual constellation of advantages and disadvantages that come with this category (which is resisted by many as an inappropriate misnomer). The lack of secure intergenerational positioning translates into present uncertainties and anxieties about the future. From a different context in the USA, Westover (2018, pp. 235–236) observes how financial precarity has a pervasive impact on possibilities for learning:

> Curiosity is a luxury reserved for the financially secure: my mind was absorbed with more immediate concerns, such as the exact balance of my bank account, who I owed how much and whether there was anything in my room I could sell for ten or twenty dollars . I submitted my homework and studied for my exams, but I did so out of terror – of losing my scholarship should my GPA [grade point average] fall a single decimal – not from real interest in my classes.

It is also pertinent that democratisation in South Africa has coincided with increasing bureaucratisation and corporatisation of higher education around the world. This context means increased access for the emergent middle class, working class and poor students comes at a time that funding for higher education is universally under pressure, exacerbated by our position as a developing economy. The demand for market-related qualifications is also increasingly impacting on the purpose of higher education and is shaping the knowledge that students and their families consider relevant and useful (Long, 2013). Bourdieu's (1986) three kinds of capital, economic, cultural and social, function together to perpetuate structural inequalities and constrain how we envisage possible personal and collective futures in the space of higher education.

Language(s) of decolonisation and textual worlds of possibility

The role of language is central to socialisation, particularly in the institutions of family and education, conveying both the contents of knowledge and meaning-making practices, and the patterns of cultural life creatively established by previous generations. In this way, the contours of social life are naturalised and encountered by each new generation of learners or developing children as simply the "way things are" in the world. Without requiring conscious attention, we move through the social world in the stuff of language in much the same automated way that our bodies move through air and across ground. Language (and by extension, culture and the law) is always imposed from the outside. In the context of access to university study, the language in question is almost always English (with the exception of a few Afrikaans medium universities who are now in the process of shifting their language policies in favour of English). Academic development programmes often focused on the difficulties of "second-language" English speakers and language was used as a marker for race and class, specifically as manifest in the hierarchies of apartheid in schools. (See for example, my own writing about this period, Bradbury, 2000; Bradbury & Miller, 2011; Miller & Bradbury, 1999.) It is disturbing to note that in the many changes to the school curriculum in the decades post-1994, hardly any attention has been given to the development of African languages for disciplinary areas or in materials and texts, and matriculants are not required to study or even demonstrate basic competency in an African language. What has changed in the curriculum tells the same story from a different angle: new subjects or learning areas, such as "business studies", "tourism" and "consumer studies", have been introduced, indicating the kind of world of work for which schooling is preparing learners. Likewise, graduates from public universities can exit into the world of work without being able to speak, read or write an indigenous language. When this graduate is a psychologist or psychotherapist, she will only be able to practise the "talking cure" with English speakers, likely predominantly middle class and white. In a multilingual country that prides itself on official language status for 11 languages, this is bizarre to put it mildly! The question of language is tied up with our colonial and racist histories.

The project of decolonisation (in all domains of cultural life but in South Africa most immediately and pressingly currently expressed in relation to higher education) might be understood as resistance to the "flattening" effects of monolingualism (Derrida, 1998, see the discussion in Chapter 4). It is impossible for a single (colonial) language to capture and contain all meaning, and what we "know" is perpetually unravelled and rewoven in multiple tongues by all people across all domains of life. The language question is therefore not simply one among many; it is central to the role of education and research in response to current and future questions of human life within and beyond the South African context. Alexander (2003, 2004, 2011, 2012) consistently argued for mother-tongue instruction, particularly in the early phases of education for pedagogical reasons. But his rationale went beyond the patently obvious observation that children learn best when they understand the medium of instruction! Indigenous languages are repertoires of representation and conceptualisation that enable alternative constructions of selves and worlds. The politically liberating effects and possibilities of writing and thinking in indigenous languages have been powerfully argued for by Freire (1972, 1973) and wa Thiong'o (1986). However, the potential value of multiple languages lies not only in the experiential zones of individual learning and collective local political action. In the vortex of the natural and political crises that seem all-pervasive across the globe, the limits of our current knowledge bases in the natural and social sciences are all too evident. New conceptual languages are required to complicate, twist, deepen and change the dominant languages of research and knowledge-production.

Other regulation, creative selves

While the imposition of meaning from the outside is most clearly visible in contexts where the language that is learned is literally the language of the other, a colonial language, *all* language learning serves to insert children into the language of others, into meanings derived not from the child's own engagement with the world but through others. To put this idea into the psychological language of development, into Vygotskian language, the world of the child is mediated. In Derrida's terms, the child's mind is "colonized" by an-other, usually, in the first instance, the maternal other but also beyond the home, most critically in the terrain of education where children's thought is "schooled" in the "traditions" (Gadamer, 1975) of knowledge and the understandings of others. Higher education is in this sense the most rigorous and pervasive form of colonising minds, full immersion into the specialist languages of disciplines.

As I have argued elsewhere, (Bradbury, 2012) we cannot do otherwise; it is only possible for us to become ourselves through these collective frameworks of meaning, through "the long detour of the signs of human-ity deposited in cultural works" (Ricoeur, 1981, p. 143). In this way, our conscious cognising of the world is socialised, formed through shared lan-guage, shared understandings and shared meanings. But the most forceful impact of tradition lies beyond the engagements of parental influence, or individual teachers' and academics' stocks of knowledge. Children (and students) join the flow of history in ways that are less reliant on the (best) intentions of adults, developing a "narrative unconscious" (Freeman, 2010) linking them into intergenerational chains of meaning-making. This heavy baggage of collective memory creates a subterraneous mapping of the world against which experience is interpreted, determining the languages in which narratives can be articulated and constraining the tales that we can tell.

However, despite the essentially communicable character of consciousness given its creation in shared language, this process is always incomplete, "not without remainder", always open to a surplus of mutable meanings. The remarkable malleability of language is evident in the astonishing pace and creativity of children's language learning which led Chomsky (1986) to resoundingly demolish the faulty logic of behaviourist notions of imitative learning. Small children produce linguistic constructions that have never been overheard, indeed, they speak into being, things that have never been said. In the adult domain of higher education, the primary task of all students and scholars is to articulate their own individual engagements with the knowledge of others. The primary mode of knowledge construction and transmission in higher education is textual, notwithstanding the resilience of the oral lecture for undergraduates, postgraduate seminar discussions and the academic conference, all of which are strange hybrids of textual and oral forms. The paradox of text is that by fixing and preserving the meaning of the author, new possibilities for meaning-making open up "in front of" the text as it articulates with the worlds of new readers (Ricoeur, 1981, p. 143). The moral panic that plagiarism produces indicates that we never expect students to directly reproduce what they read. Writing is a "*crafting* of experience rather than a direct representation of it*" (Parker, 2015c, p. 78), remaking old ideas and releasing new conceptual configurations.

Where education is about the formation of critical subjects rather than "cloning" (Essed & Goldberg, 2002), the innate creativity and novelty of language (and its important extensions in reading, writing and visual texts) and the forms of thought it makes possible, should be nurtured and facilitated rather than closed down by the process of schooling in discip-linary languages and traditions. Whereas art or literature (and science) must always belong to tradition and use the (past) languages of others, the best art (and science) always entails innovation rather than mere replication or reproduction. The best students and intellectuals learn to read not only texts but also the world (Freire & Macedo, 1987) and in this process we may rewrite ourselves (Freeman, 1993) and our interpretation of the world may animate new actions and interactions. Historical constraints are not fully determining and, although power is asymmetrically distributed, its ubiquity is not totalising and infuses human subjects with possibilities for agency (Foucault, 1979, 1988). Somewhat ironically, in a debate with Foucault, it is Chomsky (2006a, p. 55) who captures these ambivalent articulations of power in and through education:

> I think here it's too hasty to characterize our existing systems of justice [and education] as merely systems of class oppression; I don't think that they are that. I think that they embody systems of class oppression and elements of other kinds of oppression, but they also embody a kind of groping towards the true humanly valuable concepts of justice and decency and love and kindness and sympathy, which I think are real.

Conclusion

Educational projects of transformation in the transition to democracy seem, with hindsight, to have been infused with an almost delusional optimism but were, at the time, provocative and productive in both political and pedagogical terms. For individual students the TTT programme was enormously successful in creating pathways into academia and beyond into productive and interesting work in the world. In the students' demonstrable success, there were also very important gains in relation to the university. First, ideas of merit and academic standards were problematised and challenged by the realisation of potential, demonstrating that commitments to excellence and equity are compatible rather than contradictory. Second, a group of academics, many of them established scholars in their disciplines, recognised that, while students are responsible for their own learning, the academy is also responsible for *teaching* and cannot simply relegate this to the schooling system. Third, the active political and theoretical commitments of academics can drive change but institutional structural support is critical for systemic change. Although bureaucratic and territorial battles were not averted, possibilities for change were facilitated by the seniority of academics with whom we worked and the active support of the Vice Chancellor's office (once the first cohorts of students had "proved" the approach could work!). Finally, the project was a response to the political imperatives of the context beyond the university and entailed linkages and engagement that made the boundaries of the academy more permeable. However, reflections on the past make clear that change is not linear or inevitably progressive. Even where we have "made progress" in, for example, widening access and rethinking pedagogy, "progress is never permanent, will always be threatened, must be redoubled, restated and *reimagined* if it is to survive" (Zadie Smith, 2018, p. 41). The demands of the current Student Movement make clear that earlier gains with respect to financial and epistemological access have been only partially and unevenly realised or lost altogether. In particular, universities seem to have complacently adjusted their horizons of social justice to exclude the poorest young people in marginalised communities that were the target of the TTT programme from their range of vision. Students have also shifted the debates beyond the assimilationist language of access to challenge the interactional dynamics and (physical and symbolic) colonial architecture of higher education. They have also highlighted the analytic limits of the structural categories of race and class for understanding contemporary formations of power and subjectivity. (See discussion of intersectional identity politics and possibilities for changing subjectivities in Chapters 6 and 7.) Vygotsky's ZPD may yet provide a radical concept for educators and activists who are committed to imaginative futures that do not resemble the past. Higher education entails preparing students for futures unknown and unknowable by the older generation. Responsive curricula that address these (un)imaginable future challenges may be paradoxically informed by re-reading earlier experimental pedagogical practices and curriculum transformation. While our present vantage point highlights the limitations of these engagements and the systemic intransigence of dominant knowledge systems and institutional practices, this retrospective analysis also provides seeds for reformulating notions of potential and generating innovative praxis.

Notes

1 I cannot provide a complete overview of the very many academic development projects that were developed both within and beyond South African universities during this time. *The South African journal of higher education* provides a fairly comprehensive archive of work but there are several lacunae in that record, indicative of the difficulties in balancing acting, thinking and writing, and of the ways in which momentum can be lost. This is a caution from one context of activism to another: reflection and theoretical work is a kind of activism and academics and students need to be mindful of these critical obligations that define our particular role in projects of change.

There were a number of radical and creative educational innovations happening across the country focused on access to university education both before and alongside degree programmes. For example, Khanya College a project of SACHED (Essop, 1990), The Natal Workers' College (Sitas, 1990) and Neville

Alexander's PRAESA (Project for the Study of Alternative Education in South Africa) founded in 1992. The important work of these organisations was curtailed by the advent of democracy and the concomitant reduction in NGO funding and a loss of people power into formal state institutions of various kinds. However, PRAESA and Khanya are still in operation and their work remains vitally relevant as we recognise that post-apartheid education may have shifted in policy but not in practice.

The hiatus between the period of intense political activism and creative energy in education in the dying days of apartheid, and the current dynamism of the Fallist movement, is notable across multiple domains. To a large extent, civil society and the NGO sector relinquished activity and power to the state and its institutions on the mistaken assumption that democratic governance would bring about the kinds of conditions that the ANC's campaign slogan promised: "A better life for all". For example, Nieftagodien (2018) notes that the effects of democratisation, contrary to expectations, did not lead to burgeoning scholarship in alternative histories. In the early 1990s there was a vibrant and vital field of public history, developed through collaborative linkages with political activists in the independent trade unions and popular movements. Instead of opening up new possibilities for these intellectual practices, the democratic regime asserted a new dominant historical narrative of the liberation struggle in which history serves to support state-funded heritage projects. However, as the post-apartheid generation has grown up, it has also grown tired of the state's version of both history and the present and there is a new impetus for alternative histories to be written and read through the lens of present conditions and struggles. In the educational sphere, the membership-based community "movement", Equal Education (founded in 2008) has actively campaigned for social justice in schooling. Many of these campaigns have been conducted collaboratively with Section 27, a public interest law centre that mobilises constitutional rights to address inequalities in various sectors of South African society.

2 The name of a conference hosted at the University of Johannesburg in 2018 encapsulates a focus on optics that seems to eclipse more substantive questions of transformation: "Transforming ivory towers to ebony towers" (Adebayo, 2018).

3 These predominantly white institutions previously utilised Afrikaans as the medium of instruction, with the exception of Rhodes, which still officially carries the colonial name despite Fallists renaming it UCKAR (the University-currently-known-as-Rhodes) to signal that this insulting aberration will not last.

4 Although both tragic events recounted here happened in Limpopo, the failures of basic education are not restricted to this region with some rural areas such as the Eastern Cape and northern parts of KwaZulu-Natal even more poorly resourced. Outrageously, Michael Komape is also not the only or last child to die in this vile way; in 2018 another Grade R pupil Lumka Mketwa drowned in a pit latrine toilet at her school in the Eastern Cape.

5 This debate about what IQ tests tell us is not trivial nor is it done and dusted. In 1994 Herrnstein and Murray published *The bell curve* that purported to present scientific data in support of the racist position that black people are naturally less intelligent than white people. Their "science" is so patently flawed that an undergraduate student who has just been introduced to the nature-nurture debate could demolish the argument. No translation or item refinement will rehabilitate the underlying purpose of testing: to differentiate individuals and groups according to a normative distribution. This alignment to the bell curve is an artefact of

test construction, and a test that does not produce this pattern of results is considered invalid. Further, these differences are evaluative, re-inscribing and perpetuating inequalities in the worlds of education and work and, hence, reproducing hierarchies of political power and economic reward. IQ tests are ideological tools not neutral instruments of measurement akin to rulers for height or scales for weight. But despite the authoritative refutation of evolutionary theorists such as Gould (1996), these racist views remain in circulation, fuelled by, and fuelling, right-wing popular discourse and the current violent anti-immigration politics of the United States and many other countries across the globe. The "science" of psychology remains complicit, continuing to train generations of professionals in the use of these and similar tests for diagnostic purposes.

6   At the University of the Witwatersrand, Skuy (1997) and his colleagues adapted and implemented Feuerstein's mediated learning experience for the assessment of South African children's potential, focusing on (dis)ability and multiculturalism, and combining these assessments of learning potential and instrumental enrichment with conventional psychometric assessments.

7   For a historical overview of the funding and structure of higher education in South Africa under and post-apartheid, see Bozalek & Boughey, 2012. For examples of projects of alternative selection programmes, see Griesel, 1992, 2000, 2004; Yeld & Haeck, 2006.

8   By 1995, the numbers had increased exponentially and the TTT programme became RAP (Regional Access programme) and began to teach and test applicants to all tertiary institutions in KwaZulu-Natal. This programme eventually closed as entrance to tertiary studies became "normalised" or at least ostensibly less racially skewed, and institutions began to carve out their own competitive practices in this new terrain.

9   Introductory texts were written by senior University of Natal scholars from different disciplines (e.g. *Sociology*, Maré & Sitas, 1992; *Anthropology*, de Haas, 1992). However, the texts were designed to do more than transmit introductory content. The materials design by the series editor, Hanlie Griesel, created overt models for academic engagement that are common practice for those who know how but typically opaque for those that do not. For example, the typical form of academic argument in which a position is asserted only to be undercut; reading that entails back and forth movement through the text rather than linear progression from start to finish. With Hanlie Griesel as series editor, these materials were released in many iterations, culminating in a range of texts on interdisciplinary topics such as identity, democracy and discourse, among others for the RAP pre-university preparatory programme, *Introduction to Social Studies*. (Each of these conceptual fields included texts with specific foci, e.g. *Fragmented African Identities*, Busakwe, 1997.)

10 The principles of the TTT programme were adapted for a programme of selection and academic development in the sciences (Grayson, 1996).

11 Within universities, a range of academic developments provided support for students, often in the form of an additional initial year of study to foundation or bridging courses focused on language, generic critical thinking skills, or discipline-specific content. This model was typical of STEM disciplines in which the disjuncture between schooling and university study was conceived as a "gap" to be bridged in a building-block type approach. While this idea of *prerequisite* skills and knowledge also informed pedagogical approaches in the

humanities and social sciences, particularly in later iterations, curriculum transformation tended to be more integrated into mainstream degree programmes. (See for example, Boughey, 2002, 2005; Clarence-Fincham, 1992, 2001; Miller, Bradbury & Lemmon, 2000; Miller, Bradbury & Pedley, 1998; Scott, 2009.) The National Education Policy Investigation (NEPI) Framework Report (1993), drew on this base of experience to develop proposals for educational policy in anticipation of the democratic era. While these projects lost steam and many were closed down completely as universities settled back into a view that the academic difficulties of students would be solved in schools, the field of enquiry and innovation was sustained in pockets or has been recently resuscitated. (See, for example, Luckett, 2016; Luckett & Shay, 2017; Slonimsky & Shalem, 2010.) At the University of the Witwatersrand, an action research project exploring potential for excellence was focused on developing solid academic engagement in the second year of study in ways that would increase access to postgraduate study. REAP (Reaching for excellent achievement, 2011–2014) provided a forum for experimentation in curriculum design and a provocative space for learning (Bradbury & Kiguwa, 2012a).

12 The construction of the ZPD as an asymmetrical space may seem incompatible with egalitarian politics and the ZPD has often been incorrectly reframed as a space of collaboration between peers that resonates more strongly with Montessori's exploratory learning through experience or even Piaget's cognitive constructions through transactions with the world. Vygotsky included the possibilities for learning from peers rather than adult teachers and parents but these peers need to be "more capable" with respect to the task at hand or learning will not happen. This framing does not exclude the possibility that interesting things might happen in collaborative groups, and conversations between equals always include the possibility for new insights from a different perspective. Who occupies the "more capable" role will vary depending on the task at hand and, if we accept the principle of life-long learning, we all always have several zones of potential in front of where we now find ourselves.

13 A recent BBC documentary *The Ascent of Woman* (2016) provides one partial (not very satisfactory) response to Bronowski's account.

14 Students of the Afrika Cultural Centre in Johannesburg in the 1980s named their magazine *Timbuktu*, reflecting the ways in which the project enlarged the range of reference points for young people by opening up a continental African vision beyond the boundaries of the apartheid and colonial frame (Peterson, 2014).

15 Maldonado-Torres (2016) similarly notes that the resistance of decoloniality does not come *after* colonisation but is always an active strain of action and thought simultaneous with colonisation.

16 The "missing middle" are those students whose families are not among the poorest of the poor but nonetheless cannot afford exorbitant university fees or provide full financial support their children through higher education. The threshold household income is set at R600 000 (a little over $40 000 or £30 000 at current exchange rates) per annum, which actually includes all but a small number of South African households.

6

EDUCATING (OUR)SELVES
Narratives of (un)learning and being

Introduction

This chapter addresses the problematics of education in which the inevitable asymmetrical relations between all teachers and learners are amplified by differences of class, "race" and gender. These lines of difference raise questions about what kinds of learning and change are required by whom, and what new forms of knowing and being are envisaged. The chapter reflects on shifting political positions and the motility of identities that coalesce in educational exchanges that always include voices from the past in the process of articulating young people's futures. These reflections draw on an action research project, *Fast Forward* conducted at the University of KwaZulu-Natal in the first decade of the millennium that was informed by a synergy between the notion of potential (explored in Chapter 5) and the concept of narrative imagination. Drawing together these different theoretical domains enables a praxis that recognises the intersection between epistemology and ontology, between cognition and narrative identity. The learning-teaching of new ideas entails changing selves. The hope vested in young people through investing them with knowledge is amplified in newly democratised contexts where the (re)invention of our identities or ourselves, as a nation and as individuals, is an overtly articulated project. My own work as an educator both prior to democratisation and post-apartheid has been motivated by this very force. I have always understood, as Maria Tamboukou (2000, p. 464) puts it, "teaching as a way to change the world, or at least do something about it". Perhaps the coincidence of particular points in my personal narrative and in national history makes this a fruitful moment for reflection on whether such purposes are (im)possible. In this chapter, I confront the ways in which the aim of changing "the other" through the learning-teaching encounter resonates with both the oppressive language of colonisation and the more nurturing socialisation discourses of mothering, and reflect on my own positioning as a white woman academic teacher in my commitments to "change". The learning-teaching process is asymmetrical by definition creating what Derrida calls an "aporia" with inevitable political and ethical consequences. "So there is an aporia – and let us recall that there is no political decision without going through an aporia: I have to reaffirm my difference and to respect the other's difference" (Derrida, 2001, p. 183). Or in Appiah's (2005, p. 189) words, the dilemma is: "How can we reconcile a respect for people as they are with a concern for people as they might be?" He, like Derrida, suggests that this is a conundrum that cannot be avoided: "to ignore the first term, is tyranny; to give up on the second is defeatism, or complacency".

Empirical action, intervention and reflection

In the previous chapter, we explored how Vygotsky's notion of potential might provide resources for (un)learning the contents and form of university knowledge in general, and psychology in particular. Here, I will suggest that the theoretical resources of narrative psychology might be brought to bear on the processes of learning that are woven into the university experience and scholarly life: "The educational process in a university is the site for certain ways of thinking about what matters in life, and certain ways of thinking about one-self" (Parker, 2015c, p. 75). These processes of identification (Hall, 1996) insert students into specialised fields of knowledge, preparing them for particular modes of work and positioning in the socioeconomic hierarchies of society and, in the process, they learn to be different kinds of people. The vast majority of the large numbers of students who register for undergraduate psychology courses in South African universities are planning to continue at the master's level to become either counselling or clinical psychologists. Despite the fact that only an extremely small elite group of students are finally selected for these professional postgraduate degrees, the motivations of both students and academics are primarily driven in this direction and this has a pervasive retroactive influence on research agendas and on curricula at all levels of study.

In this context, my pedagogical and political aims are to disrupt particular conceptions of the psychological as amenable to neat taxonomic description, and the conventional formulation of diagnostic interventions in terms of dichotomously defined healthy or unhealthy mental life.

Narrative theory offers one way to shift this dominant framework, emphasising the temporal and fluid construction of identities and suggesting continuities between ourselves as practitioners (teachers or psychologists) and those with whom we work, all of us always in the process of becoming who we are, rather than thinking of ourselves and others as instantiating the fixed dichotomous roles of teacher/learner or therapist/ client. By working with the theoretical concepts of narrative theory, students encounter new tools for conceptualising themselves and others, and for developing the reflexivity that enables critical practice. All people narrate the events and experiences of their lives in a perpetual flow of life in which action and meaning-making are intertwined rather than sequential processes. However, the kinds of narratives that we term "life-histories" or memoires suggest that narrative comes *after* experience and conversely, we tend to think of the dominant narratives of psychological theory as coming *before* practice. By the time students have reached postgraduate studies in psychology these disconnections between life and meaning-making, between theory and practice, are entrenched.

Decolonising knowing and being: contextual relevance

In an early response to the theoretical and practical demands of the post-apartheid context, De la Rey (1997) argued that the links between psychology and political activism are incontrovertible. She was sceptical about the relevance and utility of discourse analysis where the immediate needs were (and still are) for "houses, water and jobs" (De la Rey, 1997, p. 191). Instead, she argued for a contextually relevant psychology informed by participatory action research (Fine, 2018) and critical versions of "community psychology"[1] (and associated liberatory, emancipatory or African psychologies). I share De la Rey's gut response to theory from the North that can sometimes appear to be discursive playfulness for its own sake with little relevance for our context. When these analytic tools are severed from material realities they may, at best, facilitate little more than self-referential tautologies and, at worst, feed an extreme relativist scepticism about "truth", providing for the fake news phenomenon of our era that emboldens climate change denialism and can conjure "weapons of mass destruction" from desert sands. However, discourse analysis and deconstruction may be put to progressive political use and, although we have yet to solve the ongoing crises of "jobs, houses and water", they have been productively utilised as research methodologies in critically reframing psychology and other social sciences in South Africa.

A robust psychosocial engagement with the complex problems of our times will entail more than "a kind of political immediatism that becomes antipathetic to theoretical reflection" (Maldonado-Torres, 2011, p. 4). Recently, Wahbie Long (2013) has argued that interpreting the decolonial project as primarily about making knowledge contextually relevant and applicable is problematic as it fails to acknowledge how the context itself is always changing and how the boundaries of local contexts are extremely permeable, increasingly so in the digital era. Tying ourselves too closely to our immediate contexts may lock us and those with whom we work into the very patterns and practices that require resistance but, conversely, retreating from the demands of life into abstract universals is untenable epistemologically and politically. In any case, it is erroneous to cast theory developed in the past and in other places as "universal" rather than contextually relevant as knowledge is always generated in relation to the historical lines of ideas that precede it and individual thinkers are always working in relation with others. Notions of academic freedom that resist societal pressures conceal the rather narrow constraints within which such intellectual projects are framed and the interdependence of the academy and wider society. Scheibe (1986) refers to intellectual work as a kind of "serious adventure" in which scientists and artists are supported by society to do work whose impact and value may not be immediately obvious. However, there is an anticipated "payback" for these societal costs through the reproduction of knowledge and skills for work that will sustain collective life, potentially enhancing the quality of this life in multiple ways, most obviously through technologies for communication or travel or health. In increasingly precarious times, the turn-around for this payback is accelerated and the interest demanded is inflated. This may particularly affect disciplines that do not appear to have immediate material utility such as literature or philosophy. But if education is shaped solely by the supply-and-demand model, we cede the framing and direction of human production to the forces of the market and it is in this context that Long's critique of the demands for relevant education should be taken seriously. If the way the world is structured now is not the form that we would like it to take in the future, a reductionist notion of relevance will not have emancipatory effects and will stunt the possibilities for meaningful humane forms of life. We need to recognise that "we are always educating for a world that is or is becoming *out of joint*" (Arendt, 1961, p. 192, emphasis added).

The task of decolonisation, then, will entail "redefining relevance" (Ndebele, 1991) to stretch across temporal and spatial zones. Recognising that contexts are multiple, fragmentary and fluid makes the question of context and relevance *more* rather than less important. New forms of theorising must emerge from these contextual demands created both by history and by imagined futures. The unknown futures for which education is preparing young people and the futures for which they are fighting need to be informed by long and flexible narrative arcs of memory and imagination, and by engaging the intergenerational present in both wider and more focused ways. In this way, relevant education is reframed as encompassing life beyond the here-and-now, prefiguring new ways of being as well as knowing:

> The fact is that it is not by learning yet more facts, yet more information about what already exists for us in our surroundings, that we change the way we live our lives. Our task is to change the ways in which we relate ourselves to our surroundings, and to do that, we must learn new ontological skills, *new ways of being a person.*
>
> *(Shotter, 2000, p. 25, emphasis added)*

Rewinding *Fast Forward* and articulating new forms of practice

The *Fast Forward* programme run at the University of KwaZulu-Natal (2004–2009) illustrates how a narrative approach may creatively articulate theory and practice in educating (our)selves and working with questions of youth identities. The design of the programme incorporated multiple modalities of meaning-making across temporalities: engaging the inherited legacies of apartheid and colonialism in memory and forgetting; confronting the present problems and possibilities of young people in their daily lives; and imagining individual and collective futures.[2] University students worked as facilitators on an intensive programme of activities with young people from two disadvantaged schools, one urban and one rural. The name of the programme entails a metaphorical allusion to technologies that allow us to project forward in the stories that we read, listen to and view, suggesting that we can make similar imaginative leaps across time in the construction of our own life stories. This moment in these young people's lives offers particular fluidity and uncertainty, a kind of hinge between childhood and adulthood, what is typically referred to since Erikson (1968) as a time for resolving the "crisis" of identity.

The programme was multifaceted, challenging participants to think beyond the confines of their worlds and to envisage a range of possible alternative paths their lives could follow. The primary pedagogical approach entailed using various representational cultural forms (music, dance, photography) to create alternative narratives or storylines for participants, questioning and extending their existing horizons. As McAdams (2001, p. 114) notes, "It is painfully clear that life stories echo gender and class constructions in society and reflect, in one way or another, prevailing patterns of hegemony in the economic, political, and cultural contexts wherein human lives are situated". The programme attempted to engage these structural underpinnings of narrative by presenting alternatives to enable young people to interpret their worlds and themselves in new ways, questioning taken-for-granted versions of who we are and who it is possible to become. In this way, it engaged in the development of what Césaire termed "poetic know-ledge" that enables us "to transcend the immediate everyday realities that confine our capacity to dream, imagine and hope" (Ginwright, 2008, p. 20). The approach was underpinned by two different theoretical threads to argue for the interpretive task as an appropriate way to engage young people in processes of learning and change, including the process of identity construction: first, Ricoeur's (1981) notion of the text as a model for human action and the potential for the "enlargement of the self" by appropriating new meanings across the distance generated by textuality; and second, Freire's (1972, 1973) conceptualisation of literacy (or education more broadly) being about "learning to read the world" or as a potential form of conscientisation.

Framing possibilities for new narrative lines

Although the programme eschewed didactic instruction in favour of activities that provoked interpretation and reflection on the part of participants, this does not mean that the process was content-less or learner-driven in the conventional sense. On the contrary, we worked with a very clear sense of the kinds of discourses in current circulation in our context (racism, xenophobia, homophobia, sexism) and deliberately attempted to create alternative narratives and representations from which learners could draw in the making of their identities. For example, ideas of cultural and national heritage that question the boundaries of inclusion and exclusion; women's narratives of work in traditionally male roles; dialogue about sexuality that recognises the multiplicities of desire. This agenda is far from neutral and critics could argue that it simply substitutes one "hidden curriculum" (Illich, 1971) for another, failing to respect and validate the understandings of others. In particular, many of these ideas may be rejected as not culturally appropriate. Indeed, they were often resisted by articulate learners who assertively made such claims as "homosexuality is not part of our culture" or "in our culture, women are expected to ...". Appiah (2005, p. 177) recognises that education of this kind entails far more than the simple transmission of new information:

> The decision to hew to a traditional gender role does not lend itself to such redescription. It is not affected by the correction of a few flatly factual errors. ... To get the woman to change her mind here,

you could either erase the social stigma (which would require erasing other people's presumably benighted, commitment to values it subsists upon) or you could somehow produce in her a new brazenness, or reflective disregard of that stigma. Either way you would be involved in soul making, refashioning ethical projects and ethical identities.

Such "ethical projects" are complex and require disentangling the multiple threads of historical oppression. The architecture of apartheid was explicitly built on racist ideology and constructions of "race" classification, but the maintenance of "race" boundaries was also always simultaneously sexualised (Ratele, 2006) and gendered (Shefer, 2010). Lines of difference, otherness and marginality served to reinforce and maintain one another. The unravelling and reconstruction of identities will, therefore, likewise entail engaging these multiplicities simultaneously rather than sequentially (Hassim, 2003), recognising the nuanced ways in which each might reframe the particular experiences of individual people; "race" complicated by gender and sexuality, gender complicated by "race" and sexuality, sexuality complicated by gender and "race". While the notion of intersectionality (Crenshaw, 1991) is well established in critical theory (e.g. Josselson & Harway, 2012; Weedon, 1997) "race" was the almost exclusive focus in the initial reconstruction of South African society. More recent writing across a range of disciplines (e.g. Jones & Dlamini, 2013; Ndlovu, 2012; Ratele, 2006; Shefer, 2010) is beginning to adopt the wide-angle lens of intersectionalities of power to focus both its visible field of critique and its visions of possibility. The activist agenda of the *Fast Forward* programme was premised on this notion of intersectionality, employing multiple foci of engagement, to find ways in which one form of dominance might be undercut by another to create fissures of possibility, developing "conscious awareness of the contradictory nature of subjectivity" (Weedon, 1997, pp. 83–84).

Educating for nation-building or democratic citizenship

Perhaps some would argue that these kinds of interventionist programmes go where angels fear to tread, into territory that is not the rightful or proper domain of education and rather should be left to the "private" spheres of the family and cultural institutions such as religion. Education should "stick to the facts"; the teacher's role is to impart knowledge and skills that will enable students and learners to live competently and autonomously in the world. There are at least two obvious problems with this argument: first, education is never apolitical, always entails an agenda of some kind, even where this agenda is explicitly stated as to avoid "politics" or to embrace "multiculturalism"; second, the domains of the family and religion are not "private" in the sense of being outside of politics and the kinds of socialisation that happen in these other spaces are as value-laden or political as those which take place in classrooms. Appiah (2005) argues that this is indeed the proper role of state education, educating children to develop their identities and values, understanding the languages (both "natural" and academic or political languages) that will enable them to participate fully as part of the national polity and the wider global world.

> Governments do, for example, provide public education in many countries that help children who do not yet have any settled identity or projects, hopes, and dreams. This is more than negative liberty, more than government's getting out of the way. You may say that parents could do this; in principle they could. But suppose they won't or can't? Shouldn't society step in, in the name of individuality, to insist that children be prepared for life as free adults? And, in our society, won't that require them to be able to read? To know the language or languages of their community? To be able to assess arguments, interpret traditions? And even if the parents are trying to provide all these things, isn't there a case to be made that society, through the state, should offer them positive support?
>
> *(Appiah, 2005, p. 29)*

This, however, raises the problem of who governs and therefore what (political) language children learn in school. Authoritarian systems recognise all too well the pivotal role of education in creating people who will quite literally govern themselves, internalising the surveillance of teachers and adopting appropriate approved "truths" as self-evident. Schooling may be little more than an elaborate mechanism for developing such "technologies of the self" (Foucault, 1988). In South Africa, the central role of education in maintaining and extending governmental control was elaborately expressed in the not-too-distant history of the ideological configuration of apartheid education or "Christian National Education". This system explicitly aimed to prepare children in both "national" and "moral" terms for a racially stratified future. The current South African education department must, therefore, address not only inequalities of service delivery in the provision of basic educational necessities such as infrastructure and skilled teachers but also the content and form of education in terms of "new" notions of the nation and, hence, citizenship. Two key examples encapsulate the parameters of this task: first, quite literally, rewriting history; and second, attending to issues of language in relation to constitutional multilingual rights in a context where 11 languages have official status. South African history textbooks, like all histories throughout history, tell the victor's story. In our context, this victorious story was of colonial conquest as a "righteous" campaign that culminated in the establishment of white supremacist rule. The displacement of the apartheid state means that new victors have stories to tell, versions of the world seen through the eyes of historical victims. However, this task of re-interpretation entails more than the mere substitution of rights and wrongs or the inversion of the roles of victims and victors, and presents an opportunity for analysis that will enable progressive future histories to emerge in which the intersectionalities of power are recognised and resisted. The constitutional framework for language rights has enormous implications for education, raising questions about the cognitive and political benefits of mother-tongue instruction (Alexander, 2004, 2012; Freire, 1972, 1973). Decisions about additional language learning, which languages should be learned by whom and to what level of competence, are significant in relation to both the possibilities for individual socioeconomic mobility and the development of new forms of collective social coherence (Alexander, 2004). As discussed in Chapters 4 and 5, there is a pressing imperative to extend and elaborate the conceptual lexicons of indigenous languages (Alexander, 2012) not only to increase access to existing knowledge domains but, further, to create and support alternative epistemological trajectories in the production of knowledge (Garuba, 2001; Peterson, 2011).

Furthermore, a very explicit focus on issues of identity development is evident in the compulsory course for all secondary school learners, "life orientation", in which the standard career counselling function of guidance teachers that emphasises personal routes to further study and successful working life is extended to offer instruction "for life" more broadly conceptualised. In this way, the education of young people explicitly incorporates attention to the "project of the self" (Giddens, 1991) or personal identity development and, further, includes considerations of the ethics and politics of relations with others. The progressive implementation of this project is reliant on the conscientisation of teachers[3] and (re)formulations of national policy. A contentious proposal by the then Minister of Education, Naledi Pandor, was to introduce a "School Pledge"[4] as an attempt to recruit learners to national and "moral" commitments by invoking the South African constitution that, as Pandor (2008) asserted at the time, encapsulates those "universal values that you would want any human being to attach themselves to". The South African Constitution is certainly internationally recognised as one of the most progressive in the world and includes the explicit formulation of a "non-racist and non-sexist society".[5] The contentiousness of the proposal was less to do with the contents of the pledge than the troublesome didactic assumptions that repetitive recitation could create new moral sensibilities and practices. Although the pledge was never formally instituted, it is indicative of a general sentiment about the inculcation of civic responsibilities entailed in educating and being educated. South African higher education institutions, in their formulations of their "vision and mission", now typically include "community service" or "community engagement" as a central task alongside the traditional roles of teaching and research. Academics and students are (at least on paper) required to demonstrate the links and value of their knowledge-making to the national community through active application and practice.

It is thus evident that education is understood as a primary site for the construction and development not only of individual young people's knowledge and skills but also for the (re)construction of a (new) sense of national identity or for redefining the politics of belonging (Yuval-Davis, 2011). The exclusionary effects of any identity project of this kind but perhaps particularly one which emphasises "national" identity are always immanent but in the newly democratic South Africa, it may be possible to harness inclusionary effects by cutting across other lines of division, particularly "race", but also entailing multiple intersectional dimensions of difference, including gender, sexuality, class and (dis)ability (Bradbury & Ndlovu, 2011). The hopes of older generations may always be vested in the young to "make the world a better place" but these hopes are exaggerated in contexts of conflictual histories, as epitomised in the case of South Africa (Bradbury, 2012). The articulation of these hopes in the educational process entails ethical and political commitments of care for both the world and young people, as beautifully expressed in the words of Hannah Arendt (1961, p. 196):

> Education is the point at which we decide whether we love the world enough to assume responsibility for it and by the same token save it from that ruin which, except for renewal, except for the coming of the new and young, would be inevitable. And education, too, is where we decide whether we love our children enough not to expel them from our world and leave them to their own devices, nor to strike from their hands their chance of undertaking something new, something unforeseen by us, but to prepare them in advance for the task of renewing a common world.

Recognising "the other" or the task of re-cognising the "universal"

This may all amount to little more than attempting to "make children in our own image", albeit substituting more democratic images for those of the past and projecting a new national collective in which children (and students) will, as adults, participate. However, this project of inventing the future does not happen *de novo* and, in complicated ways, we must rework our past in the dynamism of the present. This means that we work in the confluence of the long history of colonialism, the shorter explicitly racist history of apartheid, and in the multilingual, multicultural contemporary South Africa. This places exceptional demands on educators to recognise the ways in which education, in the process of changing understandings, validates and transgresses identities – both of ourselves and those we teach. This notion of "identity" is constructed through what Taylor (1992) has called "webs of interlocution" arguing that "[w]e define our identity in ways always in dialogue with, sometimes in struggle against, the things our significant others want to see in us" (Taylor, 1994, p. 33). Individual "identity" is thus relationally (Fay, 1996) constructed, always inevitably partly narrated by others and the way they interpret who we are. As Taylor (1994, p. 25) further elaborates:

> our identity is partly shaped by recognition[6] or its absence, often by the *mis*recognition of others, and so a person or group of people can suffer real damage, real distortion, if the people or society around them mirror back to them a confining or demeaning picture of themselves. Nonrecognition or misrecognition can inflict harm, can be a form of oppression, imprisoning someone in a false, distorted, and reduced mode of being.

This demand for recognition is imperative in a context where those with whom we work have been subjected to various oppressive forms of non- and mis-recognition and I understand part of our task to be this: the validation and recognition of others for who they are, thereby increasing their own agentic possibilities. To return to the empirical example of the *Fast Forward* programme, for many young participants, this sense of "recognition" from the student facilitators and academics on the programme, in dialogue across boundaries of race and class (and perhaps less obviously from our perspective, but critical for these learners, age), is remarkable, liberating.

However, equally important, for my pedagogic purposes, the experience of confronting "the other" in this intense up-close-and-personal way also provokes the university student facilitators to rethink themselves and their context. Although interventions aimed at developmental opportunities for marginalised youth are of critical importance, transformative education must also address the lacunae in understanding particular to the ignorance of the privileged (as discussed in Chapter 4, Steyn, 2012). Michelle Fine alerts us to attend to this typical "blind spot":

I worry that by keeping our eyes on those who gather disadvantage, we have failed to notice the micropractices by which White youth, varied by class and gender, stuff their academic and social pickup trucks with goodies not otherwise available to people of color. ... Whiteness accrues privilege and status within schools; how whiteness grows surrounded by protective pillows of resources and second chances; how Whiteness – of the middle-class and elite variety, in particular – provokes assumptions of and then insurance for being seen as "smart".

(Fine, 2004, p. 245)

While all learners on the *Fast Forward* programme were black, the majority of the student facilitators in the cohort were white and all, by virtue of their elite insider status as postgraduate psychology students, might be understood to occupy class and cultural positions characterised by "whiteness" as defined by scholars such as Fine (2004), Soudien (2007, 2012b) and Steyn (2012). These students had grown up post-apartheid but in a society that remains divided, spatially segregated by race and by increasingly unequal class stratification. They had of course read and written about theories of inequality and difference many times in the course of their university studies but, for many psychology students, their participation in the programme was a critical learning experience in which "Consciousness [was] put into question by a face" (Levinas, 1963, p. 352).

As discussed earlier in Chapter 4, contact across lines of difference does not inevitably transform relations of power and may even entrench them. In order for these contact zones (Torre & Fine, 2008) to effectively transform relationships and identities, multiple bidirectional zones of (un)learning need to be created in which all participants alternate in the roles of teacher and learner. Reconceptualising Vygotsky's ZPD along these lines entails opening ourselves to others in ways that challenge our existing (mis)understandings of them, the world and our-selves: "The relationship with another puts me into question, empties me of myself, and does not let off emptying me – uncovering for me ever new resources" (Levinas, 1963, p. 350). Taylor (1994) acknowledges that the "politics of recognition" are complex and fraught with tension: how can one truly recognise the other; in what terms? If recognition is to be on the terms of the other as other, this implies an appreciation of and understanding of the other's meanings and world, the language and cultural resources on which they draw to be who they are. And of course, if this were fully the case, the other would cease to be other!

It seems that the argument for recognition must in the end be premised on some reference to what is usually treated with suspicion and scepticism that is, "universals" of some kind. (See discussion in Chapter 5.) The demand for equal dignity seems premised on a notion of "*universal human potential*, a capacity that all humans share. This potential, rather than anything a person may have made of it, is what ensures that each person deserves respect" (Taylor, 1994, p. 41). This idea of individual personal potential resonates with Vygotsky's theory of potential human consciousness as developed through other-regulation, internalisation and self-regulatory agency (Miller, 2011; Vygotsky, 1987). Probably all of us who work with young people find it difficult not to indulge in the romantic expectation of possibility, of potential waiting to happen! However, Burman (2008) alerts us to the ways in which psychological theories of children's development towards adulthood are appropriated in language used to describe the potential of "developing" nations or "other" cultures, problematically asserting the "developed" world or "Western" culture as the destination or end-point of this process of development.

This opposition of the "West" and Africa (or "the rest") is the taken-for-granted framing of liberal colonising discourses that understand the task of education (or "development") as assimilation to "Western" knowledge forms (religion, language and cultural practices). An anecdote exemplifies my own ignorance of other long histories of meaning-making and forms of knowledge. As a very young junior academic while working on the TTT programme (see Chapter 5), I was engaged in animated conversation (perhaps an argument!) about the power of science and technology with a colleague in the Zulu department in his office. This was no ordinary colleague, although his office was down the corridor from mine and his door was always open. Prof. Mazisi Kunene, who had recently returned home after more than three decades in exile, was the poet laureate of Africa (1993) and later of South Africa (2005), and author of many volumes of poetry and prose, including his masterpiece, *Emperor Shaka the Great: A Zulu Epic* (1979). He was old and already quite ill, a great bear of a man, he shuffled across to his bookshelves, declaring, "I have just the book you need to read!" and then glancing over his shoulder as he reached to get it, asked, "You do read Chinese, don't you?" To this day, I am uncertain whether he really was intending to offer me an insightful Chinese text to disrupt my arrogant edifice of knowing, or was simply putting me in my place by confronting me with the limits of my confident knowledge. Either way, this memory makes me cringe and lambaste my young self but I am also filled with gratitude and humility by the generosity of a great scholar who willingly shared his time, took me more seriously than I deserved, and provoked me to think differently.

The recollection of this encounter has been repeatedly triggered in the context of the contemporary demands for decolonisation and makes me aware of the multiple threads of human knowledge-making that have been neglected and from which we can draw to enrich the academy. Mbembe (2016) captures this process as the transformation of the university into a "pluriversity". However, articulations of the decolonial project are often less multiple in formulation. The binary between the West and Africa (or the rest) is not disrupted by a framing of the project as the substitution of one tradition of knowledge by another in which the dominance of the "West" (whiteness and the colonial language of English) is unintentionally re-inscribed as the reference point for resistance. While oppositional constructions may be politically appropriate and strategically harnessed for change in the current moment, despite his fervent commitment to multilingualism and the development of indigenous knowledges, Neville Alexander's (pers. comm., 2011) oft repeated critique is pertinent: "We give too much away by ceding certain knowledges to the 'west' – all knowledge is ours, all knowledge is human knowledge!".

Recognising the potential of others to be like us is quintessentially a *mis*recognition. Recognition must entail the anticipation of worth and value to be found in the other, not in potential form, but actualised in its own terms, different from that which is familiar.

> I would like to maintain that there is something valid in this pre-sumption, [that there is something equally valuable in all cultures] but that the presumption is by no means unproblematic, and involves something like an act of faith. As a presumption, the claim is that all human cultures that have animated whole societies over some considerable stretch of time have something important to say to all human beings.
>
> *(Taylor, 1994, p. 66)*

But this act of recognition or taking this leap of faith does not dispense with critique. Cultures are not homogenous nor hermetically sealed and therefore to speak of "recognition" of others cannot mean the acceptance of some statically encoded form of life to which individuals blindly and uniformly adhere. This would imply, for example, that "Western" culture and its knowledge systems are homogenously expressed and experienced through time and across place. In binary terms, it would also assume the inverse of a romantically projected future, a nostalgia that in postcolonial language is often formulated as a pristine "African" past, untainted by colonialism.

The politics of recognition is not simply an expression of solidarity with the other, which Taylor (1994, p. 70) rightly dismisses as "breathtaking condescension" on the part of the dominant, but must assume the possibility for genuine dialogue, for mutual exchange that opens up possibilities for movement and change. Education, in our context (and although perhaps less overtly and in more convoluted ways, in all other places in the contemporary globalised world) is inextricably tied to our colonial heritage and cannot possibly proceed on the basis that the traditions of Africa need replacing. In the specific context of the *Fast Forward* programme, the reconstruction of the identities of these young people does not entail a kind of education by substitution. But neither can we approach the educational task as an elaborate form of validation, accepting differences as inevitable and immutable. Worthwhile educational encounters may disrupt or challenge the definitions of self with which people live and may offer alternative resources to enable young people to live lives that are ethical, interesting and productive. Besides, there is no sense in which the *Fast Forward* participants can be thought of as living in a world divorced from the global, neoliberal "culture" that dominates the South African landscape: designer clothing, American media of all forms including digital worlds; language crossings and reworkings, are all part of young people's "culture". Neither is it inevitably the case that different "cultures" are characterised by "different" values. In the most hopeful sense, all cultures provide members with ways to "live together" and systematised ways of recognising one another. Sadly, the less hopeful correlate is that it is also the case that sexism and homophobia have found, and continue to find, fertile ground in multiple cultural worlds. It is thus this hybrid cultural world and the mobile articulations of identity within it with which we must engage – respectfully *and* critically. bell hooks (1994) argues for a version of "multiculturalism" that, unlike the metaphorical "rainbow nation" or the "melting pot", is inevitably conflictual and challenging. This must require of us a willingness to shift positions as teachers and learners and a recognition not only of difference but also paradoxically of sameness, a recognition not only of the other, but also, an acknowledgement of who we ourselves are in the light of this encounter: "Respect of the other is an essential component of human rights, where the 'other' can also be 'I', and 'I' can also be the 'other'" (Egéa-Kuehne, 2001, p. 189).

Education is, by definition, interventionist, at its best, transformatory. If change is anathema to us or to those with whom we work, we cannot act. Whereas to act is risky and inevitably takes both learners and teachers onto dangerous and unstable ground, failing to act seems the most unethical option of all or, at least, not an option legitimately available to educators:

> We could argue that the only way to do justice to the other, the other whom we dare to educate, is by leaving the other completely alone. It is not difficult to see that this neglect (which would not even count as a border-case of education) would make the other unidentifiable and unrecognizable. This would definitely block the invention for the other and would be therefore utterly unjust. For education not to be unjust some form of recognition of the other as other is needed. But as we have already seen, any form of recognition, although necessary, is at the very same time a mis-recognition, and for that reason, violent. This seems to be the aporia of any education that does not want to be unjust. It is, however, the aporia with which education has to reckon. Can this be done? How can this be done?
>
> *(Biesta, 2001, p. 51)*

Educating (our)selves in a postmodern, postcolonial world?

I want to conclude by turning reflexively and specifically to my-self and my positioning in this process of educating "selves". Given my blind spots, the ways in which I am implicated in historical forms of knowing and patterns of power, and the incomplete processes of my own (un) learning and change, can the projects in which I am engaged be considered critical feminist practice? Can this educational praxis have emancipatory effects? Or is it simply the expression of colonial expansiveness, missionary proselytising or traditional mothering? These are serious not flippant questions and are indeed very specifically pertinent to my own self, my own context of practice: can a white middle-class, middle-aged, English-speaking woman still teach in Africa?[7] However, I think that while these issues of diversity, difference and otherness may be exaggerated in my case, they are characteristic features of all educational relations. Perhaps women educators, especially if we are committed to emancipatory agendas, are particularly prone to anxieties in relation to the exercise of power in the learning-teaching situation. Tamboukou's (2000) article, "The paradox of being a woman teacher", explores these ambivalences with such remarkable insight that reading it made me feel as if I were looking in a mirror! However, bell hooks (1994, p. 33) argues that such prevarications may be problematic and inadvertently retrogressive: "If we fear mistakes, doing things wrongly, constantly evaluating ourselves, we will never make the academy a culturally diverse place where scholars and the curricula address every aspect of that difference". While definitely littered with such "mistakes", the educational practice that I have reflected on here is an attempt to teach in a way that "enables transgressions – a movement against and beyond boundaries" (bell hooks, 1994, p. 12).

It is imperative that as educators we attend to our own boundaries, our own entrenched ideas and ways of being, and open ourselves up to the possibilities for these to be challenged, unravelled and reconfigured in dialogue with learners. However, it also remains incumbent upon us to challenge learners' boundaries, to create new frameworks of understanding. As a feminist academic teacher who grew up white and was educated under apartheid, perhaps I can do little more than offer new theoretical concepts, new ways to talk about the world and ourselves. But then again perhaps this little is enough. Mark Freeman is cautiously hopeful that teachers can create possibilities for others through narratives or stories but neither he nor I think that, "we, academic researchers and theorists, ought to be in the business of telling others how to live. Our own lives are often troubling enough" (Freeman, 1993, p. 229).

Angela Davis recently gave the 2016 annual Steve Biko Memorial Lecture, which she entitled, "Unfinished Activisms". She drew parallels between the US civil rights movement of the 1960s (and to a lesser extent, with the struggle against apartheid) and the contemporary "Black Lives Matter" campaign in America and the Fallist Student Movement in South Africa. She outlined how these movements may be understood to represent the unfinished business of earlier battles against racism, and economic and cultural inequalities. Despite the attainment of political freedoms in both contexts, the younger generation view these as hollow victories, and many of the older generation feel that "this is not the future we were fighting for" (Davis, 2016). The older generation, although living alongside the youth in the same time zone, do not live in the same *world* as the youth, and their futures are foreshortened. However, while the young may critique the older generation for giving in or up too soon, for failing to finish the fight, they did not live in the worlds of overt racism and brutal state power in which their parents had to survive. It could be argued that contemporary youth's interpretations of these earlier times is as legitimate as the understandings of those who lived through those events. In much the same way that the novelist's account of her narrative becomes simply another version alongside that of other literary critics, past protagonists do not have sole purchase on the meanings of historical events, particularly in terms of their later impact in the future-of-now. But, conversely, it could also be suggested that the perspective of the older generation is not irrelevant to current events in which the youth are the main actors. Davis is insistent that the youth should be "left to make their own mistakes" even when they seem to be repeating the errors of previous historical moments. However, successive generations do not operate from a blank slate; this is both the beauty and the terror of human life. In this sense, the mistakes (and new victories) of the youth are never entirely and solely their "own" but those of all living (and dead) generations. The older generation needs to acknowledge this complicity and, despite our making of messy history, dare to offer suggestions for tackling the complexities of life in the present and imagining futures.

> But surely it is not outside the bounds of possibility to suppose that some of the work we do, even if its primary role is but an exemplary one – i.e. "This is what a life can be like", "This is how someone can be defeated or rendered unconscious", "This is how someone can reclaim his or her history", and so on – might be of value to someone besides ourselves.
>
> *(Freeman, 1993, p. 229)*

While the autobiographical past experiences of the older generation are quite literally consigned to history by the young, and the older generation will not live into their extended futures, the present is a shared, overlapping space. This space is a multi-dimensional chronotope (Bakhtin, 2010) in which elements of both the past and future exist in a complex interface. Present actions are informed by vibrant threads of remembering and imagining, even (or perhaps especially) when these are not conscious processes. In this sense, the present is a space of shifting sands, processes of activity and understandings that are always in motion. This sense of flux and uncertainty cannot be contained in assertions of fixed standpoints or by privileging the vantage point of either the past or the future. To draw on Gadamer's metaphor of the horizon:

> as human beings we can never come to an overview of the whole which would allow us to systematize it but instead find ourselves *under way* within an entirety of speaking and thinking which always exceeds the horizons of our perspective.
>
> *(Smith's introduction to Gadamer, 1980, xiii, emphasis added)*

In the 10th annual Helen Joseph Memorial lecture at the University of Johannesburg, Njabulo Ndebele (2016) spoke of his sense of the deep fissures in South African society, and an "intergenerational dissonance" in understanding both past and present events. The provocative title of his talk "They are Burning Memory" points primarily to conceptions of decolonisation as a project of erasing the past (as encapsulated in the cultural objects of oppressive histories, such as statues, commemorative naming of spaces and buildings, artworks or even books). Ndebele is highly sceptical about the possibility (and desirability) of this project of erasure and asks us to reflect on the collateral damage of such actions. He argues that in the process what is lost is not just past knowledge or opportunities to learn from history but, more critically, attempts to erase the past may entail a loss of agentic visions of the future, a burning of potential memories. He suggests that what is occurring is a temporal inversion, looking back in the hopes of recuperating a utopian future that never happened and, in the process, negating the possibilities contained in present conditions.

Paradoxically, without the constraining parameters of past meanings and actions, it would not be possible to develop new forms of action and understanding. Intergenerational knowledge makes it possible for both the past and the future to inform the present. The question is whether generations who do not speak one another's languages can find common meanings in translation and forge ways to participate in multilingual conversations. The exigencies of this present moment mean that it is imperative to ensure the inclusion of multiple traditions and contradictory voices, voices that speak from the past and echoes from as yet unformed futures. The mythical Ghanaian Sankofa bird represents an inspirational metaphor of the tensed narrative subject who flies forward while looking backward to collect the wisdoms of the past, creating new storied trajectories and lines of flight. The famous aphorism from Kierkegaard (cited in Crites, 1986, p. 165) captures a similar sense of the contra-flows of action and narrative understanding: "Life must be lived forwards but can only be understood backwards". We are compelled (or perhaps even condemned) to be propelled forward in action on the understandings of others, acting in advance of our own understanding which cannot but come after the fact. As parents and teachers, we may build nests to nurture the young and prepare for the future and, as intellectuals and researchers, we may pursue new lines of thinking in the hopes of transforming the world, but we do so precariously perched in the messy present, on the tensile high-wire, where the past remains electrically alive.

Notes

1 An innovative example of a participatory action research project that crosses the boundaries between political activism, higher education and the disciplinary practices of psychology is the recent University of East London project in the Calais camp for migrants (mostly but not only from the Syrian war), named

by residents themselves, "the Jungle". The multi-pronged approach was to (1) provide opportunities for migrants to study a foundational higher education course; (2) press for improvements in the living conditions in the camp and for resolution to their status as "illegal" migrants; (3) offer psychosocial support; and (4) collaboratively research and document the experiences of people living in the Jungle. The camp was subsequently demolished but a published collection of narratives tells how people acted creatively to humanise themselves and their relationships in this dehumanising place (Godin, Moller Hansen, Lounasmaa, Squire & Zaman, 2017).

2 The programme has been written about in more detail elsewhere (see Bradbury & Clark, 2012; Bradbury & Miller, 2010). I would like to acknowledge the intellectual, soul and embodied energies of my UKZN colleagues who worked with me on this innovative programme, particularly Jude Clark, Tarryn Frankish, Kerry Frizelle and the late Siyanda Ndlovu. In the decade since, I have been involved in other similar participatory action projects focused on narrative identity. In the initial phase of The Africa Gender Institute project at the University of the Witwatersrand, Witsies (Women Intellectuals Transforming Scholarship in Education), Peace Kiguwa and I worked together with photographer, Iris Dawn Parker, who coined the acronym that framed our action and thinking. Young women students became co-researchers with us, documenting their ambivalent experiences of articulating new versions of themselves as university students. They captured their daily experiences of alienation, assimilation and aspiration in images and text (Bradbury & Kiguwa, 2012b). Currently, NEST (Narrative Enquiry for Social Transformation) at Wits is working in partnership with YOTS (Youth of the South) in Soweto, under the leadership of Hayley Haynes-Rolando and Phethile Zitha, to create dynamic, bidirectional flows of narrative research and practice between young people in the community, and students and researchers in the university.

3 An incident reported in the local press is indicative of the ways in which multiple identity struggles are playing themselves out in the sites of schooling. A lesbian learner was informed by a teacher that she could not bring her same-sex partner to the matric dance (the South African equivalent of the American prom) because "same-sex couples had behaved 'inappropriately' in the past by 'holding hands'" (Govender, 2013). The immorality act of apartheid that prohibited sex across the "colour line" may be abolished and freedom from discrimination on the basis of sexual orientation may be enshrined in the constitution but "transgressive" sexualities are still clearly the subject of censure and continue to be overtly policed. However, the teacher's position was successfully challenged by a supportive mother, some indication of societal shifts and optimistic possibilities for change.

4 The proposed School Pledge:

"We the youth of South Africa, recognising the injustices of our past, honour those who suffered and sacrificed for justice and freedom.

We will respect and protect the dignity of each person, and stand up for justice.

We sincerely declare that we shall uphold the rights and values of our Constitution and promise to act in accordance with the duties and responsibilities that flow from these rights."

5 The inclusion of the term "non-sexist" alongside "non-racist" was not a foregone conclusion, pointing to the precarious nature of these commitments. One of the participants in the drawing up of the constitution who was later to become one of

the first judges of the Constitutional Court, Albie Sachs (2011), provides us with a (black!) humorous account of how his initial proposal of the phrase was met with bemusement and even incomprehension by fellow team-members and was dropped in various interim iterations before finally being accepted.

6 The standard greeting in isiZulu, Sawubona, translated as "hello" in English, literally means "I see you" as in "I recognise you" in the full sense in which Taylor uses the term of "recognition".

7 From a different identity positioning as a young black middle-class student, Chikane (2018) asks a similar question: "Can Coconuts be trusted with the revolution?" For many in the Student Movement, the answer to both Chikane's question and mine (Can a middle-class, middle-aged white woman still teach in Africa?) would be a resounding no. However, I think that different answers might emerge by reframing these questions. What is it that "coconuts" can (and cannot) contribute to the revolutionary moment? It is often angrily observed that the democratic state neglected the student crisis and institutional recalcitrance with regard to transformation for decades, only responding once the protests hit the elite universities of Cape Town and the Witwatersrand. This re-inscribes the lack of state accountability to the majority poor and working class, and bolsters the "whiteness" of these institutions and those who learn and teach within them. It is this that produces Chikane's questioning of himself in acknowledging that he deserves the derogatory label of "coconut". But instead of lamenting the fact that government were only provoked into a response when student protests challenged the centres of historical privilege, recognising this political leverage creates new demands for accountability and integrity on the part of those with access to these spaces and the power of these knowledge-making processes. Coconuts cannot be solely entrusted with the revolution but that does not mean they have no role to play. Likewise, the dominant narratives of colonial education must be challenged and white academics decentred. However, side-lining the older generation and those with disciplinary knowledge and power may provide license to renege on our commitments and obligations to the world and the younger generation in ways that may benefit no one except those intended to be penalised.

7

HISTORIES AND HOPE

Acting, thinking and being in the present

Introduction

This final chapter will explore the possibilities for change towards hopeful futures in relation to the ways in which the traumatic past infuses the present.[1] The temporal structure of human experience that spans past and future enables a dialogical engagement with present tensions and creates possibilities for intentional action and individual and social change. However, this temporal line is not inevitably progressive or developmental and neither are the consequences of our actions predictably contained in our intentions. A historical narrative that consigns trauma and conflict to the past and hopeful imaginative possibilities to the future is hopelessly over-simplified. The warp and weft of time-space bends the narrative lines of personal memory and imagination, and creates oscillating movements in the longer durations of human life. In the first few decades of the 21st century, these shifts, twists and turns seem to occur at ever increasing speeds, threatening both the retention of memory and past traditions, and the possibilities for planning or intentional action. The question is how to engage with, respond to and act thoughtfully in the flow of these accelerated frames of experience by "reflect[ing] on the process we are going through now: the process of becoming, of making sense of all the noises" (Ndebele, 2007, p. 156). From the perspectives of both Vygotskian and narrative psychology, intergenerational longitudinal trajectories coalesce in this process of meaning-making which is at once personal and political. As the Sankofa bird reminds us, flying forward without looking back is both foolish and dangerous even though it may seem ostensibly the safest, most efficient way to reach a future destination. However, the process of constructing a meaningful life in the present cannot rely solely on the traditions of the past, even when these traditions are recuperated from outside of dominant knowledge systems, and demands a dialectic between the recollected past and the imagined future. Arendt (1961, p. 193) reminds us that generating these lines of vision requires open dialogue across generational vantage points:

> Our hope always hangs on the new which every generation brings; but precisely because we can base our hope only on this, we destroy everything if we so try to control the new that we, the old, can dictate how it will look.

Traumatic histories and present day violences

The post-apartheid generation has now come of age, both the young people who were "born free" and the state and its institutions: the imagined future of our past has arrived and it is now clear that the rainbow was a mirage. For the younger "hinge generation" (Hoffman, 2004), the legacy of apartheid, the weight of history is substantial and systemic; entrenched in the racialised economic hierarchy, inscribed in the spatial architecture of "separate development" and in the transmission of the psychic scarring of the older generation. At a global level, the hopes that unfurled in an Obama campaign that declared "Yes, we can!", the possibilities of an Arab Spring or a socialist Venezuela are dashed, and violent conflicts continue around the globe. While some things are better for some people, most things are not for most people and this is particularly true for the African continent.

In 2016, eight staff members of the South African Broadcasting Corporation (SABC) were summarily fired by the Director for resisting instructions not to broadcast footage of violent service delivery protests which were (and are) an everyday occurrence across South Africa. These protests by ordinary people declare the failures of the democratic state to deliver the basic facilities of life: housing, water, electricity, education and health, and disrupt the ruling party's election slogan, "We have a good story to tell!". After years of "waiting lists" and the recognition that "change cannot happen overnight", the dignity of political freedom has been eroded by the material indignities of poverty in the face of continuing and accelerating wealth by the white minority and the new black elite. It has become widely accepted that such protests must employ an element of "violence" (such as destruction of infrastructure, burning of tyres, blocking roads) to have any hope of attracting the attention of those with the power to do anything about the situation. People gathering on the streets is a way of refusing invisibility and interrupting the silencing of policies that paper over the cracks of lived experiences. The SABC policy directive was premised on concealing this activism from the wider public, to smooth the national storyline of progress and development, consigning the poor to a "normalised absence/pathologised presence" (Phoenix, 2002, p. 505).

One of the SABC Eight (as they became known) was Lukhanyo Calata, son of the struggle hero, Fort Calata, who was murdered by apartheid security police over 30 years earlier, on 27 June 1985. Fort Calata and his comrades, the Cradock Four, were intercepted at a road block, tortured, killed and, in the particularly gruesome violence of the apartheid era, their bodies burnt. When Nomonde Calata (Fort's widow and Lukhanyo's mother) testified at the TRC, her memories were unleashed in a scream of psychic pain (Gobodo-Madikizela, 2018). Although the firing of the son is not comparable to the murder of the father, the blow to his life is delivered by the very democratic state for which his father fought and died, in a futile attempt to conceal its own failure to create a just and equal society. His mother's scream seems to resonate silently in the intergenerational family story as the traumatic past actively mutates in the present.

We are living through what is described by Berlant (2011, p. 200) as a historical "impasse", in the aftermath of catastrophe and in the tedious repetitions of action and thought without "traction" for change. In language that anticipates Christina Sharpe's (2016) remarkable text *In the Wake*, Berlant (2011, p. 10) describes how, in the crisis of the impasse, "being treads water; mainly, it does not drown. Even those whom you would think of as defeated are living beings figuring out how to stay attached to life from within it". Sharpe (2016) explores contemporary articulations of racism and xenophobia both on the ground of America and in the waves of migrants crossing seas and borders, demonstrating the ways in which oppression is perpetuated "in the wake". She works the metaphor in its multiple meanings "as a means of understanding how slavery's violences emerge within contemporary conditions" (Sharpe, 2016, p. 14). First, and most prominently, the wake refers to the dragging, churning agitated currents of water behind slave ships. But the word also evokes other associations in the enactment of a wake at the bedside of her dying brother, a simultaneous mourning and celebration of life, and, echoing Fanon (1963), refers to the state of wakefulness or anxious insomnia that makes sleep and rest impossible.

Through powerful visual and word images, Sharpe concentrates the oppressive sweeps of history in individual narratives of loss. The text opens with the piling up of her own family's losses and how these reflect the multiple lines of marginalisation of African Americans in the present. The narrative form of the text moves the reader back and forth between personal experience and political systems, maintaining a "critical bifocal" approach (Fine, 2018) that ranges across temporal and spatial zones of racist exploitation and oppression to undercut the simple version of historical progress. She juxtaposes the ships of slavery and of African migrants drowning in waters within sight of European shores, forces us to look into the face of a little girl rescued in the Haitian earthquake of 2010 with the label "ship" above her vacantly staring eyes and, as we do so, to read the account of the slave auctioning of Phyllis Wheatley as a little girl of similar age, both children ripped from their families, isolated, alone and dehumanised.

Sharpe's text creates the sense of the all-pervasive foul "weather" of oppressive conditions within and against whose powerful currents life must be navigated. The present patterns of systemic racism and material inequalities throughout the world mean that traumatic histories are not deeply buried but entangled in the living surfaces of experience, creating "holding" patterns of repetitive trauma. #Black Lives Matter emerged not through feats of historical imagination but because people "are already experiencing trauma *from their material, lived violence*", (Sharpe, 2016, p. 88). In the South African context, the violence of apartheid is perpetuated in current patterns of unequal distribution of the material and political "goods" of democratic life, creating precarious forms of contemporary citizenship.

> Whether explicitly stated or not, every political effort to manage populations involves a tactical distribution of precarity ... regarding whose life is grievable and worth protecting, and whose life is ungrievable or marginally or episodically grievable.
>
> (Butler, 2012, p. 170)

It is in this national and international context that the South African Student Movement took shape in 2015, in its two primary (inter-related) articulations: #Rhodes Must Fall (engaging symbolic violence and initiating the urgent imperatives of the decolonisation project) and #Fees Must Fall (focusing on the material exclusions of the majority of young South Africans from a range of citizenship rights, including, specifically, participation in higher education and the economy). These contemporary political movements are responses to dehumanising histories that are actively animating present conditions, producing what Manganyi (1973, p. 10) refers to as conditions that are "unhygienic" for mental health, generating "existential insecurity" resulting in "helplessness" and despairing "nauseous anxiety".

Hope for change: an optimistic vision?

In a context where the majority are living precarious lives of survival, the narrative of hope most often takes the shape of a story of possible escape. We have already explored the ways in which the myth of meritocracy (see Chapter 5) works to assimilate people to the expectations of a hierarchical system that is sustained through increasing levels of exclusions. "Today's optimism in undergoing education seems exclusively driven by our present need (and fear) to secure individual success above all else" (Di Paolantonio, 2016, p. 152). The provision of basic goods and services, including access to education that is the promised route to attain these things and more, is being implemented at an excruciatingly slow pace but in a context of conspicuous consumption by the rich and in a (digital) world without limits, offering remarkable remakes of the "American dream" for all. Berlant (2011, p. 2) describes these conditions of late capitalism as characterised by "cruel optimism" in which people develop

> a sustaining inclination to return to the scene of fantasy that enables you to expect that *this* time, nearness to *this* thing will help you or a world to become different in just the right way. ... such that a person or a world finds itself bound to a situation of profound threat that is, at the same time, profoundly confirming.

She argues that the project of assimilation or incorporation into the narrative of progress is an apocalyptic vision, a repetition in Marxist terms of "farce after tragedy". Although she wrote this work before recent troubling global developments, the xenophobic exclusionary politics being played out in Europe, in the endlessly deferred Brexit escape plan, and in the United States in its un-united state under Trump, these events might be understood as the consequences of a continually unravelling narrative of universal progress. Hopeful aspirations are disfigured and "freedom is reduced to a market strategy and citizenship either is narrowed to the demands of the marketplace or becomes utterly privatised" (Giroux, 2008, p. 130). Berlant (2011, p. 1) suggests that being co-opted into this narrative of individual achievement creates a "cruel optimism" in that what "you desire is actually an obstacle to your flourishing". The forms of life that are supported and demanded by late capitalism promise possibilities for this flourishing, "by the incoherence with which alienation is lived as exhaustion plus saturating intensity" (Berlant, 2011, p. 166).

Within the horizons of human and planetary finitude, hope mutates into striving for individual access to privatised public goods that might deliver future benefits for one's children. In one sense, this hope for the next generation is the most universal, most human, most ordinary sustaining force of life, and those of us who already have ownership of these private goods, including comfortable armchairs (mine, Berlant's and Giroux's!) from which to offer this critique, should proceed with caution in asserting alternative visions. In some places in the world (South Africa included) generational mobility is a very real prospect for some (though of course not all). It is, however, also very clear that our inherited structural frameworks both entice and frustrate individual strivings for better futures, and the routes for mobility are along narrow pathways across treacherous terrain rather than multi-lane speedy highways. Personal success happens in a context of collective misery. It is difficult to think creatively and productively about collective possibilities for change in the mire of despair. But Eagleton (2016, p. 122) reminds us that despair is not hopelessness:

> As long as calamity can be given a voice, it ceases to be the final word. Hope would stumble to a halt only when we could no longer identify cruelty and injustice for what they were. To speak of hopelessness must logically presuppose the idea of hope. It is when meaning collapses that tragedy is no longer possible.

The future holds out the potential of not-yet-realised worlds and triggers our imaginations for alternatives even when the meaning of the present seems perpetually on the verge of collapsing and people are living "illegible lives" (Phoenix, 1991), incomprehensible to others and themselves. "[B]eing able to imagine an alternative future may distance and relativise the present, loosening its grip upon us to the point where the future in question becomes more feasible. ... True hopelessness would be when such imaginings were inconceivable" (Eagleton, 2016, p. 85). However, in responding to and rethinking conditions of despair, hopeful resources may counterintuitively be found not only in the imagined future but also in the re-imagining of the past and in present activism.

Backward-looking hope: resources in the past

Sharpe (2016, p. 19) imagines the astonishment of slave ancestors who were "thrown, jumped, dumped overboard in Middle Passage" to find their descendants still here, still breathing, still living in the wake. The components of hydrogen and oxygen that constitute the water that drowns are also the stuff of the air that we breathe, that enlivens and aspirates us. Aspirational desire for achievement is usually thought of as an unequivocal good, motivating study and "hard work", and driving purposeful forms of life. But Sharpe (2016, p. 113) again alerts us to the ambiguous and ambivalent implications of aspiration for black life in the wake as a process of "imagining and for keeping and putting breath back in the Black body in hostile weather". Forcing breath into dying bodies, enabling them to live on into futures that may not be of their choosing, is both "violent and life-saving" (Sharpe, 2016, p. 113). As I have argued above, the possibilities for these futures are constrained by the past of multiple near-drownings that have been survived. But the paradox of human life is that even within the most brutal passages of history, human resistance and creativity persists. People not only survive but live, generating cultural resources for themselves and for future generations (Mama, 1995).

Mourning and nostalgia for what is lost may, therefore, be intertwined with a kind of backward-looking hope. As opposed to restorative nostalgia that entails attempts to restore the "truth" in the recovery of the past, *reflective* nostalgia has the capacity to remake memory in ways that are generative for the present (Boym, 2001, 2007). This form of nostalgic longing is not so much for a particular time or place but for earlier identities (senses of self) and cultural resources that recuperate human dignity and enable new practices of ethics and aesthetics in the present. "[I]t is not nostalgia for the ideal past, but for the present perfect and its lost potential" (Boym, 2001, p. 21), entailing a process of "inventing memory in the future tense" (Sanders, 2010, p. 121). From this perspective, precolonial forms of life and art are not lost remnants of past life; they provide imaginative frames for present life and aspirational imagined possibilities of social coherence generated through bonds of obligation[2] and care:

> A time is posited when there *will have been* ubuntu. If this were merely a time in the past, one could call this a remembering. But strictly speaking the phrasing is in the future perfect: the time of Ubuntu that is posited has never had an actual existence, rather it exists at the level of possibility.
>
> *(Sanders, 2010, p. 120)*

The continuities across the ostensible radical ruptures of history through colonisation and in post-colonial social formations mean that the traumatic *and* creative processes of the past simultaneously actively animate the present. These creative possibilities are overshadowed but not eclipsed by the obsession with the accumulation and spread of facts and figures in the ether of the information age. Global connectivity offers resources for scientific control of personal, embodied and planetary futures but, conversely, those with financial and technological power are also able to monopolise and manipulate knowledge systems in extenuated ways in the production of fake news and the insinuation of homogenous frames of reference, language and culture. In the face of these pervasive neo-colonial forces, the cultural resources of long histories and the vibrancy of culture in everyday life are essential for the generation of alternative futures. Appiah (1992) expresses faith in the potential of African resilience and resistance beyond the walls of the academy, in relational cultural life on the ground rather than in the ether.

> And what happens will happen not because we pronounce upon the matter in theory, but out of the changing everyday practices of African cultural life. For all the while, in Africa's cultures, there are those who will not see themselves as Other. Despite the overwhelming reality of economic decline, despite unimaginable poverty; despite wars, malnutrition, disease and political instability, African cultural productivity grows apace: popular literatures, oral narrative and poetry, dance, drama, music, and visual art all thrive.
>
> *(Appiah, 1992, p. 254)*

Raging hope in the present

The challenges of the present cannot be met by avoiding, minimising or silencing the catastrophic effects of the past. The terrain of potential development or the imagined future horizons of life are anchored in or tethered to the past. As Eagleton (2016, p. 24) notes:

> If the past cannot be deleted … it is not least because it is a vital constituent of the present. We can progress beyond it, to be sure, but only by means of the capabilities with which it has bequeathed us. The habits bred by generations of supremacy and subservience, arrogance and inertia, are not to be *un*learned overnight. Instead they constitute [a] … legacy of guilt and debt which contaminates the roots of human creativity, infiltrating the bones of and bloodstream of contemporary history and entwining itself with our more enlightened, emancipatory impulses.

In contemporary South Africa, working-class muscle is being newly flexed, strengthened not only by recollection of past injustices that people refuse to forget but in direct response to the repetitive actions of elites that entrench conditions of structural violence and inequality in the present. The decades of "waiting" post the first democratic elections of 1994 have betrayed people's hope in yet another of the governing party's catchy slogans, promising "a better life for all". In these circumstances, rage is not an irrational response but rather "a productive force for freedom from oppression" (Canham, 2018, p. 320), expressing "affective commitments to self and community" (Canham, 2018, p. 325). Rage indicates that people *know* the world does not need to be organised in this way, and they *understand* that the elite has both the power and the financial resources necessary to change things but not the political will to do so.

In this sense, rage may be read as an indicator of hope, a belief that the future need not resemble either the past or the present. In Canham's analysis, the affect of rage is conjoined with a term that sounds antiquated and anachronistic by comparison: indignation. However, this somewhat mild-sounding term refers not to an impolite slight but to an assault on human dignity. Although material poverty undermines the dignity[3] of personhood, the question of recognition is also critical. Questions of the sociological, political and economic dimensions of human life cannot be abstracted from the peculiarly dehumanising effects of racialisation that permeate South African society, nor from contestations about gendered and sexual identities, or the dynamics of global conflicts around citizenship and belonging. "From this perspective, the concept of reparation is not only an economic project but also a process of reassembling amputated parts, repairing broken links, relaunching forms of reciprocity without which there can be no progress for humanity" (Mbembe, 2017, p. 182).

Canham argues that the affective response of rage need not translate into violent action; however, it most often does and it is in any case difficult to imagine its effectiveness as a political tool for change in conditions of structural violence unless it is externally expressed in some way. In the face of intransigent authorities who remain impassive to the legitimate, pressing demands of citizens particular forms of disruptive protest (that may include actions such as blockading roads or the destruction of public property, often by burning) have become commonplace in South Africa. While the machinery of the state may sometimes be moved to provide partial responses to these demands (re-inscribing these forms of protest as the only effective way to gain attention) these responses are also typically accompanied by overt, sometimes violent, policing that may serve to exacerbate rather than contain violence. Aggressive activism or violent forms of protest may be analytically sensible and politically defensible under conditions of structural violence but rendering these patterns "normal" is also part of the problematics of change in a context characterised by pervasive (hyper)masculine forms of interpersonal violence in everyday life.[4] Rage may be triggered by "commitments to self and community" but violent expressions of rage may not always be effective in the face of repressive institutional and state violence. Further, it may not provide the impetus for *sustaining* selves or communities in constructing hopeful futures, sometimes acting back on the actor/s, inflicting self-harm and further fraying already fragile community bonds, with the deepest and most critical wounds being inflicted by and on black youth.

The Student Movement is the loud voice of young people challenging the optimistic narrative of their parents' generation and protesting the ways in which their inheritance is mostly manifest as a burden of debt, sometimes adopting and adapting similar methods of raging protest from the streets. In the "best" moments of the protests, the students (who are by definition a relatively advantaged group) and the desperate needs of the working poor were recognised as inextricably linked. For example, in several confrontations with the police (called onto campuses by university management[5]), students appealed to them to recognise that this fight for access to higher education was in their interests as it would be impossible for them to send their children to university on a police salary. The campaign against the inhumane and exploitative system of outsourcing workers at universities was integrated with the Student Movement's demands and won on many campuses (Motimele, 2019). In these processes of protest, it is clear that "[f]reedoms calcify and have to be rejected and/or adapted by the young" (Zadie Smith, 2018, p. 339) but the question of the older generation's accountability cannot be ducked and requires ongoing intergenerational dialogue.

> Nor can it be easy for children, heroically transformed into adults overnight, to be their own redemptive metaphor because the experience of compassion and the nurturing of conscience have not been a consistently informing aspect of their growth in recent times. Can they succeed in effecting a strategic distance from themselves for the purpose of moral reflection? That we need their energy is beyond dispute. And so do we need their fearlessness and questioning attitude, which, under the circumstances, are the strange gifts of these terrible times. But where will the visionary authority come from that will harness that energy and assign a proper role to it in a new and infinitely challenging society?
>
> *(Ndebele, 2007, p. 43)*

In the wake, in the aftermath, in the impasse, in a present haunted by traumatic histories, we will need to grapple with the question of how rage and righteous indignation might be harnessed for imaginative hopeful futures. Psychoanalysis and other therapeutic practices might offer some resources for surviving the chaos of "the ordinary as a zone of convergence of many histories, where people manage the incoherence of lives that proceed in the face of threats to the good life they imagine" (Berlant, 2011, p. 10). These practices of care are surely necessary in the face of extraordinary psychosocial strains for individuals and communities and part of the immediate demands on the discipline of psychology is to find appropriate responses to the pervasive everyday crises of ordinary people. On university campuses, the mental health impact on students active in the Student Movement, and on those who are not, has been immense, including alarmingly unusually high suicide rates. Beyond these immediate imperatives, the task of a critical psychology is to "think ahead of the burning fires" (Canham, 2018, p. 328) and the task of education is to create zones of potential development that enable people to engage in social and inner dialogues that animate agency and imagination, hoping for a world of imaginative, productive joy rather than resilient survival against the odds. We need to nurture a kind of hope that is "mobilising rather than therapeutic" (Giroux, 2008, p. 139).

Articulations of meaningful hope

The context of higher education should provide an ideal environment for generating this meaningful activating hope, crossing the domains of past and future in a parenthetical present. Human agency in the present is enabled by the temporal quality of subjectivity that incorporates past and future. The haunting effects of the past in the present are accompanied by whispers from the future so that present concrete realities are always infused with these alternative temporalities. Although it is always subject to contestation, the past may be rendered legible through public records and archives, through the practices of tradition, science, art and socialisation. Future storylines are similarly present to consciousness but are less clearly articulated, requiring improvisation, flexibility and creativity.

> We cannot know the future directly, but ... we can feel its ghostly pull all the same, like a force that warps spaces out of true. It is to be found in the unfinished nature of the actual, discernible as a hollow at its heart. Potentiality is what articulates the present with the future, and thus lays down the material infrastructure of hope.
>
> *(Eagleton, 2016, p. 52)*

Realising these potent possibilities (potentiality) for the future requires an articulation of what Eagleton (2016), in a book by this title, calls "hope without optimism". Meaningful hope for alternatives is to be differentiated from optimism which demands nothing of us in the present in the passive assumption that "things will get better" and progress is inevitable. In this way, optimism offers no more resources than its ostensible opposite, pessimism, which similarly implies that there is nothing to be done as things can only get worse, and they will! Optimism for a perfect utopian future cannot redeem the grievous effects of the past and articulations of hope must confront, rather than deferring to the future, the challenges of the present. The antithesis of hope is thus not rage or despair but cynicism. "One has faith in the future precisely because one seeks to confront the present at its most rebarbative" (Eagleton, 2016, p. 7).

Hope creates "a crack in the present through which the future can be glimpsed" (Eagleton, 2016, p. 44). Critical psychological praxis, whether in the domain of therapeutic interventions or in the world of teaching and learning, entails the creation or widening of such cracks in edifices of certainty. This is of course a risky business, whether the edifice in question is the carefully constructed coherent self, or the structural foundations of collective culture life and meaning-making, and the traditions of knowledge that have served (some of) us well up to this point. It is not only those who currently benefit from these structural formations or identity categories that resist their unsettling but also those whose precarious grip on the world is under constant threat who desire this certainty for their future selves. Working with young people whose futures have longer trajectories than our own requires simultaneous strategies of affirmation and unsettling. As explored in Chapters 5 and 6, university education functions at a unique nexus between the past and future.

A key role of public educational institutions is to prepare graduates for the world of work and the requirements of professional life are quite firmly framed, sometimes in the "hidden curriculum" of conformity to the "culture" of corporate life, and sometimes in the explicit codes of professional regulatory bodies such as the HPCSA (Health Professions Council of South Africa) that governs the training of psychologists. The goal of the vast majority of students is to gain a qualification that will offer them a "degree of distinction" in the workplace that they will inhabit in the very near future where they will be expected to demonstrate mastery of particular skills, including appropriate modes of conceptual thinking and problem solving. University mission and vision statements throughout the world increasingly use a language of recruiting staff in the service of students as "paying" customers towards these purposes. In this frame, university education is reduced to "maintaining a society of quiet ones, of mere 'job-holders and consumers'" (Greene, 1982, p. 5). The focus is on the transmission of information or, at best, providing guidelines for the gathering of volumes of information via the internet that, like fast-food outlets, serves up "precooked" material for quick and filling consumption. The nutritional value of such information is questionable, leave aside the more time-consuming processes of learning to cook things up oneself. Maxine Greene (1982, p. 5) cautions that to "rear a generation of spectators is not to educate at all". In the context of these global trends, the disruptive protest politics of the South African Student Movement can be understood as a refusal to remain on the sidelines of the practices of knowledge production and as resistance to the regimentation of the academic calendar and the established institutional conventions of that work to "render black subjects quiet" (Motimele, 2019, p. 205). The anxieties of academic staff and particularly of university management in response to the disruption of the Student Movement centred around the completion of the academic year to produce the "output" of students progressing through their degrees and graduating on time.[6] The aim (shared by many students) was to get things to "quieten down" and return to "normal".

Individual aspirations that assimilate to the status quo, and the routine cycles of teaching and learning that are repetitive for teachers but fresh for each new cohort of students, are the target of the decolonising project. However, this abstract position of critique is not fully adequate to frame our response in the face of the young people on the cusp of adulthood in our classrooms, and it is unethical to negate the often remarkable sacrifices that their families have made to facilitate their studies. "For hope to be more than an empty abstraction, it must be firmly anchored in the realities and contradictions of everyday life and have some hold on the present" (Giroux, 2008, p. 138). We have responsibilities for equipping students with the languages and forms that have made for our success and will make for theirs, not because they are paying customers nor because we are beholden to the market but because we have relational commitments to them as people, recognising the legitimacy of their choices even when they do not coincide with our own. In the highly diversified global landscapes of work, we all of us need the benefits of skilled expertise that can only be developed through extended high-level study across a range of disciplines of which we ourselves remain largely or entirely ignorant. This is perhaps most clearly evident in the application of the sciences in everyday technologies such as cars and planes, laptops and cell phones that we so take for granted that we forget they are the products of human thought and labour. However, it is also a feature of the arts where audiences need not have the knowledge or skills that musicians, visual artists, writers and choreographers inscribe in their works. In all domains of knowledge and work, our present practices are articulated in the tension between past and future in the contesting dialectics of change and continuity. In relation to the discipline of psychology, it is incumbent upon us to equip graduates to thoughtfully practise the work of psychological support or healing. However, our existing repertoires of specialist knowledge are strained to their limits in response to the pervasive psychic stresses of our times. It is imperative that we develop new concepts for analysis and potential modes of practice and this will entail contestations about the canon. As I have argued throughout this book, Vygotskian theory and narrative psychology provide some such conceptual resources for rethinking personhood as mutable, temporal and relational. These frameworks might be fruitfully combined with other critical psychology and interdisciplinary insights and, in particular, largely untapped reservoirs of meaning in African languages and the art of life beyond the academy.

Beyond mastering the content of disciplinary knowledge, university study is an apprenticeship in the traditions, forms and practices of enquiry and knowledge-making. These forms of engagement are most often what we mean when we claim that what we teach and what graduates develop is "critical thinking". This thinking is valuable beyond the domain of specialist applications and the best education should enable students to deploy these new languages of description, theoretical concepts and the rigorous processes of gathering supportive evidence or developing rich idiosyncratic detail, in work and life. Contemporary life requires the capacity to read between the lines to differentiate truth from fake news, the ability to range across disciplines to think through large-scale "wicked" problems such as climate change and poverty, and full democratic citizenship cannot be articulated without learning the languages of others and learning to read the structures of power within which we live. If democracy is to have any future life, it needs to find new vital expressions beyond traditional ballot boxes or parliamentary spaces that, in many places in the world, increasingly feel like circus arenas. New ligaments of strength for democratic practice may be developed through new textual horizons that challenge established world views and through the exchange of ideas that happens in conversation. Conversations with provocative potential to change subjects and worlds are not necessarily characterised by politeness and tolerance, and the most productive exchanges often entail conflict and contestation, challenging participants in their claims to truth and commitments to ethical judgements. Others may provoke us to see and listen (to reflectively think) from positions (both temporally and spatially) other than our own ... the world calls me out to attend to not only those others who are present, but also those who are no longer here or not yet here, leading me to sense the world as more than me.

(Di Paolantonio, 2016, pp. 154–155)

The skill of talking across difference with heat but not hostility is in short supply in the world and the academic context should provide scope for practising this art.

However, the importance of face-to-face learning and teaching is being increasingly challenged by digital platforms that have transformed the old modes of correspondence or distance learning into immediate real-time exchanges with human or avatar others across remote ether worlds. The explosion of information and the acceleration of communication across geographical, cultural, linguistic and other boundaries has empowering effects and, regardless, it is impossible for those of us in it to reimagine an existence without this dimension of the world. However, perhaps because I am not a digital native, I would argue that this virtual world can supplement but not supplant embodied face-to-face interaction in the space of the therapeutic room, in the classroom, in political gatherings or live performances, across family dining room tables and over coffee or wine with friends. In his insightful interpretation of Berlant's "cruel optimism", Di Paolantonio (2016) sketches the possibilities for a hopeful praxis that counters the precarious effects of loneliness and alienation that characterise contemporary life. Reading, thinking and talking in zones of potential development "implies the 'beautiful risk' of human interaction, the relational encounter where human beings come together to influence each other with words and interpretations that work to forge and sustain a common world" (Di Paolantonio, 2016, p. 149).

While the massification of higher education, in South Africa and around the world, is critical on grounds of both human rights and economic imperatives, it has most often been implemented through increasing corporatisation of higher education in which the market place determines the worth of qualifications. This produces a divide between the purposes of "training" and "education" that cuts at the heart of the idea of the university, distinguishing between the traditions of research and developing scholarship, and the preparation of students for the workplace. The vast majority of students, and courses that command high registration rates, are treated as "cash cows" (a term used without approbation in South African university management discourse), suggesting that students and lecturers have a limited commercial contract with one another. Relations defined in this way erode the hope that graduates may leave their studies equipped for meaningful work and social life, contracting their future horizons to work that entails performing repetitive practices on known ground. The tension between the demands of the marketplace and the imaginative domain of scholarship and enquiry requires that educators creatively conjoin the ostensibly contradictory aims of education and training. Flexible responsive curricula and pedagogies should inculcate disciplinary knowledge and practices while simultaneously provoking creative leaps that will enable us to invent new languages and forms, and encourage students to participate in these intellectual adventures with us. University life should provide spaces for experimentation and innovation, reflection and imagination, time for living inside our heads in positive quietness. In the solitary practices of reading and writing and in the collective dialogues of seminars or tutorials, the cultivation of scholarship entails giving "time to what is not here – to the past and to the future" (Di Paolantonio, 2016, p. 150) in ways that will enable us to cultivate a "less anxious creativity" (Appiah, 1992, p. 254). Our world is in dire need of rigorous critical analysis of political and economic systems but it is also essential that we cultivate practices of "improvisation and playfulness, pleasure and independence … humour [that] recognises ironies, impossibilities, and disproportions … driven by imaginations as *supple as art* rather than as stiff as dogma" (Solnit, 2016, p. 44, emphasis added). Hope without critique is reduced to optimism and critique without hope is reduced to pessimism and neither eviscerated forms have the potency to effect change.

> Combining the discourse of critique and hope is crucial to affirming that critical activity offers the possibility for social change and to viewing democracy as a project and a task, as an ideal type that is never finalised and has a powerful adversary in the social realities it is meant to change.
>
> *(Giroux, 2008, p. 141)*

Productive work to change subjects and worlds will require the relinquishment of ourselves and a willingness to question established certainties in traditions of knowledge. Hopeful futures take the "shape of water" rather than following the contours of solid ground and are not amenable to design by fixed blueprints or plans. "Hopefulness lies in its unfinishedness, its openness to improvisation and participation. … [When] hope is no longer fixed on the future: it becomes an electrifying force in the present" (Solnit, 2016, p. 95).

Concluding thoughts

Particularly in periods of sociopolitical change, narratives of the past cannot provide clear storylines for the future, and the usually incremental, silent and invisible formation of human subjectivity becomes accelerated, articulated and visible, although no less easy to grasp. We may resist the imposition of the monolingual formulation of the past and the ways in which this makes us feel "out of place" but speaking the language of the future entails moments in which of all of us will feel "lost in translation". We live tensed and tense lives, in which the present is a moment of tension between past and future. This tension entails precarious balance, poised at the moment in which we navigate the lifting of the one foot still in the past before the other can yet be placed in the future. We may never have both feet on present ground but nevertheless, we cannot have both in the air simultaneously either. Navigating the demands of the present transformational moment to create more equitable futures is a process steered by those with whom we converse, by the narrative histories, both silenced and voiced, which we are willing to hear, sometimes in fraught translation, and through which we must weave new versions of ourselves and the world.

> Stories trap us, stories free us, we live and die by stories. … Hope is the story of uncertainty, of coming to terms with the risk involved in not knowing what comes next, which is more demanding than despair and, in a way, more frightening. And immeasurably more rewarding.
>
> *(Solnit, 2016, p. 7)*

To realise these potential narrative subjectivities, it is imperative to open ourselves to voices not only from the past but from the future too, so as to become what Xolela Mangcu (2011) terms "worthy ancestors". In as much as successive generations need to learn from history, the future horizons of the young are beyond our reach and their vantage point is therefore critical in informing the present. The argument of the book has been that the same psychosocial processes and forms of intergenerational life that make it impossible to escape the past simultaneously orientate us towards imagined not-yet-present futures. The question of change entails the challenge of how to live ethically in the present, in relationship with others, creating collective future histories that will be conceptually and politically transformative. We are impelled to live innovatively rather than repetitively, with an aesthetics and humour, entailing relational care not only towards those with whom we live but also those beyond our spatial borders; to the memories of those in the past whom we have lost, often through our own violence and ethical failure; and towards the imagined futures of those who will inherit the earth, the consequences of our actions, and our fragments of meaning and cultural threads from which to weave new more humane forms of life.

Notes

1 Some of the ideas in this final chapter were first explored in a previous article, *Narrative Possibilities of the Past for the Future* (Bradbury, 2012) and then further developed in a paper presented at the first NEST (Narrative Enquiry for Social Transformation) international conference, *Narrative Subjects: Tense (in)tension and (im)possibilities for change*.

2 The term "obligation" in English implies negative bonds of duty to be fulfilled on the basis of social respectability rather than motivated by desire. However, we sometimes express our thanks by saying "much obliged" acknowledging the reciprocal "debt" created by someone's kindness towards us and revealing a more positive etymology, as evident in the Spanish term for "thank you", *obligado*. From the worldview of ubuntu, (see Chapter 3), relations of obligation and duty serve to consolidate filial affection and community cohesion.

3 This focus on the dignity of personhood is central in the analyses of a wide range of contemporary authors from multiple disciplinary backgrounds and varying political perspectives, for example, Appiah (2018); Fukuyama (2018); Peterson (2012). (In a particularly interesting twist, Fukuyama utilises the notion of dignity and its expression in identity politics to account for the rise of the (working-class) right in the United States that propelled Trump into the presidency, catching many political analysts and left intellectuals by surprise.)

4 South African society is characterised by pervasive violence: gender-based violence, rape and femicide, xenophobic and homophobic violence, gang- and drug-related murders, the excessive use of physical violence in petty crimes such as theft or mugging, cyber- and physical bullying in schools. While (white) middle-class fear of crime is most visible, the victims of violence are mostly black and poor. I do not mean to conflate violent tactics in protest action with these more generalised forms of interpersonal violence but this wider context indicates a milieu of violence shaped by the dehumanising effects of colonial oppression and apartheid brutality, rather than aberrant or exceptional acts.

5 For those of us who were students in the 1980s when apartheid police often forcibly occupied campuses, the notion that police would be *invited* onto campuses by university management in a democratic state was unthinkable until it happened. Although the situation was complex, tense and difficult to manage, the argument that this was unavoidable reflects an alarming bankruptcy of intellectual and political resources at the heart of the very institutions charged with developing these resources in the next generation. The SERI (Socio-economic Rights Institute of South Africa) report (Rayner, Baldwin-Ragaven & Naidoo, 2017) provides a detailed account of how the strategies of securitisation and

policing were deployed by the University of Witwatersrand. While vast sums of money were expended on these strategies, no provisions were made for medical or psychological support for students or staff in the midst of violent clashes with private security forces and police.

6 The irony is that we are not very good at even this routine process. Throughput rates at South African universities are notoriously low, with the "average" student taking five years to complete a three-year degree.

BIBLIOGRAPHY

Abe, T. (2014). Transitional justice destined to be criticized as failure: Understanding its uniqueness from African cases. *African Study Monographs*, 50, pp. 3–23.

Achebe, C. (1988). *Hopes and impediments*. London: Heinemann.

Adebayo, A. (2018). *Transforming ivory towers to ebony towers*. Conference at the University of Johannesburg, 17–18 August 2018. Retrieved from www.uj.ac.za/new andevents/Pages/transforming-ivory-towers-to-ebony-towers-adekeye-adebajo. aspx.

Alexander, N. (2003). Language policy, symbolic power and the democratic responsibility of the post-apartheid university. *Pretexts, Literary and Cultural Studies*, 12 (2), p. 179–190.

Alexander, N. (2004). The politics of language planning in post-apartheid South Africa. *Language Problems & Language Planning*, 28 (2), pp. 113–130.

Alexander, N. (2011). The value of multilingualism in higher education in post-apartheid South Africa. Paper presented at the symposium, *Language and Cultural Capital: High potential youth in marginalised communities*, University of the Witwatersrand, Johannesburg, South Africa, 9–10 November 2011.

Alexander, N. (2012). The centrality of the language question in the social sciences and humanities in post-apartheid South Africa. Paper presented as the *Inaugural EB van Wyk Honorary Public Linguistics Lecture*, University of Johannesburg, Johannesburg, South Africa, 22 February 2012.

Alexander, N. (2013). *Thoughts on the New South Africa*. Johannesburg: Jacana.

Ally, S. (2009). *From servants to workers: South African domestic workers and the democratic state*. Ithaca, NY: Cornell University Press.

Anderson, B. (1983). *Imagined communities: Reflections on the origins and spread of nationalism*. London: Verso.

Andrews, M. (2014). *Narrative imagination and everyday life*. Oxford: Oxford University Press.

Andrews, M. (2018). The narrative architecture of political forgiveness. Keynote address, 4th international *NEST* (*Narrative Enquiry for Social Transformation*) conference, University of the Witwatersrand, Johannesburg, South Africa, 22–24 March 2018.

Appadurai, A. (1990). Disjuncture and difference in the global cultural economy. *Theory, Culture & Society*, 7, pp. 295–310.

Appiah, K. A. (1992). *In my father's house: Africa in the philosophy of culture*. London: Methuen.

Appiah, K. A. (2005). *Ethics of identity*. Princeton: Princeton University Press.

Appiah, K. A. (2006). *Cosmopolitanism: Ethics in a world of strangers*. New York: W. W. Norton & Company.

Appiah, K. A. (2018). *The lies that bind: Rethinking identity: Creed, country, colour, class, culture*. London: Profile Books.

Archer, M. (2000). *Being human: The problem of agency*. Cambridge: Cambridge University Press.

Archer, M. (2003). *Structure, agency and the internal conversation*. Cambridge: Cambridge University Press.

Arendt, H. (1961). *Between past and future*. London: Faber & Faber.

Baerveldt, C. (2014). The ontology of the "in-between" and the genetic legacy in psychology. *Theory & Psychology*, 24 (4), pp. 542–560.

Bakhtin, M. (2010). *The dialogic imagination*. Translated by C. Emerson & M. Holquist. Austin: University of Texas Press.

Baldwin, J. (1993). (1962/1963) *The fire next time*. New York: Vintage Books.

Baumann, Z. (1996). From pilgrim to tourist – or a short history of identity. In S. Hall & P. Du Gay (Eds.). *Questions of cultural identity* (pp. 18–36). London: SAGE.

Baumann, Z. (2000). *Liquid modernity*. Cambridge: Polity Press.

BBC (1992). *7 up South Africa*. Directed by A. Gibson.

BBC (2016). *The ascent of woman*. Written and presented by A. Foreman.

Benjamin, W. (1940). On the concept of history. In H. Eiland, & M. W. Jennings (Eds.) E. Jephcott (trans.). 2003. *Walter Benjamin: Selected writings, volume 4, 1938–1940* (pp. 389–400).

Berlant, L. (2011). *Cruel optimism*. Durham, NC: Duke University Press.

Bertau, M.-C. (2014). The need for a dialogical science: Considering the legacy of Russian-Soviet thinking for contemporary approaches in dialogic research. In A. Yasnitsky, R. van der Veer, & M. Ferrari (Eds.). *The Cambridge handbook of cultural-historical psychology* (pp. 9–44). Cambridge: Cambridge University Press.

Biesta, G. J. J. (2001). "Preparing for the incalculable": Deconstruction, justice, and the question of education. In G. J. J. Biesta & D. Egéa-Kuehne (Eds.). *Derrida & education* (pp. 32–54). London: Routledge.

Biko, S. B. (1978). *I write what I like*. Oxford: Heinemann.

Böhmke, W. & Tlali, T. (2008). Bodies and behaviour: Science, psychology and politics in South Africa. In C. Van Ommen & D. Painter (Eds.). *Interiors: A history of psychology in South Africa* (pp. 125–151). Pretoria: UNISA Press.

Booysen, S. (Ed.) (2016). *Fees must fall*. Johannesburg: Wits University Press.

Boughey, C. (2002). "Naming" students' problems: An analysis of language-related discourses at a South African university. *Teaching in Higher Education*, 7 (3), pp. 295–307. DOI: 10.1080/13562510220144798.

Boughey, C. (2005). Epistemological access to the university: An alternative perspective. *South African Journal of Higher Education*, 19 (3), pp. 230–242.

Bourdieu, P. (1986). The forms of capital. In E. Richardson (Ed.). *Handbook of theory of research for the sociology of education* (p. 46–58). Westport, CT: Greenwood Press.

Bourdieu, P. (2006). Understanding. In P. Bourdieu (Ed.). *The weight of the world* (pp. 607–626). Oxford: Blackwell.

Bourdieu, P. & Wacquant, L. J. D. (1992). *An invitation to reflexive sociology*. Chicago, IL and London: University of Chicago Press.

Boym, S. (2001). *The future of nostalgia*. New York: Basic Books.

Boym, S. (2007). Nostalgia and its discontents. *The Hedgehog Review*, Summer, pp. 7–18.

Bozalek, V. & Boughey, C. (2012). (Mis)framing higher education in South Africa. *Social Policy & Administration*, 46 (6), pp. 688–703.

Bradbury, J. (Ed.) (1995). *Psychology I: Resource package*. Cape Town: Juta & Company Ltd.

Bradbury, J. (2000). *The questioning process in the development of knowledge*. Unpublished PhD thesis, University of Natal, South Africa.

Bradbury, J. (2012). Narrative possibilities of the past for the future. *Peace and Conflict: Journal of Peace Psychology*, 18 (3), pp. 341–350.

Bradbury, J. & Clark, J. (2012). Echoes of the past in imaginings of the future: The problems and possibilities of working with young people in contemporary South Africa. *Global Studies of Childhood*, 2 (3), pp. 176–189.

Bradbury, J. & Kiguwa, P. (2012a). Fish out of water: Swimming upstream. Paper presented at the SACHES (South African Comparative Education) conference, *Education and societal dynamics: possibilities for educational change in the Southern African region*, Nelson Mandela Metropolitan University, 30 October–1 November 2012.

Bradbury, J. & Kiguwa, P. (2012b). Thinking women's worlds. *Feminist Africa*, 17, pp. 28–47.

Bradbury, J. & Miller, R. (2010). Narrative possibilities: Theorizing identity in a context of practice. *Theory and Psychology*, 20 (5), pp. 687–702.

Bradbury, J. & Miller, R. (2011). A failure by any other name: The phenomenon of underpreparedness. *South African Journal of Science*, 107 (3/4), pp. 1–8.

Bradbury, J. & Ndlovu, S. (2011). Dangerous liaisons: Ties that bind and lines that divide. *Psychology & Society (PINS)*, 42, pp. 3–20.

Brockmeier, J. (2002). Remembering and forgetting: Narrative as cultural memory. *Culture & Psychology*, 18 (1), pp. 15–43.

Brockmeier, J. (2009). Reaching for meaning. *Theory & Psychology*, 19 (2), pp. 213–233.

Bronowski, J. (1973). *The ascent of man*. London: British Broadcasting Corporation.

Bruner, J. (1986). *Actual minds, possible worlds*. Cambridge, MA: Harvard University Press.

Bunn, D. (1998). Whited sepulchres: On the reluctance of monuments. In H. Judin & I. Vladislavic (Eds.). *Blank: Architecture, apartheid and after* (pp. 93–118). Rotterdam: NAi Publishers.

Burman, E. (1994/2008/2017). *Deconstructing developmental psychology* (1st, 2nd & 3rd eds.). London: Routledge.

Burman, E. (2008). *Developments: Nation, child and image.* London: Routledge.

Burr, V. (1995/2003/2015). *An introduction to social constructionism* (1st, 2nd & 3rd eds.). London: Routledge.

Burr, V. (1998). Overview: Realism, relativism, social constructionism and discourse. In I. Parker (Ed.). *Social constructionism, discourse and realism* (pp. 13–26). London: SAGE.

Busakwe, D. (1997). *Fragmented African identities.* Cape Town: Juta & Company Ltd.

Butler, J. (1997). *The psychic life of power: Theories in subjection.* Stanford, CA: Stanford University Press.

Butler, J. (2012). Post two, in Puar, J. (Ed.) (2012) Precarity talk: A virtual roundtable with Lauren Berlant, Judith Butler, Bojana Cvejić, Isabell Lorey, Jasbir Puar, and Ana Vujanović. *The Drama Review,* 56 (4), pp. 163–177.

Canham, H. (2018). Theorising community rage for decolonial action. *South African Journal of Psychology,* 48 (3), pp. 319–330.

Cerbone (1999). Composition and constitution: Heidegger's hammer. *Philosophical Topics,* 27 (2), pp. 309–329.

Chikane, N. (2018). *Breaking a rainbow, building a nation: The politics behind #MustFall movements.* Johannesburg: Picador Africa, Pan Macmillan.

Chinguno, C., Kgoroba, M., Mashibini, S., Masilela, B. N., Maubane, B., Moyo, N., Mthombeni, A., & Ndlovu, H. (Eds.) (2017). *Rioting and writing: Diaries of wits fallists.* Johannesburg: SWOP (Society, Work and Development Institute).

Chisholm, L. (2013). The textbook saga and corruption in education. *Southern African Review of Education,* 19 (1), pp. 7–22.

Chomsky, N. (1986). *Knowledge of language: Its nature, origin, and use.* New York: Praeger.

Chomsky, N. (2006a). Human nature: Justice vs power: A debate between Noam Chomsky and Michel Foucault. In N. Chomsky & M. Foucault. *The Chomsky-Foucault debate on human nature* (pp. 1–67). New York: The New Press.

Chomsky, N. (2006b). Politics. In N. Chomsky & M. Foucault. *The Chomsky-Foucault debate on human nature* (pp. 68–116). New York: The New Press.

Clarence-Fincham, J. (1992). Language, power and voices of a university: The role of critical linguistics in curriculum development. *Journal of Literary Studies,* 8 (3–4), pp. 145–161. DOI: 10.1080/02564719208530012.

Clarence-Fincham, J. (2001). Responding to academic discourse: Developing critical literacy at a South African University. In B. Comber & A. Simpson (Eds.). *Negotiating critical literacies in classrooms* (pp. 273–286). London: Routledge.

Cliff, A. (2015). The National Benchmark test in academic literacy: How might it be used to support teaching in higher education? *Language Matters,* 46 (1), pp. 3–21.

Cock, J. (1980). *Maids and madams: Domestic workers under apartheid.* Johannesburg: Ravan Press.

Cohen, J. (2013). *Private lives: Why we remain in the dark.* London: Granta.

Cole, M. (1995). *Cultural psychology: A once and future discipline.* Cambridge, MA: The Belknap Press of Harvard University Press.

Craig, A. P. (1992). Defamiliarisation as a learning-teaching strategy. *Quality and Equality in higher education, SAARDHE Conference proceedings,* pp. 218–221.

Crenshaw, K. (1991). Mapping the margins: Intersectionality, identity politics, and violence against women of color. *Stanford Law Review,* 43 (6), pp. 1241–1299.

Crites, S. (1986). Storytime: Recollecting the past and projecting the future. In T. Sarbin (Ed.). *Narrative psychology: The storied nature of human conduct* (pp. 152–173). New York: Praeger.

Cromby, J. & Nightingale, D. J. (1999). What's wrong with social constructionism? In D. J. Nightingale & J. Cromby (Eds.). *Social constructionist psychology: A critical analysis of theory and practice* (pp. 1–15). Buckingham: Open University Press.

Cromby, J., Newton, T., & Williams, S. J. (2011). Neuroscience and subjectivity. *Subjectivity,* 4 (3), pp. 215–226.

Crossley, M. L. (2000). Narrative psychology, trauma and the study of self/identity. *Theory & Psychology,* 10, pp. 527–546.

Daniels, H. (2001). *Vygotsky and pedagogy.* London: Routledge Falmer.

Daniels, H., Cole, M., & Wertsch, J. V. (Eds.) (2007). *The Cambridge companion to Vygotsky.* Cambridge and New York: Cambridge University Press.

Danziger, K. (1990). *Constructing the subject: Historical origins of psychological research.* Cambridge: Cambridge University Press.

Davis, A. (2016). The 17th annual Steve Biko Memorial Lecture, UNISA, Pretoria, 9 September 2016. Retrieved from www.enca.com/south-africa/catch-it-live-angela-davis-delivers-the-17th-annual-steve-biko-lecture.

de Haas, M. (1992). *Anthropology.* In H. Griesel & J. Withers (Eds.). *Foundation series.* Durban: TTT Programme, University of Natal.

De la Rey, C. (1997). On political activism and discourse analysis in South Africa. In A. Levett, A. Kottler, E. Burman, & I. Parker (Eds.). *Culture, power and difference: Discourse analysis in South Africa* (pp. 189–198). London: Zed Books.

Derrida, J. (1998). *Monolingualism of the other or the prosthesis of origin.* Translated by P. Mensah. Redwood City: Stanford University Press.

Derrida, J. (2001). Talking liberties: Jacques Derrida's interview with Alan Montforte. In G. J. J. Biesta & D. Egéa-Kuehne (Eds.). *Derrida & education* (pp. 176–185). London: Routledge.

DHET, (2018). *Statistics on post-school education and training in South Africa 2016.* Department: Higher Education and Training, Republic of South Africa. Retrieved from www.dhet.gov.za/Research%20Coordination%20Monitoring%20and%20Evaluation/6_DHET%20Stats%20Report_04%20April%202018.pdf.

Di Paolantonio, M. (2016). The cruel optimism of education and education's implication with 'passing-on'. *Journal of Philosophy of Education,* 50 (2), pp. 147–159.

Dick, A. (2018). How the apartheid regime burnt books in their tens of thousands. *The Conversation,* 24 October 2018. Retrieved from. https://theconversation.com/how-the-apartheid-regime-burnt-books-in-their-tens-of-thousands-102355.

Dowdall, T. L. (1991). Repression, health care and ethics under apartheid. *Journal of Medical Ethics,* 17, pp. 51–54.

Du Bois, W. E. B. (1903). *The souls of black folk*. Chicago, IL: A.C. McClurg & Co.

Eagleton, T. (2000). *The idea of culture*. London: Blackwell.

Eagleton, T. (2016). *Hope without optimism*. New Haven, CT: Yale University Press.

Eco, U. (2004). *Mouse or rat: Translation as negotiation*. London: Phoenix.

Edwards, D., Ashmore, M., & Potter, J. (1995). Death and furniture: The rhetoric, politics and theology of bottomline arguments against relativism. *History of the Human Sciences*, 8 (2), pp. 25–49.

Egéa-Kuehne, D. (2001). Derrida's ethics of affirmation: The challenge of educational rights and responsibilities. In G. J. J. Biesta & D. Egéa-Kuehne (Eds.). *Derrida & education* (pp. 186–216). London: Routledge.

Enriquez, V. G. (1992). *From colonial to liberation psychology: The Philippine experience*. Quezon City: The University of the Philippines Press.

Equal Education. Retrieved from https://equaleducation.org.za/.

Erasmus, Z. (2017). *Race otherwise: Forging a new humanism for South Africa*. Johannesburg: Wits University Press.

Erikson, E. H. (1968). *Identity, youth and crisis*. New York: Norton.

Erikson, E. H. (1970). Autobiographic notes on the identity crisis. *Daedalus*, 99 (44), pp. 730–759.

Essed, P. & Goldberg, D. T. (2002). Cloning cultures: The social injustices of sameness. *Ethnic Racial Studies*, 25 (6), pp. 1066–1082.

Essop, A. (1990). Khanya college: A critical assessment. In C. Hemson (Ed.). *Educational development in the South African universities: Is an intermediate tertiary college the solution?* (pp. 82–85). Conference Proceedings. Durban: University of Natal.

Fanon, F. (1963). *The wretched of the earth*. London: Penguin Books.

Farber, T. (2017). Read it and weep: SA kids struggle with literacy. *Times Live*, 6 December 2017. Retrieved from. www.timeslive.co.za/news/south-africa/2017-12-06-read-it-and-weep-sa-kids-struggle-with-literacy/.

Fay, B. (1996). *Contemporary philosophy of social science: A multicultural approach*. Oxford: Blackwell.

Feuerstein, R., Rand, Y., & Hoffman, M. B. (1979). *The dynamic assessment of retarded performers: The learning potential assessment device, theory, instruments, and techniques*. Baltimore, MD: University Park Press.

Feuerstein, R., Rand, Y., Hoffman, M. B., & Miller, R. (1980). *Instrumental enrichment*. Baltimore: University Park Press.

Fine, M. (2004). Witnessing whiteness / gathering intelligence. In M. Fine, L. Weis, L. Powell Pruitt, & A. Burns (Eds.). *Off white: Readings on power, privilege, and resistance* 2nd edition (pp. 245–256). New York and London: Routledge.

Fine, M. (2018). *Just research in contentious times: Widening the methodological imagination*. New York: Teachers College Press.

Foucault, M. (1970). *The order of things*. London: Routledge.

Foucault, M. (1979). *Discipline and punish: The birth of the prison*. Harmondsworth: Penguin Books.

Foucault, M. (1988). *Technologies of the self*. Cambridge, MA: University of Massachusetts Press.

Foucault, M. (2006). Human nature: Justice vs power: A debate between Noam Chomsky and Michel Foucault. In N. Chomsky & M. Foucault. *The Chomsky-Foucault debate on human nature* (pp. 1–67). New York: The New Press.

Foxcroft, C. & Davies, C. (2008). Historical perspectives on psychometric testing in South Africa. In D. Van Ommen & D. Painter (Eds.). *Interiors: A history of psychology in South Africa* (pp. 152–181). Pretoria: UNISA Press.

Freeman, M. (1993). *Rewriting the self: History, memory, narrative.* London: Routledge.

Freeman, M. (2010). *Hindsight.* Oxford: Oxford University Press.

Freeman, M. (2014). *The priority of the other.* Oxford: Oxford University Press.

Freire, P. (1972). *Pedagogy of the oppressed.* New York: Herder and Herder.

Freire, P. (1973). *Education for critical consciousness.* New York: The Continuum Publishing Company.

Freire, P. & Macedo, D. (1987). *Literacy: Reading the word and the world.* South Hadley, MA: Bergin & Garvey.

Fukuyama, F. (2018). *Identity: The demand for dignity and the politics of resentment.* London: Profile Books.

Gadamer, H. (1975). *Truth and method.* London: Sheed and Ward.

Gade, C. B. N. (2013). What is Ubuntu? Different interpretations among South Africans of African descent. *South African Journal of Philosophy*, 31 (3), pp. 484–503.

Garuba, H. (2001). Language and identity in Nigeria. In S. Bekker, M. Dodds, & M. M. Khoza (Eds.). *Shifting African identities* (pp. 7–20). Pretoria: Human Sciences Research Council.

Gergen, K. J. & Gergen, M. M. (1986). Narrative form and the construction of psychological science. In T. R. Sarbin (Ed.). *Narrative psychology: The storied nature of human conduct* (pp. 22–44). Westport, CT: Praeger Publishers/Greenwood Publishing Group.

Gergen, M. (2001). *Feminist reconstructions in psychology: Narrative, gender & performance.* Thousand Oaks, CA and London: SAGE.

Giddens, A. (1991). *Modernity and self-identity: Self and society in the late modern age.* Cambridge: Polity Press.

Gillespie, K. & Naidoo, L. (2019). Between the cold war and the fire: The student movement, antiassimilation, and the question of the future in South Africa. *South Atlantic Quarterly*, 118 (1), pp. 226–239.

Ginsburg, H. & Opper, S. (1979). *Piaget's theory of intellectual development: An introduction* (3rd ed.). Engelwood Cliffs, NJ: Prentice Hall.

Ginwright, S. (2008). Collective radical imagination. In J. Cammarota & M. Fine (Eds.). *Revolutionizing education: Youth participatory action research in motion* (pp. 13–22). New York and London: Routledge.

Giroux, H. (2008). *Against the terror of neoliberalism: Politics beyond the age of greed.* Boulder, CO: Paradigm Publishers.

Gobodo-Madikizela, P. (2009). Working through the past: Some thoughts on forgiveness in cultural context. In P. Gobodo-Madikizela & C. van der Merwe (Eds.). *Memory, narrative and forgiveness: Perspectives on the unfinished journeys of the past* (pp. 148–169). Newcastle upon Tyne: Cambridge Scholars Publishing.

Gobodo-Madikizela, P. (2012). Nostalgia, trauma and the legacy of apartheid. *Peace and Conflict: Journal of Peace Psychology*, 18 (3), pp. 252–267.

Gobodo-Madikizela, P. (2013). Acting out and working through. In M. Linden & K. Rutkowski (Eds.). *Hurting memories and beneficial forgetting* (pp. 217–224). London: Elsevier.

Gobodo-Madikizela, P. (2016). *What does it mean to be human in the aftermath of trauma? Re-envisioning the sunflower and why Hannah Arendt was wrong.* Uppsala: The Nordic Africa Institute and Uppsala University.

Gobodo-Madikizela, P. (2018). Why memories of the truth and reconciliation commission still ache. *The Conversation*, 29 November 2018. Retrieved from. https://theconversation.com/why-memories-of-the-truth-and-reconciliation-commission-still-ache-107721.

Godin, M., Moller Hansen, K., Lounasmaa, A., Squire, C., & Zaman, T. (Eds.) (2017). *Voices from the "Jungle": Stories from the Calais refugee camp.* London: Pluto Press.

Gould, S. J. (1996). *The mismeasure of man* (2nd ed.). New York: W.W. Norton & Company.

Govender, P. (2013). Lesbian matric dance drama. *Sunday Times*, 22 September. Retrieved from http://times-e-editions.newspaperdirect.com/epaper/viewer.aspx.

Govender, P. (2017). Three years on and no compensation for Limpopo family whose child died like a dog. *Mail and Guardian*, 16 February. Retrieved from https://mg.co.za/article/2017-02-16-00-three-years-on-and-no-compensation-for-limpopo-family-whose-child-died-like-a-dog.

Govender, P. (2019). Matatiele school's "huge problem" with segregation. *Times Live*, 13 January. Retrieved from. www.timeslive.co.za/sunday-times/news/2019-01-13-matatiele-schools-huge-problem-with-segregation/.

Grayson, D. (1996). A holistic approach to preparing disadvantaged students to succeed in tertiary science studies. Part I. Design of the Science Foundation Programme (SFP). *International Journal of Science*, 18 (8), pp. 993–1013. DOI: 10.1080/0950069960180810.

Greene, M. (1982). Public education and the public space. *Educational Researcher*, 11 (6), pp. 4–9.

Griesel, H. (1992). A developmental selection procedure. *SAAAD / IDT Symposium on admissions.*

Griesel, H. (2000). Paradoxes of policy: The case of higher education in South Africa. *South African Journal of Education* 25, pp. 90–108.

Griesel, H. (Ed.) (2004). *Curriculum responsiveness: Case studies in higher education.* Pretoria: SAUVCA (South African Universities Vice-Chancellors Association).

Griesel, H. (n.d.). Appendix one: The teach-test-teach paradigm. In J. Bradbury (2000), *The questioning process in the development of knowledge*, (pp. 309–310). Unpublished PhD thesis. Durban: University of Natal.

The Guardian (2018). South African musician Musa Manzini plays guitar during brain surgery, *The Guardian*, 23 December. Retrieved from www.theguardian.com/world/2018/dec/23/south-african-musician-musa-manzini-plays-guitar-during-brain-surgery.

Hacking, I. (1999). *The social construction of what?* Cambridge, MA: Harvard University Press.

Hall, S. (1996). Who needs identity? In S. Hall & P. Du Gay (Eds.). *Questions of cultural identity* (pp. 1–17). London: SAGE.

Harré, R. (1998). *The singular self.* London: SAGE.

Harré, R. (2000). Personalism in the context of a social constructionist psychology: Stern & Vygotsky. *Theory & Psychology*, 10 (6), pp. 731–748.

Harré, R. (2010). Hybrid psychology: The marriage of discourse analysis with neuroscience. *Athenea Digital*, 18, pp. 33–47.

Harré, R. & Secord, P. F. (1972). *The explanation of social behaviour.* Lanham: Rowman & Littlefield.

Hassim, S. (2003). The gender pact and democratic consolidation: Institutionalizing gender equality in the South African state. *Feminist Studies*, 29 (3), pp. 504–528.

Hayes, G. (1986). Intervening with the political psyche. *Proceedings of Apartheid & Mental Health. OASSSA National Conference*, University of the Witwatersrand, Johannesburg, 17–18 May 1986, pp. 44–48.

Hayes, G. (2000). The struggle for Mental Health in South Africa: Psychologists, apartheid and the story of Durban OASSSA. *Journal of Community & Applied Social Psychology*, 10, pp. 327–342.

Heffernan, A. & Nieftagodien, N. (Eds.) (2016). *Students must rise: Youth struggle in South Africa before and beyond Soweto 76.* Johannesburg: Wits University Press.

Henriques, J., Holloway, W., Urwin, C., Venn, C., & Walkerdine, V. (1984). *Changing the subject: Psychology, social regulation and subjectivity.* London: Methuen.

Hermans, H. (2001). The dialogical self: Toward a theory of personal and cultural positioning. *Culture & Psychology*, 7, pp. 243–281.

Herrnstein, R. J. & Murray, C. (1994). *The bell curve: Intelligence and class structure in American society.* New York: Free Press.

Hoffman, E. (2004). *After such knowledge: A meditation on the aftermath of the Holocaust.* London: Secker and Warburg.

Hoffman, E. (2009). *Time.* London: Profile Books.

hooks, b. (1994). *Teaching to transgress: Education as the practice of freedom.* New York and London: Routledge.

Hustvedt, S. (2012). *Living, thinking and looking.* London: Spectre.

Hustvedt, S. (2016). *A woman looking at men looking at women: Essays on art, sex, and the mind.* London: Sceptre.

Illich, I. (1971). *Deschooling society.* London: Harper & Row.

James, W. (1962). *Psychology: Briefer course.* New York: Collier Books.

Jameson, F. (1975). *The prison-house of language: A critical account of structuralism and Russian formalism.* Princeton: Princeton University Press.

Jameson, F. (1982). *The political unconscious: Narrative as a socially symbolic act.* Ithaca, NY: Cornell University Press.

Jansen, J. (2017). *As by fire: The end of the South African university.* Cape Town: Tafelberg.

Jones, M. & Dlamini, J. (Eds.) (2013). *Categories of persons: Rethinking ourselves and others.* Johannesburg: Picador Africa.

Josselson, R. (2004). Hermeneutics of faith and the hermeneutics of suspicion. *Narrative Inquiry*, 14 (1), pp. 1–28.

Josselson, R. & Harway, M. (Eds.) (2012). *Navigating multiple identities: Race, gender, culture, nationality, and roles*. Oxford: Oxford University Press.

Jovanović (2015). Vygotsky's cultural theory of subjectivity and Habermas's critical theory of society. In J. Cresswell, A. Haye, A. Larraín, M. Morgan, & G. Sullivan (Eds.). *Dialogue and debate in the making of theoretical psychology* (pp. 163–172). Concord, ON: Captus University Publications.

Kallaway, P. (Ed.) (2002). *The history of education under apartheid, 1948–1994: The doors of learning and culture shall be opened*. Cape Town: Pearson Education South Africa.

Kaminer, D. & Eagle, G. (2010). *Traumatic stress in South Africa*. Johannesburg: Wits University Press.

Kaplan, R. (2001). The Aversion project – Psychiatric abuses in the South African defence force during the Apartheid era. *South African Medical Journal*, 91 (3), pp. 216–217.

Kessi, S. & Kiguwa, P. (2015). Social psychology and social change: Beyond western perspectives. *Papers on Social Representations*, 24, pp. 1.1–1.11.

Khunou, G. (2015). What middle class? The shifting and dynamic nature of class position. *Development Southern Africa*, 32 (1), pp. 90–103. DOI: 10/1080/0376835X.2014.975889.

Kros, C. (2012). A new monumentalism? From public art to freedom park. *Image and Text: A Journal for Design*, 19, pp. 34–51.

Kunene, M. (1979). *Emperor Shaka the great: A Zulu epic*. London: Heinemann.

Lacan, J. (1977). Écrits, a selection. A. Sheridan (trans.). London: Tavistock.

Laher, S. & Cockcroft, K. (2014). Psychological assessment in post-apartheid South Africa: The way forward. *South African Journal of Psychology*, 44, pp. 303–314.

Laher, S. & Cockcroft, K. (2017). Moving from culturally biased to culturally responsive assessment practices in low resource, multicultural settings. *Professional Psychology: Research and Practice*, 48 (2), pp. 115–121.

Langa, M., Ndelu, S., Edwin, Y., & Vilakazi, M. (2017). *#Hashtag: An analysis of the #FeesMustFall Movement at South African universities*. Centre for the study of violence and reconciliation (CSVR). Retrieved from www.africaportal.org/pub lications/hashtag-an-analysis-of-the-feesmustfall-movement-at-south-african-universities/.

Larrain, A. & Haye, A. (2012). The discursive nature of inner speech. *Theory & Psychology*, 22 (1), pp. 3–22.

Levinas, E. (1963) *The trace of the other*, (La Trace de l'Autre), A Lingis, (Ed. and trans.), pp. 345–359. Retrieved from http://jst.ufl.edu/pdf/dragan2001.pdf.

Livholts, M. & Tamboukou, M. (2015). *Discourse and narrative methods*. London: SAGE.

Long, W. (2013). Rethinking "relevance": South African psychology in context. *History of Psychology*, 16 (1), pp. 19–35.

Long, W. (2016). Psychology in South Africa and the end of history. *History of Psychology*, 19 (3), pp. 220–228.

Long, W. (2018). Postcolonial theory and the strong arm of identity. *Africa Is a Country*, 26 November. Retrieved from. https://africasacountry.com/2018/11/postcolonial-theory-and-the-strong-arm-of-identity.

Luckett, K. (2016). Curriculum contestation in a post-colonial context: A view from the South. *Teaching in Higher Education*, 21 (4), pp. 415–428. DOI: 10.1080/13562517.2016.1155547.

Luckett, K. & Shay, S. (2017). Reframing the curriculum: A transformative approach. *Critical Studies in Education*. DOI: 10.1080/17508487.2017.1356341.

Luister. (2015). *Luister: A documentary about the power of language at Stellenbosch University*, produced by Contraband. Retrieved from www.youtube.com.

Maldonado-Torres, N. (2011). Thinking through the decolonial turn: Post-continental interventions in theory, philosophy and critique – An introduction. *Transmodernity: Journal of Peripheral Cultural Production of the Luso-Hispanic World*, 1 (2), pp. 1–15.

Maldonado-Torres, N. (2016). Outline of ten theses on coloniality and decoloniality. *Fondation Frantz Fanon*, (pp. 1–37). Retrieved from http://fonda tion-frantzfanon.com/outline-of-ten-theses-on-coloniality-and-decoloniality/.

Mama, A. (1995). *Beyond the masks: Race, gender and subjectivity*. London: Routledge.

Mamdani, M. (2002). Amnesty or impunity? A preliminary critique of the report of the truth and reconciliation commission of South Africa (TRC). *Diacritics*, 32 (3/4), pp. 32–59.

Mamdani, M. (2009). Response by Mahmood Mamdani. *International Journal of Transitional Justice*, 3 (3), pp. 472–473.

Manganyi, N. C. (1973). *Being Black in the world*. Johannesburg: Ravan Press.

Mangcu, X. (2003). The state of race relations in post-apartheid South Africa. In J. Daniel, A. Habib, & R. Southall (Eds.). *State of the nation: South Africa 2003–2004* (pp. 105–117). Pretoria: HSRC Press.

Mangcu, X. (2011). Evidentiary genocide: Intersections of race, power and the archive. In X.Mangcu,X. (Ed.). *Becoming worthy ancestors: Archive, public deliberation and identity in South Africa* (pp. 1–16). Johannesburg: Wits University Press.

Maré, G. & Sitas, A. (1992). *Sociology*. Durban: TTT Programme, University of Natal.

Marschall, S. (2010). *Landscapes of memory: Commemorative monuments, memorials and public statutory in post-apartheid South Africa*. Leiden: Brill.

Marx, K. (1852). The eighteenth Brumaire of Louis Bonaparte. Retrieved from www.fulltextarchive.com/pdfs/The-Eighteenth-Brumaire-of-Louis-Bonaparte.pdf.

Mbembe, A. (2016). Decolonizing the university: New directions. *Arts & Humanities in Higher Education*, 15 (1), pp. 29–45.

Mbembe, A. (2017). *Critique of Black reason*. Johannesburg: Wits University Press.

McAdams, D. P. (2001). The psychology of life stories. *Review of General Psychology*, 5 (2), pp. 100–122.

Meintjies, F. (2013). The TRC and CODESA failed South Africa: It's time we reflected on this. The South African Civil Society information service, 12 September. Retrieved from http://sacsis.org.za/site/article/1783.

Merleau-Ponty, M. (2013). *The phenomenology of recognition*. London: Routledge.

Metz, T. (2007). Ubuntu as a moral theory: Reply to four critics. *South African Journal of Philosophy*, 26 (4), pp. 369–387.

Metz, T. (2011). Ubuntu as a moral theory and human rights in South Africa. *African Human Rights Law Journal*, 11, pp. 532–559.

Miller, R. (1989). Critical psychology: A territorial imperative. *Psychology in Society (PINS)*, 12, pp. 3–18.

Miller, R. (1992). Double, double, toil and trouble. *The South African Journal of Higher Education*, 6 (1), pp. 98–104.

Miller, R. (2011). *Vygotsky in perspective*. Cambridge: Cambridge University Press.

Miller, R. (2014). Introducing Vygotsky's cultural-historical psychology. In A. Yasnitsky, R. van der Veer, & M. Ferrari (Eds.). *The Cambridge Handbook of cultural-historical psychology* (pp. 9–44). Cambridge: Cambridge University Press.

Miller, R. & Bradbury, J. (1999). Academic performance of first and second language students: Selection criteria. *South African Journal of Science*, 95, pp. 30–34.

Miller, R., Bradbury, J., & Lemmon, G. (2000). Justifying means with ends: Assessment and academic performance. *South African Journal of Higher Education*, 14 (1), pp. 166–173.

Miller, R., Bradbury, J., & Pedley, K. (1998). Academic performance of first and second language students: Disadvantage and under-preparedness. *South African Journal of Science*, 94, pp. 103–107.

Mills, C. W. (1997). *The racial contract*. Ithaca, NY and London: Cornell University Press.

Mills, C. W. (2013). An illuminating blackness. *The Black Scholar: Journal of Black Studies and Research*, 43 (4), pp. 32–37.

Mkhize, N. (2004). Psychology: An African perspective. In N. Duncan, K. Ratele, D. Hook, N. Mkhize, P. Kiguwa, & A. Collins. *Self, community and psychology* (pp. 4.1–4.29). Cape Town: UCT Press.

Morrow, W. (2009). *Bounds of democracy: Epistemological access in higher education*. Pretoria: HSRC Press.

Motimele, M. (2019). The rupture of neoliberal time as the foundation for emancipatory epistemologies. *South Atlantic Quarterly*, 118 (1), pp. 205–214.

Mphahlele, E. (2002). *Es'kia: Education, African humanism and culture, social consciousness, literary appreciation*. Johannesburg: Kwela Books.

Murray, M. (2016). *Jacques Lacan: A critical introduction*. London: Pluto Press.

Muruthi, T. (2006). Practical peacemaking wisdom from Africa: Reflections on Ubuntu. *The Journal of Pan African Studies*, 1 (4), pp. 25–33.

Nabudera, D. W. (2005). Ubuntu philosophy, memory and reconciliation. Texas Scholar Works. Retrieved from https://repositories.lib.utexas.edu/bitstream/handle/2152/4521/3621.pdf.

Ndebele, N. S. (1986). The rediscovery of the ordinary: Some new writings in South Africa. *Journal of Southern African Studies*, 12 (2), pp. 143–157.

Ndebele, N. S. (1991). *Rediscovery of the ordinary: Essays on South African literature and culture*. Johannesburg: COSAW (Congress of South African Writers).

Ndebele, N. S. (2007). *Fine lines from the box: Further thoughts about our country*. Johannesburg: Umuzi.

Ndebele, N. S. (2016). They are burning memory. The 10th annual Helen Joseph Memorial lecture, University of Johannesburg, Johannesburg, South Africa, 14 September. Retrieved from www.youtube.com/watch?v=5EBEz7f_bRM.

Ndlovu, S. (2012). "I am more (than just) Black": Contesting multiplicity through conferring and asserting singularity in narratives of blackness. In R. Josselson &

M. Harway (Eds.). *Navigating multiple identities: Race, gender, culture, nationality, and roles* (pp. 143–166). Oxford: Oxford University Press.

NEPI (1993). *National Education Policy Investigation (NEPI): The Framework Report.* Cape Town: National Education Co-ordinating Committee/Oxford University Press.

Nieftagodien, N. (2018). *Public history in times of decolonisation: Reflections on the past and present.* Inaugural lecture, University of the Witwatersrand, 23 August.

Nkrumah, K. (1998). Consciencism. In E. C. Eze (Ed.). *African philosophy: An anthology* (pp. 81–93). London: Blackwell.

Ntesebeza, L. (2005). *Democracy compromised: Chiefs and the politics of land in South Africa.* Leiden: Brill.

Nwoye, A. (2015). What is African psychology the psychology of? *Theory & Psychology,* 25, pp. 96–116. DOI: 10.1177/0959354314565116.

Ommen, V. & Painter, D. (Eds.) (2008). *Interiors: A history of psychology in South Africa.* Pretoria: UNISA Press.

Ong, W. J. (1982). *Orality and literacy: The technologizing of the word.* London and New York: Methuen.

Painter, D. (2012). Speaking in tongues: A report on the second Marxism and psychology conference, Morelia, Mexico, 9–11 August. *Pins,* 43, pp. 72–75.

Pandor, N. (2008). Pandor unveils school pledge. *News 24 Archives,* 12 February. Retrieved from www.news24.com/SouthAfrica/News/Pandor-unveils-school-pledge-20080212.

Parker, I. (2002). *Critical discursive psychology.* London: Palgrave.

Parker, I. (2015a). *Psychology after deconstruction: Erasure and social reconstruction.* London: Routledge.

Parker, I. (2015b). *Psychology, after discourse analysis: Concepts, methods, critique.* London: Routledge.

Parker, I. (2015c). *Psychology after the crisis: Scientific paradigms and political debate.* London: Routledge.

Peterson, B. (2011). The language question in Africa. In A. Quayson (Ed.). *The Cambridge History of postcolonial literature* (pp. 681–702). Cambridge: Cambridge University Press.

Peterson, B. (2016). Modernist at large: The aesthetics of native life in South Africa. In J. Remmington, B. Willan, & B. Peterson (Eds.). *Sol Plaatje's native life in South Africa: Past and present* (pp. 18–36). Johannesburg: Wits University Press.

Peterson, B. (2019a). Spectrality and inter-generational Black narratives. *Social Dynamics,* 45 (3), pp. 73–97.

Peterson, B. (forthcoming). The art of personhood: Kinship and its social challenges. In J. Ogudu (Ed.). *Ubuntu and the reconstitution of community.* 45 (3) Bloomington, IN: Indiana University Press.

Peterson, P. (2012). Dignity, memory and the future under siege: Reconciliation and nation-building in post-apartheid South Africa. In S. Opondo & M. Shapiro (Eds.). *New violent cartographies: Geo-analysis after the aesthetic turn* (pp. 214–232). London: Routledge.

Philips, A. & Taylor, B. (2009). *On kindness.* New York: Picador.

Phoenix, A. (1991). *Young mothers?* Cambridge: Polity Press.

Phoenix, A. (2002). Mapping present inequalities to navigate future success: Racialisation and education. *British Journal of Sociology*, 23 (3), pp. 505–515.

Piketty, T. (2015). *The economics of inequality*. Boston, MA: The Belknap Press of Harvard University Press.

Plotkin, H. (1994). *Darwin machines and the nature of knowledge: Concerning adaptations, instinct and the evolution of intelligence*. London: Penguin Books.

Poland, M. & Hammond-Tooke, D. (2003). *Abundant Herds: A celebration of the Nguni cattle of the Zulu people*. Artwork: L. Voigt. Cape Town: Fernwood Press (an imprint of Penguin Random House).

PRAESA. Retrieved from www.praesa.org.za/.

Price, M. (2019). The UCT and Wits strategies on #FeesMustFall were different for good reason. *Daily Maverick*, 12 March. Retrieved from www.dailymaverick.co.za/article/2019-03-12-the-uct-and-wits-strategies-on-feesmustfall-were-different-for-good-reasons/.

Ramose, M. (2015). Ecology through Ubuntu. In R. Meinheld (Ed.). *Environmental values emerging from cultures and religions of the ASEAN region* (pp. 69–77). Bangkok: Konrad-Adenauer Siftung & Guna Chakra Research Centre.

Ramphele, M. (2008). *Laying ghosts to rest: Dilemmas of the transformation in South Africa*. Cape Town: Tafelberg.

Ratele, K. (2006). Ruling masculinity and sexuality. *Feminist Africa*, 6, pp. 48–64.

Ratele, K. (2017). Four (African) psychologies. *Theory & Psychology*, 27 (3), pp. 313–327.

Rayner, M., Baldwin-Ragaven, L., & Naidoo, S. (2017). *A double harm: Police misuse of force and barriers to necessary Health Care Services Responses to student protests at the University of the Witwatersrand, September to November 2016*. Johannesburg: SERI (Socio-economic rights institute of South Africa).

Ricoeur, P. (1978). The metaphorical process as cognition, imagination and feeling. *Critical Inquiry*, 5 (1), pp. 143–159.

Ricoeur, P. (1981). *Hermeneutics and the human sciences*. J.B. Thompson, (Ed. & trans.). Cambridge: Cambridge University Press.

Ricoeur, P. (1992). *Oneself as another*. Chicago: University of Chicago Press.

Ricoeur, P. (2004). *Memory, history and forgetting*. K. Blamey & D. Pellauer, (Ed. & trans.). Chicago: University of Chicago Press.

Riesen, J. (2015). American Psychological Association Bolstered C.I.A. Torture Program, Report Says. Retrieved from www.nytimes.com/2015/05/01/us/report-says-american-psychological-association-collaborated-on-torture-justification.html.

Rose, S. (1976). Scientific racism and ideology: The IQ racket from Galton to Jensen. In H. Rose & S. Rose (Eds.). *The political economy of science* (pp. 112–141). New York: Springer.

Rutherford, A. (2018). *The book of humans*. London: Weidenfeld & Nicolson.

Sachs, A. (2011). *The soft vengeance of a freedom fighter* (3rd ed.). London: Souvenir Press.

Sacks, O. (2014). Luria and "romantic science". In A. Yasnitsky, R. van der Veer, & M. Ferrari (Eds.). *The Cambridge handbook of cultural-historical psychology* (pp. 517–528). Cambridge: Cambridge University Press.

Sacks, O. (2017). *The river of consciousness*. London: Picador.

Said, E. (1993). *Culture and Imperialism*. London: Chatto & Windus.

Sankofa. Retrieved from https://en.wikipedia.org/wiki/Sankofa.

Sampson, E. E. (1989). The deconstruction of the self. In J. Shotter & K. Gergen (Eds.). *Texts of identity* (pp. 1–19). Thousand Oaks, CA: SAGE.

Sanders, M. (2002). Ethics and interdisciplinarity in philosophy and literary theory. *Diacritics*, 32 (3/4), pp. 2–16.

Sanders, M. (2010). *Complicities: The intellectual and apartheid*. Pietermaritzburg: Natal University Press.

Scheibe, K. E. (1986). In T. R. Sarbin (Ed.). *Narrative psychology: The storied nature of human conduct* (pp. 129–151). New York: Praeger.

Scott, I. (2009). Academic development in South African higher education. In E. Bitzer (Ed.). *Higher education in South Africa: A scholarly look behind the scenes* (pp. 21–50). Stellenbosch: SUN Press.

Shange, N. (2019). Parents fume as black and white grade R children are "separated" in North West classroom. *Times Live*, 9 January. Retrieved from www.timeslive. coza.

Sharpe, C. (2016). *In the wake: On blackness and being*. Durham, NC and London: Duke University Press.

Shefer, T. (2010). Narrating gender and sex in and through apartheid divides. *South African Journal of Psychology*, 40 (4), pp. 382–395.

Shefer, T. (2012). Fraught nearness: Narratives on domestic workers in memories of apartheid. *Peace and Conflict: Journal of Peace Psychology*, 18 (3), pp. 307–317.

Shotter, J. (2000). Seeing historically: Goethe and Vygotsky's "enabling theory-method". *Culture & Psychology*, 6 (2), pp. 233–252.

Shotter, J. (2006). Vygotsky and consciousness as *Con-scientia*, as witnessable knowing along with others. *Theory & Psychology*, 16 (1), pp. 13–36.

Shweder, R. A. (1991). *Thinking through cultures: Expeditions in cultural psychology*. Cambridge, MA: Harvard University Press.

Simons, D. J. & Chabris, C. F. (1999). Gorillas in our midst: Sustained inattentional blindness for dynamic events. *Perception*, 28, pp. 1059–1074.

Sitas, A. (1990). Labour colleges and the university – A comment. In C. Hemson (Ed.). *Educational development in the South African universities: Is an intermediate tertiary college the solution?* (pp. 86–88). Conference Proceedings. Durban: University of Natal.

Skutnabb-Kangas, T. (1998). Human rights and language wrongs – a future for diversity. *Language Sciences*, 20 (1), pp. 5–27.

Skutnabb-Kangas, T. (2002). Language policies and education: The role of education in destroying or supporting the world's linguistic diversity. World Congress on Language Policies, Barcelona, 16–20 April.

Skuy, M. (1997). Cross cultural and interdimensional implications of Feuerstein's construct of mediated learning experience. *School Psychology International*, 18 (2), pp. 119–135. DOI: org/10.1177/0143034397182002.

Slonimsky, L. & Shalem, Y. (2010). Reading below the surface: Students' organisation of content and form. *HE Monitor*, pp. 81–109. Retrieved from www.che.ac.za/sites/default/files/publications/Higher_Education_Monitor_10.pdf. Pretoria: Council of Higher Education.

Smith, P. C. (1980). Translator's introduction. In H.-G. Gadamer (Ed.). *Dialogue and dialectic: Eight hermeneutical studies on Plato* (pp. ix–xv). Translated and with an Introduction by P. C. Smith. New Haven, CT: Yale University Press.

Smith, Z. (2018). *Feel free: Essays*. London: Hamish Hamilton, Penguin.

Solnit, R. (2016). *Hope in the dark: Untold histories, wild possibilities*. Edinburgh: Canongate.

Soudien, C. (2007). Democracy and higher education in South Africa: A dialogue in tension. *South African Journal of Higher Education*, 20 (6), pp. 941–949.

Soudien, C. (2008). The intersections of race and class in South African higher education. *South African Journal of Higher Education*, 22 (3), pp. 662–678.

Soudien, C. (2012a). The promise of the university: What it's become and where it could go. In B. Leibowitz (Ed.). *Higher education for the public good: Views from the South* (pp. 31–44). Stoke-on-Trent: Trentham Books & Stellenbosch: SUN MeDIA

Soudien, C. (2012b). *Realising the dream*. Pretoria: Human Sciences Research Council.

Spence, D. P. (1986). Narrative smoothing and clinical wisdom. In T. R. Sarbin (Ed.). *Narrative psychology: The storied nature of human conduct* (pp. 211–232). New York: Praeger.

Stam, H. (2001). Introduction: Social constructionism and its critics. *Theory & Psychology*, 11 (3), pp. 291–296.

Stam, H. (2002). Varieties of social constructionism and the rituals of critique. *Theory & Psychology*, 12 (5), pp. 571–576.

Stevens, G., Duncan, N., & Hook, D. (Eds.) (2013). *Race, memory and the apartheid archive: Towards a transformative psychosocial praxis*. Johannesburg: Wits University Press.

Steyn, M. (2012). The ignorance contract: Recollections of apartheid childhoods and the construction of epistemologies of ignorance. *Identities: Global Studies in Culture and Power*, 19 (1), pp. 8–25.

Steyn, M. (2015). Critical diversity literacy: Essentials for the twenty-first century. In S. Vertovec (Ed.). *Routledge international handbook of diversity studies* (pp. 379–389). London: Routledge.

Tamboukou, M. (2000). The paradox of being a woman teacher. *Gender and Education*, 12 (4), pp. 463–478.

Taylor, C. (1992). *Sources of the self: The making of the modern identity*. Cambridge: Cambridge University Press.

Taylor, C. (1994). *Multiculturalism: Examining the politics of recognition*. Princeton: Princeton University Press.

Teo, T. (2010). What is epistemological violence in the empirical social sciences? *Social and Personality Psychology Compass*, 4 (5), pp. 295–303. DOI: 10.1111/j.1752-9004.2010.00265.x.

Torre, M. E. & Fine, M. (2008). Participatory action research in the. In C. Zone, J. Cammarota, & M. Fine. *Revolutionizing education: Youth participatory action research in motion* (pp. 23–44). New York and London: Routledge.

Tutu, D. (1999). *No future without forgiveness*. London: Rider.

Tutu, D. (2004). *God has a dream: A vision of hope for our time*. New York: Doubleday.

Tutu, D. (2010). Foreword. In M. Maharaj (Ed.). *Reflections in prison* (pp. 1–3). Johannesburg: Penguin, Random House.

Vally, S. (2015). The education crisis and the struggle to achieve quality public education in South Africa. *Education as Change*, 19 (2), pp. 151–168. DOI: 10.1080./16823206.2015.1085616.

Valsiner, J. (2015). The place for synthesis: Vygotsky's analysis of affective generalization. *History of the Human Sciences*, 28 (2), pp. 93–102.

Valsiner, J. & van der Veer, R. (2014). Encountering the border: Vygotsky's *zona blizhaishego razvitia* and its implications for theories of development. In A. Yasnitsky, R. van der Veer, & M. Ferrari (Eds.). *The Cambridge handbook of cultural-historical psychology* (pp. 148–173). Cambridge: Cambridge University Press.

Van der Veer, R. (1996). The concept of culture in Vygotsky's thinking. *Culture & Psychology*, 2, pp. 247–263.

Van der Veer, R. & Valsiner, J. (1991). *Understanding Vygotsky: A quest for synthesis*. Oxford: Blackwell.

Vogelman, L. (1987). The development of an appropriate psychology: The work of the organisation of appropriate social services in South Africa. *Psychology in Society*, 7, pp. 24–35.

Vygotsky, L. S. (1978). *Mind in society: The development of higher psychological processes*. M. Cole & S. Scribner Eds. & trans. Cambridge, MA: Harvard University Press.

Vygotsky, L. S. (1986). *Thought and language*. Edited by A. Kozulin. Cambridge, MA: The MIT Press.

Vygotsky, L. S. (1987). *The collected works of L.S. Vygotsky. Vol. 1: Problems of general psychology*, R. W. Rieber & A. S. Carton (Eds.). New York: Plenum Press.

Vygotsky, L. S. (1994). The methods of reflexological and psychological investigation. In R. Van der Veer & J. Valsiner (Eds.). *The Vygotsky reader* (pp. 27–45). Oxford: Blackwell.

Vygotsky, L. S. (1997). *The collected works of L.S. Vygotsky. Vol. III: Problems of the theory and history of psychology*, R. W. Rieber & J. Wollock (Eds.). New York: Plenum Press.

Vygotsky, L. S. (1998). *The collected works of L.S. Vygotsky. Vol. V: Child psychology*, R. W. Rieber (Ed.). New York: Plenum Press.

Vygotsky, L. S. (1999). *The collected works of L.S. Vygotsky. Vol. VI: Scientific legacy*, R. W. Rieber (Ed.). New York: Plenum Press.

wa Thiong'o, N. (1986). *Decolonising the mind: The politics of language in African literature*. London: James Currey.

Webster, E. (1986). The role of social scientists in the current South African crisis. *Apartheid & Mental Health*, Proceedings of the OASSSA National Conference, University of the Witwatersrand, Johannesburg, South Africa, 17–18 May, pp. 38–43.

Weedon, C. (1997). *Feminist practice & poststructuralist theory* (2nd ed.). London: Blackwell.

Wertsch, J. V. (1998). *Mind as action*. Oxford: Oxford University Press.

Wertsch, J. V. (2007). Mediation. In H. Daniels, M. Cole, & J. V. Wertsch (Eds.). *The Cambridge companion to Vygotsky* (p. 178–192). Cambridge: Cambridge University Press.

Westover, T. (2018). *Educated*. London: Hutchinson.

Wood, D., Bruner, J. S., & Ross, G. (1976). The role of tutoring in problem solving. *Journal of Child Psychology & Psychiatry*, 17, pp. 89–100.

Yasnitsky, A. (2012). Revisionist revolution in Vygotskian science: Toward cultural-historical gestalt psychology. *Journal of Russian and East European Psychology*, 50 (4), pp. 3–15. DOI: 10.2753/RPO1061-0405500400.

Yeld, N. (2007). Critical questions? Some responses to issues raised in relation to the national benchmark tests project. *South African Journal of Higher Education*, 21 (5), pp. 610–616.

Yeld, N. & Haeck, W. (2006). Educational histories and academic potential: Can tests deliver? *Assessment & Evaluation in Education*, 22 (1), pp. 5–16. DOI: 10.1080/0260293970220101.

Yuval-Davis, N. (2011). *The politics of belonging: Intersectional contestations*. Thousand Oaks, CA: SAGE.

Žižek, S. (2005). Philosophy is not a dialogue. In A. Badiou & S. Žižek. *Philosophy in the present*. P. Engelmann (Ed.), P. Thomas & A. Toscano (trans.) London: Polity Press. Oaks, CA: SAGE.

INDEX

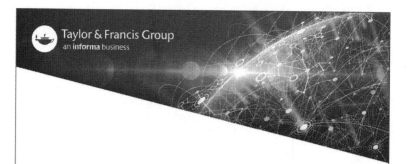